ROCK OF AGES

In the series *Religious Engagement in Democratic Politics*,
edited by PAUL A. DJUPE

ALSO IN THIS SERIES:

Brian R. Calfano and Nazita Lajevardi, eds., *Understanding Muslim Political Life in America: Contested Citizenship in the Twenty-First Century*

Jeanine Kraybill, *One Faith, Two Authorities: Tension between Female Religious and Male Clergy in the American Catholic Church*

Paul A. Djupe and Ryan L. Claassen, eds., *The Evangelical Crackup? The Future of the Evangelical-Republican Coalition*

Jeremiah J. Castle

ROCK OF AGES

Subcultural Religious Identity and Public Opinion among Young Evangelicals

TEMPLE UNIVERSITY PRESS
Philadelphia • Rome • Tokyo

TEMPLE UNIVERSITY PRESS
Philadelphia, Pennsylvania 19122
tupress.temple.edu

Copyright © 2019 by Temple University—Of The Commonwealth System
 of Higher Education
All rights reserved
Published 2019

Library of Congress Cataloging-in-Publication Data

Names: Castle, Jeremiah J., author.
Title: Rock of ages : subcultural religious identity and public opinion among young
 evangelicals / Jeremiah J. Castle.
Description: Philadelphia : Temple University Press, 2019. | Series: Religious engagement in
 democratic politics | Includes bibliographical references and index. |
Identifiers: LCCN 2018054757 (print) | LCCN 2019018912 (ebook) | ISBN 9781439917237
 (E-book) | ISBN 9781439917213 (cloth : alk. paper) | ISBN 9781439917220
 (pbk. : alk. paper)
Subjects: LCSH: Evangelicalism—United States. | Christianity and politics—
 United States. | Public opinion—United States.
Classification: LCC BR516 (ebook) | LCC BR516 .C38 2019 (print) |
 DDC 277.3/0830842—dc23
LC record available at https://lccn.loc.gov/2018054757

∞ The paper used in this publication meets the requirements of the American National
Standard for Information Sciences—Permanence of Paper for Printed Library Materials,
ANSI Z39.48-1992

Printed in the United States of America

9 8 7 6 5 4 3 2 1

Contents

Acknowledgments ... vii

Introduction: Two Big Questions about Young Evangelicals ... 1

Part I Trends in Public Opinion among Young Evangelicals

1 A Subcultural Theory of Public Opinion among Evangelicals ... 17

2 Winds of Change or Still the Same? Political Identities and Issue Attitudes among Young Evangelicals ... 37

3 Inside Out or Outside In: Explaining Change among Young Evangelicals ... 70

Part II Methods of Understanding Public Opinion among Young Evangelicals

4 How the Evangelical Subculture Influences Public Opinion ... 99

5 Testing Subcultural Immersion's Impact on Public Opinion ... 131

6 Public Opinion among Liberal Young Evangelicals ... 146

Conclusion ... 172

Appendix: Coding Religious Tradition	*181*
Chapter 3 Appendix	*183*
Chapter 5 Appendix	*185*
Chapter 6 Appendix	*189*
Notes	*193*
References	*199*
Index	*215*

Acknowledgments

I'm often asked how I started studying religion and politics. Having grown up in a socially and politically conservative rural area north of Indianapolis, I knew from a young age that there was an important relationship between religion and political attitudes. Although I didn't yet consider myself a social scientist, I was interested in why my friends who attended church seemed to think differently about politics than my friends who slept in on Sunday mornings. My personal interest in religion transitioned into formal academic study during my time as an undergraduate at Hanover College. It seemed like every semester I wound up writing at least one term paper about religion's relationship with politics. Around that time, I had a series of conversations with trusted advisers that convinced me to continue studying political science by attending graduate school and pursuing a career in academia. In a lot of ways, then, the roots of this project could be traced back to the musty classrooms in the Faculty Office Building or the empty third floor of Duggan Library on a Friday night.

Therefore, the many debts of gratitude I owe also begin at Hanover. I am particularly thankful to Bill Kubik, who accompanied me to the Midwest Political Science Association and the Southern Political Science Association conferences to present some of my early research, including my senior thesis. I am also grateful to Bill Bettler, Keith Roberts, Ron Smith, Ruth Turner, and numerous other members of the Hanover College faculty for the careful mentorship I received during my time there. I can only hope to be as effective a mentor and guide for my students as these scholars have been for me.

I am also grateful for the opportunity to study political science as a graduate student at the University of Notre Dame. This is where the project really came to life. As I was struggling to come up with a viable dissertation topic, it was David Campbell who first suggested I look into the political attitudes of young evangelicals. The idea immediately appealed to both my academic interest in public opinion and my lived experience growing up in rural Indiana. Throughout the dissertation process, Peri Arnold, David Campbell, and Geoff Layman provided valuable comments that substantially improved the project. The Rooney Center for the Study of American Democracy generously provided funding for the interviews that informed the dissertation and now add so much to the second half of this book. In addition, I am thankful for the Dissertation Year Fellowship that provided me a service-free year, which proved vital to completing this project, as well as several research articles. Finally, I am thankful for the peer community that offered important early feedback on this project. Colleagues including Todd Adkins, Andre Audette, Patrick Schoettmer, Greg Shufeldt, Chris Weaver, and others read and commented on parts of this book.

My dissertation, while passable, had its share of problems. Much of the data were from 2007, my attempt at an original panel study of evangelicals was too small for reliable analysis, and the writing was stiff and, at times, disorganized. Therefore, wholesale changes were needed before the project would stand up to the rigors of the peer review process. I wrote (and rewrote) most of the manuscript while a postdoctoral fellow at Central Michigan University. Again, I was tremendously lucky to land at a position with so many great colleagues. I am thankful to Prakash Adhikari, Ted Clayton, Thomas Greitens, Tim Hazen, Soo He Jeon, David Jesuit, Sterling Johnson, Sharon Kukla-Acevedo, Emma Powell, Cherie Strachan, Larry Sych, and the many others who provided support and encouragement while I was writing this book. I am particularly thankful to Jill Prior, Lara Raisanen, and Kyla Stepp, who generously provided feedback on parts of the manuscript.

Of course, this project would not have been possible without the staff at Temple University Press. Paul Djupe, editor of the *Religious Engagement in Democratic Politics* series, first encouraged me to send the manuscript to Temple University Press. Paul also provided assistance that was above and beyond the call of duty during the editorial process, including valuable feedback on the figures. In addition, the reviewers chosen by the press provided helpful feedback on the manuscript, and the final result provides a clearer and more complete picture of the politics of young evangelicals because of this input. Most of all, I thank Aaron Javsicas and the staff of Temple University Press for their efforts in bringing this project to completion.

I also thank the various individuals and organizations who provided data for this project, including the Pew Research Center, Robbie Jones and the Public Religion Research Institute, the National Opinion Research Center (which conducts the General Social Survey), and Stephen Ansolabehere and Brian Schaffner (who lead the team that conducts the Cooperative Congressional Election Studies). By making their data publicly available, they do a tremendous service for other social science researchers. I'm deeply thankful for their generosity. In addition, Greg Smith at the Pew Research Center was particularly helpful in responding to a few emails soliciting data sets. I am grateful for his time and effort in helping me access the valuable data used in this book.

Finally, I owe gratitude to my friends and family, who have encouraged me throughout this journey. My parents, Mark and Jan Castle, were supportive as I grew (and, occasionally, regressed) throughout my college and graduate school years. Ashleen and Vince Bagnulo, Lauren Brown, Lauron Haney, Cameron O'Bannon, Jessica and Robert Spencer, and many others tried to get me to socialize and stop talking about political science. I'm most grateful to my wife, Kira. When we met, this project was in its infancy, and she has patiently listened to my theories and proofread much of my work. She also spent far too many weekends watching our infant daughter, Carson, alone while I was at the office writing. I am thankful for them both; they make life worth living.

ROCK OF AGES

Introduction

Two Big Questions about Young Evangelicals

In 2004, the dominance of the Republican coalition in presidential elections was becoming conventional wisdom. After all, when the smoke cleared in November 2004, the Republicans had won five of the last seven contests. Furthermore, although Democrat Bill Clinton won the Electoral College (and therefore the presidency) in 1992 and 1996, in both elections he failed to win a majority of the popular vote. Among the most important constituencies that enabled the Republican Party's electoral dominance was religiously committed evangelicals. Motivated by opposition to cultural liberalism and the language of religious traditionalism, they turned out in droves to vote for like-minded candidates such as Ronald Reagan and George W. Bush (Campbell and Monson 2007; Green et al. 2007). The symbiotic relationship between evangelicals and Republicans ensured that both would remain powerful parts of American politics.

Yet by 2008, both secular and religious observers were wondering whether evangelicals might be leaving the very coalition that they had helped build. In particular, observers speculated that young evangelicals were substantially more liberal than older generations. A variety of sources also suggested that young evangelicals were more likely to vote for Barack Obama in 2008 than they had been to vote for other recent Democratic Party candidates (Edwards 2008; Zogoby 2009). Writing for ABC News, Dan Harris (2008) claimed that young evangelicals were "breaking from their parents and focusing on a broader range of issues than just abortion and gay marriage." Within the evangelical tradition, much ink has been spilled explaining how and why young evangelicals are different and what it means for the church (Kinnaman 2011; Krattenmaker 2013; Vicari 2014b; Wehner 2007).

However, other commentators deny that young evangelicals are embracing the Democratic Party or political liberalism. Russell Moore, president of the Southern Baptist Convention's Ethics and Religious Liberty Commission, depicts young evangelicals as tired of the "culture wars" rhetoric and the divisive politics of the New Christian Right, but just as conservative and countercultural as previous generations (Nazworth 2014). In her book *The New Faithful*, Colleen Carroll (2002), a former speechwriter for George W. Bush, describes a new generation of faithful Protestants and Catholics who are rejecting liberalism and returning to orthodoxy. Descriptive statistics seem to support the notion that change has been overstated, too: of the 1,329 evangelicals ages eighteen to twenty-nine in the 2016 Cooperative Congressional Election Study, just 11 percent identified themselves as "liberal" or "very liberal," while almost 54 percent identified themselves as "conservative" or "very conservative."

These conflicting accounts highlight the need for a more thorough understanding of public opinion among young evangelicals. Evangelical Protestants constitute roughly one-quarter of the population, and they have been an important factor in American politics for the past several decades. As such, any changes in public opinion among young evangelicals could reverberate throughout the American political system for years to come. In this chapter, I briefly introduce evangelical Protestants. I then ask two important questions about young evangelicals. First, are their political beliefs changing? Second, are any changes we see driven by factors internal to the church, or are they driven by factors external to the church? Finally, I highlight the need for a more thorough social scientific study of public opinion among young evangelicals. In particular, I stress the importance of using multiple data sources and grounding the analysis in a social scientific theory of public opinion. This discussion paves the way for Chapter 1, in which I introduce my own theory of public opinion among young evangelicals.

The Foundations of Religious Influence on Political Behavior

To understand religion's influence on political behavior, we must first confront the problem of conceptualizing religion itself. Religion, by its very nature, is a multidimensional concept. Researchers have attempted to capture that multidimensionality through emphasizing the three b's: believing, behaving, and belonging (e.g., Kellstedt, Green, Guth, et al. 1996; Layman

2001). Each of these dimensions of religion provides the potential for religion to influence public opinion (e.g., Kellstedt, Green, Guth, et al. 1996).

The most common way of understanding religion is in terms of belonging to one of several religious traditions. The marketplace of religion in the United States is enormous, encompassing hundreds of denominations and many thousands of nondenominational churches (Finke and Stark 2005). While researchers recognize that the social contexts of individual churches and denominations can provide powerful insight into public opinion (e.g., Djupe and Gilbert 2009), most researchers find it helpful to group denominations into a handful of religious traditions. Corwin E. Smidt writes, "A religious tradition reflects a characteristic way of interpreting and responding to the world" (2007, 30). Common schemes separate individuals into broad categories that include evangelical Protestant, mainline Protestant, black Protestant, Catholic, Jewish, and the unaffiliated (Kellstedt, Green, Guth, et al. 1996; Leege and Kellstedt 1993; Smidt, Kellstedt, and Guth 2009). Smaller traditions, like Muslims, Hindus, and nontraditional Protestants (i.e., Mormons, Christian Scientists, and so on), are often grouped together in an "other" category or left out of analyses.[1]

In this book, I follow the majority of the social science literature in understanding evangelicals as those who belong to the evangelical Protestant religious tradition. The denominations that make up evangelical Protestantism are those that pushed back against modernization and secularization in the early twentieth century. They are characterized by several theological commitments, including an emphasis on the Bible as the authoritative Word of God, a belief that Jesus Christ is the only way to salvation, and an emphasis on evangelism (spreading the faith). A long list of denominations fall under the evangelical Protestant banner, including Southern Baptists (and many other Baptists), the Lutheran Church–Missouri Synod, the Wisconsin Evangelical Lutheran Synod, the Christian Reformed Church, nearly all Pentecostals, nearly all charismatics, and many nondenominational Protestant churches (for a detailed explanation of coding for religious traditions, see Steensland et al. 2000).

Within this broad evangelical tradition, there is considerable diversity (e.g., Hunter 1983; Kellstedt, Green, Smidt, et al. 1996). In particular, history has witnessed a number of smaller religious movements within evangelicalism that emphasize specific theological and political doctrines. For example, the fundamentalist movement that arose around the start of the twentieth century responded to the growth of cultural modernism by advocating adherence to the "fundamentals," including the literal truth of the Bible, a premillennial dispensationalist eschatology, and a separationist stance toward a society that seemed increasingly hostile toward conservative

Protestant theology (FitzGerald 2017; Kellstedt and Smidt 1996).[2] Later in the history of the fundamentalist movement, influential fundamentalists, such as Jerry Falwell and Ken Ham, encouraged adherents to take a more active role in sharing their religious viewpoints with the broader society. The beginning of the twentieth century also saw the rise of the "spirit-filled" movement, which is closely affiliated with Pentecostal and charismatic churches. This subdivision of evangelicalism emphasizes the gifts of the Holy Spirit, including glossolalia (speaking in tongues), prophesy, and healing by faith (FitzGerald 2017; Smidt et al. 1996). In the 1950s, Billy Graham and other influential evangelicals triggered the "neoevangelical" movement, pushing back against the fundamentalist tendencies toward polarizing rhetoric and separatism (Strachan 2015). Neoevangelicals used institutions such as Fuller Theological Seminary and the magazine *Christianity Today* to advocate a more intellectually engaged, theologically conservative version of evangelical theology (FitzGerald 2017).

While many of these religious movements are variations of theological conservatism, there is also a sizable progressive movement within evangelicalism. Led by organizations such as Jim Wallis's Sojourners and Tony Campolo's Red Letter Christians, this nondenominational movement rejects both the harsh rhetoric and the narrow focus on cultural issues characteristic of the New Christian Right. Instead, progressive evangelicals seek to expand the evangelical issue agenda to include social justice issues like poverty, immigration, and global affairs (see Campolo 2008; Wallis 2006). Differences aside, these progressive evangelicals held much in common with other movements within evangelicalism, including a continued commitment to the authority of the Bible. Clearly, then, while the concept of an evangelical religious tradition captures the common social and theological characteristics held by evangelicals, there is also considerable diversity within the tradition.

One advantage of conceptualizing evangelicals in terms of belonging is that it facilitates recognition of evangelical Protestantism as a social group identity. A consistent finding in political science research is that the average American has relatively low levels of political knowledge (Delli Carpini and Keeter 1996). Rather than spending their time developing a sophisticated understanding of politics and policy, the public often turns to "heuristics," or logical shortcuts, to understand political phenomena (Popkin 1994; Sniderman, Brody, and Tetlock 1991). One particularly powerful heuristic is social identity. Voters evaluate parties (Campbell et al. 1960; Green, Palmquist, and Schickler 2002), candidates (Campbell, Green, and Layman 2011; Castle et al. 2017; Popkin 1994), and political issues (Kinder and Kam 2009; Sniderman, Brody, and Tetlock 1991) in terms of their relationship to and effect on a variety of social reference groups.

In the case of evangelicalism, the intense connection between evangelicalism and the Republican Party (and political conservatism) that was reinforced by the rise of the Christian Right in the 1970s and 1980s paved the way for a mass-level shift among evangelicals (e.g., Hunter 1991; Layman 2001). The Republican Party's adoption of cultural conservatism on issues like abortion made issue-based sorting possible for evangelicals concerned by the growing signs of sexual liberalism in the United States (Adams 1997; Killian and Wilcox 2008). The Democratic Party's embrace of cultural modernism, symbolized by the 1972 presidential candidacy of George McGovern, provided an out-group contrast that further sped the movement of evangelicals to the Republican Party (e.g., Layman 2001).

Another way of conceptualizing religion's influence on political behavior is in terms of behaving. Research has identified a growing gap on a number of measures of political behavior between those who are active participants in religion and those who belong to a tradition but are not as involved (Green 2010; Layman 2001; Layman and Green 2005; Smidt, Kellstedt, and Guth 2009). Religious commitment may affect political behavior for a variety of reasons. Those who attend religious services and are otherwise active in their faith are more likely to be exposed to political messages through church attendance (Guth et al. 1997; Olson 2009; Smidt 2004). Such individuals may also be more likely to develop social networks and civic skills that translate to political efficacy (Campbell 2004; Djupe and Gilbert 2009; Wald, Owen, and Hill 1988, 1990). Finally, drawing on findings that the parties are becoming increasingly polarized in terms of religious commitment, new evidence suggests that religious commitment may be becoming a social group identity in its own right. Republican candidates in particular may use religious language to build support among Republicans and social conservatives (Castle et al. 2017).

Finally, researchers might conceptualize religion in terms of religious beliefs. When writers use the terms "evangelical" and "born-again" interchangeably, they are employing a belief-based definition. Evangelicals hold a number of distinctive theological beliefs, including the importance of a personal conversion (often in the form of a "born-again" experience), a faith that the Bible is the authoritative Word of God, and a dedication to evangelism (Oldfield 1996; Smidt 2007, 2013). As I discuss throughout this book, many of these beliefs can become politically relevant given certain social conditions. For example, the evangelical tradition's stringent norms on sexual behavior are undoubtedly an important factor in evangelicalism's opposition to cultural issues such as abortion and gay marriage (e.g., Cook, Jelen, and Wilcox 1992; Jelen 2009). However, religious beliefs affect politics in terms of more than just social issues. Numerous works have tied various religious beliefs to attitudes on issues ranging from social welfare programs to foreign policy (see Guth 2009; Wilson 2009). Clearly, the multidimensional nature of religion creates numerous paths in which religion can influence politics (Castle 2018a; Leege and Kellstedt 1993; Smidt, Kellstedt, and Guth 2009).

Major Trends in Evangelicalism Today

Over the past two decades, scholars have identified several major trends that are radically altering the American religious landscape. One very important trend is that fewer Americans are associating themselves with organized religion (Castle and Schoettmer 2019; Hout and Fischer 2002; Putnam and Campbell 2010). This trend seems to be concentrated among Millennials, who are increasingly taking unconventional approaches to religion or abandoning religion altogether (Smith and Snell 2009; Wuthnow 2007). One reason for this may be the secularization that has affected all modern industrial nations. However, Michael Hout and Claude Fischer (2002) suggest that another important factor in the declining percentage of Americans who affiliate with religion is the increasingly close relationship between religion and political conservatism. In short, moderates and liberals are opting out of religion because their religious identity seems increasingly at odds with their political identity. This trend is evident among all generations, but it is particularly strong among younger Americans.

The effects of this trend are evident when looking at religious adherence over time. Figure I.1 shows, from the General Social Survey, 1972–2014 (Smith, Hout, and Marsden 2016), the percentage of respondents under thirty years of age who identify with the most common religious traditions in the United States: evangelical Protestant, mainline Protestant, black Protestant, Catholic, unaffiliated, and other faiths. To make the graph more readable, I limited the data to the time period from 1994 to 2014. From the graph, it is clear that the percentage of youth with no religious affiliation has grown steadily during this period, from 16 percent in 1994 to 33 percent in 2014. This decline has come primarily at the expense of mainline Protestantism, whose share of the youth religious market shrank from 10 percent to 5 percent, and Catholicism, whose share shrank from 32 percent to 24 percent. Evangelicals are also feeling the effects of the trend toward secularism: the percentage of evangelicals in the under-thirty population has fallen from 24 percent in 1994 to a low of 17 percent in 2014. Clearly, then, young evangelicals today are coming of age in a much different religious marketplace than previous generations.

What about the young evangelicals who are still involved in the faith? If moderates and liberals are leaving the church, it is possible that those mod-

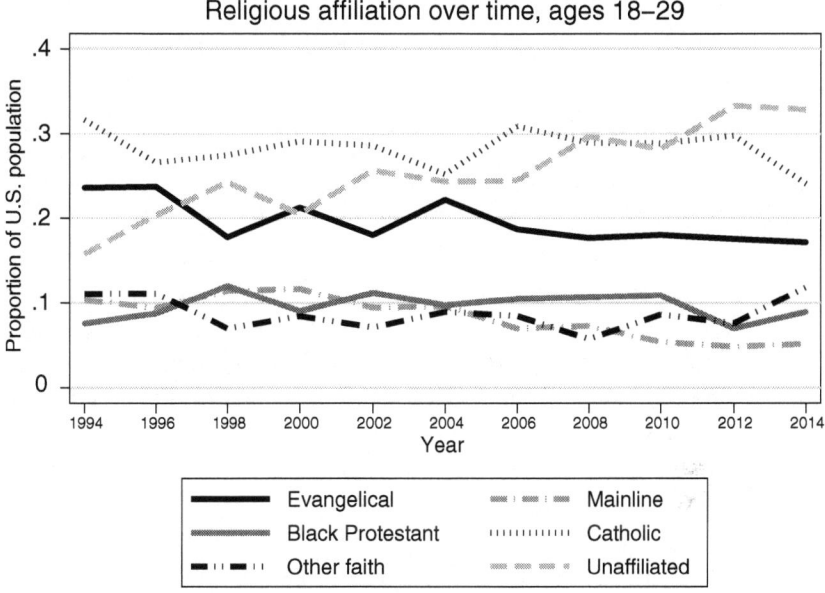

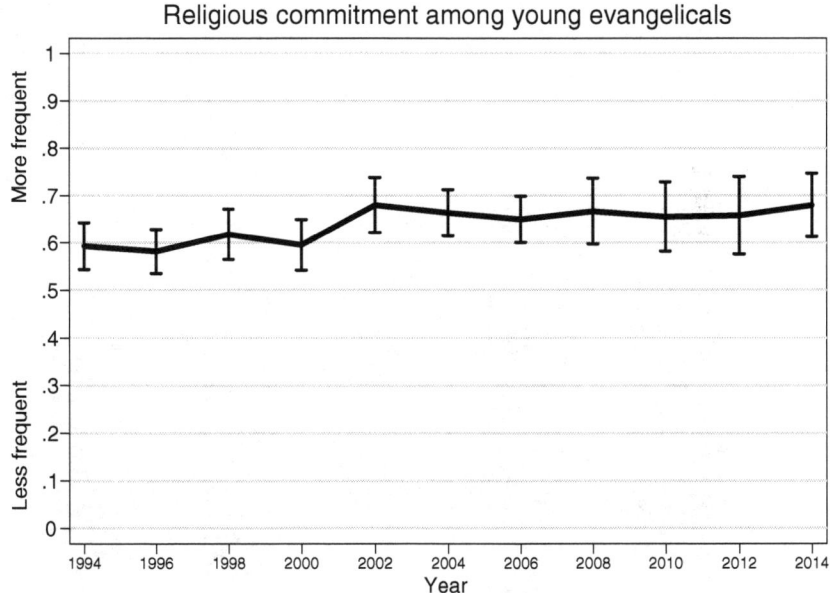

Figure I.1. Membership in religious traditions and religious commitment among young evangelicals.

Source: Weighted 1972–2014 General Social Survey.
Note: Error bars represent 95 percent confidence intervals.

erates and liberals who remain would reduce their level of commitment, thereby leading to a drop in the aggregate level of commitment. However, the data suggest that this is not the case. The bottom panel of Figure I.1 shows the mean religious commitment of evangelicals ages eighteen to twenty-nine over time, again using data from the General Social Survey.[3] Some movement is apparent in the results: religious commitment among young evangelicals bottomed out at .59 in 1996, and rose to .68 in 2002, likely due in part to the wave of religiosity that swept the country in the wake of the terrorist attacks of September 11, 2001. The mean religious commitment score for 2014 was nearly .68, essentially equaling the historical high point for this time period. In short, evidence suggests that among those young evangelicals who maintain their faith, their aggregate level of religious commitment is about the same as it has always been.

Another major trend is that American evangelicalism is becoming more racially and ethnically diverse. This should not be surprising, as America in general is becoming more diverse (Jones 2016). We can see this diversity in Figure I.2, which plots the racial diversity of evangelicals by age group using the 2016 Cooperative Congressional Election Study (CCES) (Ansolabehere and Schaffner 2017). While 95 percent of evangelicals ages sixty-five and older are white (non-Hispanic), that number falls to 83 percent among evangelicals ages eighteen to twenty-nine. The biggest source of the increasing

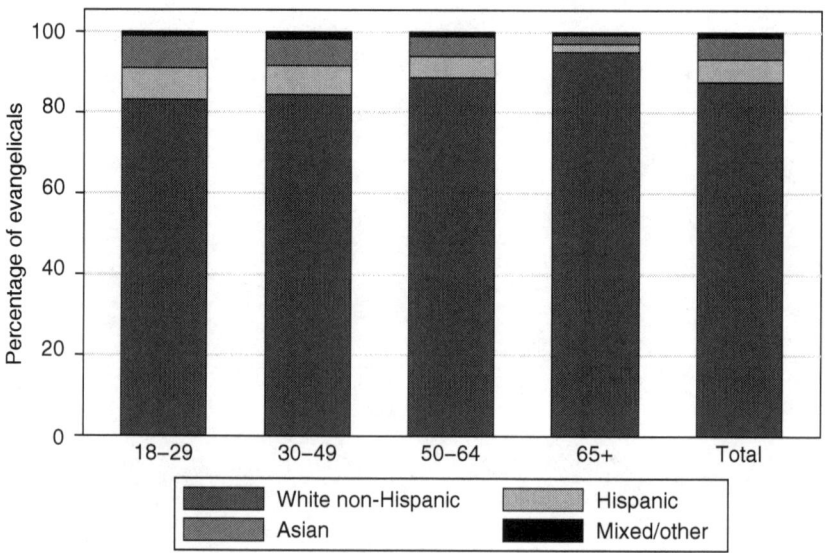

Figure I.2. Race/ethnicity among evangelicals by age group.
Source: Weighted 2016 Cooperative Congressional Election Study.

diversity is Hispanics, who make up just 2 percent of evangelicals sixty-five and older but 8 percent of evangelicals ages eighteen to twenty-nine. However, we also see about a 4 percent increase in the percentage of Asians and a slight increase among mixed-race individuals. Clearly, then, there is evidence of sociological change among young evangelicals. Young evangelicals are different from their parents in several ways, including growing up in a social context where evangelicals make up a smaller proportion of the population and where the evangelical tradition is more racially and ethnically diverse than it used to be.

The Politics of Young Evangelicals: Two Questions

Another important set of questions, addressed at the start of this chapter, concerns the political identities and issue attitudes of the youngest generation of evangelicals. Due in part to the multidimensional nature of religion, the relationship between evangelical identity and political attitudes has varied over time. While evangelicals were politically withdrawn for much of the 1930s and 1940s (Jelen 1991), the period from the 1970s to the present has seen evangelicals taking a much more active role in American politics (Hunter 1991; Putnam and Campbell 2010; Wilcox and Robinson 2010; Williams 2010). Mobilized by the growth of cultural modernism in American entertainment, media, law, politics, and public life, evangelicals became the backbone of the highly influential "New Christian Right" (Capps 1994; Leege et al. 2002; Martin 2005; Wilcox and Robinson 2010; Williams 2010). Highly committed evangelicals became an important part of the Republican Party's electoral coalition and were instrumental in the success of Ronald Reagan and George W. Bush, as well as in countless congressional, state, and local victories (e.g., Williams 2010). Thanks in part to the public visibility of the Christian Right and the prominence of evangelical candidates like George W. Bush and Sarah Palin, evangelicalism has become increasingly associated with the public image of the Republican Party and ideological conservatism in the minds of voters from all faith backgrounds (Campbell, Green, and Layman 2011; Layman 2001).

While this association between evangelicals and the Republican Party has become axiomatic in American politics, there is some question as to whether this connection is weakening among the youngest generation. Since 2006, a variety of popular commentators have in one way or another suggested that young evangelicals, those who fall into the Millennial generation, are substantially more liberal than previous generations. Commentators have suggested several potential types of change. First, observers have speculated that evangelicals are becoming more liberal in their positions on issues such as LGBT rights, poverty, the environment, and immigration (Dokoupil 2009; Wehner 2007). Second, observers have argued that evangelicals are de-emphasizing cultural issues like abortion and gay marriage and are instead embracing new issues like economic inequality, the environment, and immigration (Banerjee 2008; Harris 2008; Lee 2015; Murashko 2014). Finally, observers have speculated that young evangelicals are on the brink of abandoning their relationship with Republican Party (Edwards 2008; Zogoby 2009).

In academic terms, then, these journalistic accounts posit a "cohort effect." Scholars note that there are at least three possible ways in which time might influence public opinion: age effects, period effects, and cohort effects (Ryder 1965). Here, I use the hypothetical example of attitudes on war to help illustrate the differences between these three types of effects. Age effects occur when some age groups hold different positions than other age groups systematically over time. A typical example of age effects might be young people opposing war until they reach an age in which they are no longer eligible for the draft. Period effects occur when specific events in society at a particular point in time drive those living through the event to change their opinions, no matter their age or generation. For example, if television coverage of a war caused a drop in support for the war over time that was not concentrated among one age group or generation, that would be a period effect. Finally, cohort effects occur when a particular generation's common experiences inform their opinions. For example, if the generation of young people who turned eighteen during the time of a war remained antiwar throughout their lives as a result of the atrocities they saw on the battlefield, this would constitute a cohort effect.

This basic account leads to two important questions about young evangelicals. First, are young evangelicals' political beliefs changing? On the one hand, there are any number of important social dynamics that might be leading to change within the evangelical tradition. One of the most important changes is the continuing influence of modernization and secularization, which together decrease the public and private influence of religion and increase the reliance on science, technology, and bureaucracy. Another important change is the retirement or death of many of the leaders of the New Christian Right, including Jerry Falwell and Phyllis Schlafly, and the emergence of a new generation of evangelical leaders like Rick Warren and Joel Osteen who many say have a gentler, less abrasive rhetorical style. These changes are summarized further in the pages ahead.

On the other hand, political science theory gives us reason to be skeptical of any change. For example, given the emphasis on the relative consistency of party identity in the social-psychological tradition (Campbell et al. 1960; Green, Palmquist, and Schickler 2002), it would be surprising to find that young evangelicals are abandoning the tradition's deeply entrenched association with the Republican Party. In addition, past predictions of a more liberal generation of young evangelicals have generally been proven premature. A generation ago, James Davison Hunter (1987), the famous sociologist of religion, argued that young evangelicals were embracing theological liberalism. Calvin College political scientists James Penning and Corwin E. Smidt (2002) responded with an exhaustive profile showing that young evangelicals were as conservative as ever. Therefore, absent sufficient evidence, we should approach any claims of major change within the evangelical tradition with a healthy degree of skepticism.

This discussion leads naturally into a second, and perhaps even more interesting, question: If young evangelicals are changing, why? Are any changes we see driven by factors internal to the church, or are they driven by factors external to the church? Observers who posit a liberal-leaning cohort effect among young evangelicals disagree on the causes. In the previous generation of the debate over young evangelicals, Hunter (1987) argued that modernization and secularization were responsible for the liberalization of young evangelicals. Justin Farrell (2011) supports this narrative, arguing that a declining belief among young people that God is the source of moral authority is responsible for liberal trends among young evangelicals concerning their beliefs about pornography, cohabitation, premarital sex, and same-sex marriage. Others suggest that changes within the church, like turnover among religious elites and changing religious teachings on issues as diverse as gay marriage and the environment, are responsible for the change (Harris 2008; Mendenhall 2006; Vicari 2014a; Wear 2014).

Each of these questions could have important implications for American politics and society. If young evangelicals are becoming more liberal, it could change American politics for years to come. Despite the overwhelming Republican victories of 2014 and 2016, a long-term demographic analysis suggests that if present coalitions hold, the Democratic Party has the advantage in the long run. Whites are shrinking as a portion of the population, while racial minorities and Millennials are becoming a bigger part of the voting-age population. If young evangelicals are becoming more liberal, it would suggest that the Republican Party's long-term electoral fortunes are even more dire. Alternatively, if young Republicans are more or less as conservative as ever, it would suggest that the Republican Party might be able to focus on making incremental changes to its platform and/or constituency to remain competitive.

Likewise, the question of the source of any changes in opinion is deeply important. If the evangelical tradition is pushing members toward a more liberal perspective, it would represent an important shift from the last three decades of scholarship on religion and politics. On the other hand, if forces outside the evangelical tradition are causing any change we see, it might lead us to ask a different set of questions about the durability of the evangelical tradition in the face of social trends like secularization that have led to a breakdown of organized religion in other advanced democracies. Clearly, then, answering each of these questions is quite important for understanding the past, present, and future of American politics.

Answering the Two Questions with Social Science

Given the potential stakes, it should be surprising that to date there has been little academic research conducted on young evangelicals, and the few studies that exist yield somewhat contradictory findings. In a short research note, Buster Smith and Byron Johnson (2010) find that young evangelicals are similar to their older counterparts on issues including abortion, stem cell research, marijuana use, welfare spending, health care, and the Iraq War. Only on the environment did they find substantial evidence of liberalization among young evangelicals. However, their data are only cross-sectional, and therefore they cannot say whether young evangelicals are becoming more liberal over time. Farrell (2011) shows that young evangelicals are more liberal on same-sex marriage, premarital sex, cohabitating, and pornography. However, he finds that higher education, delayed marriage, and shifts in views on moral authority are the likely causes, rather than changes in religion itself. Most recently, Mikael Pelz and Corwin Smidt (2015) find evidence of consistency in young evangelicals' political identities and social issues but some evidence of change on nonsocial issues, like the environment, foreign policy, and government aid to the needy. Again, though, their data are entirely cross-sectional. Thus, while these works serve an important purpose in beginning to test the empirical claims being made in this debate, this scholarship highlights the need for both additional data as well as a more unified theory of public opinion among evangelicals that can help explain why we see change in some instances and continued conservatism in others.

To provide a more robust explanation of trends in public opinion among young evangelicals, several advances are necessary. First, it is clear that more data are needed to develop a more complete understanding of young evangelicals' political attitudes. Many of the stories on the liberalization of young evangelicals have relied on observations from political elites, field studies of particular events (such as the gathering of young evangelicals in New York City reported on in Harris 2008), or at best, cross-sectional data (e.g., Smith and Johnson 2010). In this book, in addition to cross-sectional data, I employ time-series cross-sectional data, including the General Social Survey

(Smith, Hout, and Marsden 2016), to examine how evangelicals' attitudes have changed over time. However, an important limitation of time-series cross-sectional data is that it cannot help us understand the causes of any observed change. Therefore, I also use panel data, including the 2010–2014 Cooperative Congressional Election Study Panel Survey, to test certain aspects of my argument. In addition, I supplement the quantitative analyses with a series of forty-two semistructured hour-long interviews with evangelical college students conducted at five universities in 2014. These interviews help provide context for the quantitative data.

Second, the existing scholarship has not attempted to explain why we see stability among evangelicals on some issues and change on others. Thus, any social scientific investigation into public opinion among young evangelicals has to break new theoretical ground if it is to help sort out the truth about their views. In particular, a satisfactory theory must be able to (1) explain why we see evidence of change on some issues but continued conservatism on others as well as (2) adjudicate between "change from the outside" and "change from the inside" to help us understand the likely source of any shift in opinion. Answering these questions is crucial to developing a fuller understanding of trends in public opinion among young evangelicals. In Chapter 1, I introduce just such a theory.

PART I

Trends in Public Opinion among Young Evangelicals

1

A Subcultural Theory of Public Opinion among Evangelicals

The Introduction begins this book by asking two questions. First, are young evangelicals becoming more liberal? Second, if they are, is that change driven by factors internal to or external to evangelicalism? In this chapter, I develop a theory that helps provide answers to these and other questions. I begin by drawing on the notion of the evangelical tradition as a subculture (Gay, Ellison, and Powers 1996; Oldfield 1996; Smith et al. 1998). I apply this concept to public opinion by emphasizing that the evangelical subculture takes part in four processes that together give it the potential to exert a substantial influence on public opinion: building evangelical social group identity, promoting the distinctive beliefs of the subculture, discrediting certain aspects of mainstream culture, and delivering explicitly political messages. However, I qualify this subcultural theory of public opinion among evangelicals by emphasizing that we should expect the evangelical subculture to exert a greater impact on public opinion (1) on issues that have been central to evangelicalism's subcultural identity and (2) among those who are most committed to and immersed in the evangelical subculture.

Finally, I emphasize that the evangelical subculture takes a particular interest in socializing young people into its religious, social, and political beliefs. Churches, families, youth groups, evangelical colleges, and evangelical student organizations on secular college campuses help communicate political messages to young evangelicals. Therefore, we should expect this theory to help explain patterns in the political attitudes of young evangelicals. This chapter explains each element of the theory in greater detail, laying the groundwork for empirical hypothesis testing in subsequent chapters.

Evangelicalism as a Subculture

An important step in building a theory of public opinion among evangelicals is recognizing what differentiates evangelicalism from other religious traditions. As the Introduction indicates, theological differences are one of the most important sources of boundaries between the major religious traditions in America today (Kellstedt, Green, Guth, et al. 1996; Leege and Kellstedt 1993; Smidt, Kellstedt, and Guth 2009). One of the key theological beliefs of evangelicals is that the Bible is the Word of God and should be taken as authority (Smidt 2007). In fact, many evangelicals argue that the Bible is meant to be taken literally, word for word. Another distinguishing characteristic of evangelicals is theological exclusivism (Smidt 2007). At a time when increasing numbers of Americans believe people of all religions are capable of reaching an afterlife (Putnam and Campbell 2010), evangelicals remain more restrictive on this question. Evangelicals also tend to emphasize a personal conversion experience, which some might describe as being "born again" (Smidt 2007). In some charismatic or Pentecostal brands of evangelicalism, this might even include speaking in tongues (see Roberts 2004). Finally, and perhaps most obviously, evangelicals emphasize the sharing of their faith (Smidt 2007).

Beyond theology, another key factor that distinguishes evangelicalism is its relationship with culture and mainstream cultural values. Scholars have characterized evangelical Protestantism as a subculture (e.g., Gay, Ellison, and Powers 1996; Oldfield 1996; Smith et al. 1998). Although the term *subcultural* may have a negative connotation to some members of the mass public, the scholarly understanding of a subculture is simply "a cultural group within a larger culture, often having beliefs or interests at variance with those of the larger culture" ("Subculture," n.d.). Sociologists have long been interested in subcultures and the values that set them apart from mainstream culture (e.g., Haenfler 2013). Sociologists have identified bikers, punk rockers, rappers, and gay men as other examples of subcultures (e.g., the readings in Gelder 2005; Hebdige 1979). Applying the subcultural label helps remind us that theological beliefs are not the only difference between evangelicalism and other religious traditions. Rather, evangelicals are also distinctive for their longstanding history of pushing back against accepted ideas in the mainstream culture that they perceive as violating their core values.

Evangelicalism's subcultural roots are evident throughout its history. Corwin E. Smidt is remarkably accurate in his observation that "evangelical Protestantism can be viewed both to have preceded mainline Protestantism as well as to have arisen out of it" (2007, 32). Although the split between the mainline and evangelical Protestant churches occurred gradually between the Civil War and the 1920s, signs of a subculture are evident throughout the history of Protestantism. Indeed, Martin Luther's fateful decision to share his Ninety-five Theses may be understood as the first subcultural action of Protestantism.[1] By publicly challenging the hegemony of the Catholic tradition, Luther was both engaging in society and criticizing widely accepted ideas that conflicted with his understanding of the Bible, as exemplified through the reformers' doctrine of *sola scriptura* (by "Scripture alone"). Thus, a subcultural element has been present in evangelicalism from its inception.

As Protestantism developed, this subcultural impulse on the evangelical side of the tradition was evident in some of its most important milestones. The Enlightenment's emphasis on reason and scientific ways of knowing led to a liberalization of religious doctrine among Puritans in the late seventeenth and early eighteenth centuries. During the 1730s, evangelical preachers responded with the religious movement known as the First Great Awakening. Influential preachers like George Whitefield and Jonathan Edwards delivered emotional sermons that reminded listeners of their need for personal salvation (Noll 1983). Perhaps the most famous work of the First Great Awakening was Edwards's "Sinners in the Hands of an Angry God," which argued God's wrath was building toward sinners, and nothing could save them from hell but the acceptance of Christ and conversion to Christianity (Kidd 2008). The emphasis on "New Birth" or a born-again experience in the works of Edwards, Whitefield, and other Great Awakeners is typical of the evangelical subcultural style of challenging accepted doctrines that contradict the theological and social core values of evangelicalism.

Likewise, the Second Great Awakening was wrapped up in fears that religion was losing its power, and Americans, especially those living on the frontier, were becoming religiously complacent. The solution, from the evangelical perspective, was to develop tools that included itinerant preachers, camp meetings, and emotional sermons in an effort to rekindle the belief in the importance of conversion experiences and individual salvation (Hatch 1989). Again, we see a pattern of both engagement with the dominant culture and criticism of certain accepted doctrines within that culture. In part because of the success of the movement, the evangelical strain of American Protestantism surpassed the popularity of mainline denominations between the Second Great Awakening and the early 1900s.

The gradual split between mainline and evangelical Protestantism became clearer and more well defined between 1900 and 1930. During this period, American religions were reacting to modernization, including an increasing reliance on science (such as Darwinian evolution) and technology. Many of the denominations that would form the foundation of mainline Protestantism incorporated aspects of modernization into their theologies, including emphasizing the poetic qualities of the account of creation in Genesis. They also embraced the Social Gospel, which encouraged Christians to take on social problems like poverty, alcoholism, and working conditions (Evans 2017). The evangelical tradition, on the other hand, took a much harder line against modernization. One key factor in this split was the publication of *The Fundamentals: A Testimony to the Truth*, a twelve-volume set that laid out the basics of a fundamentalist version of Christianity, from 1910 to 1915 (Marsden 1980). *The Fundamentals* argued for Biblical literalism and personal piety, and attacked the perceived threats of evolution and Catholicism, among others. Following these theological controversies, denominations like the Northern Baptists and the Presbyterians endured a series of painful conflicts between fundamentalist and modernist factions for control of the denomination. Ultimately, many of these conflicts resulted in the evangelical factions leaving the established traditions and founding their own separate denominations (FitzGerald 2017). This sorting effect made the theologies of both the long-established and new denominations clearer and more homogeneous.

The symbolic defining moment of the mainline-evangelical split was the Scopes "Monkey Trial" of 1925. Evangelical and fundamentalist Christians felt a tremendous cultural threat in response to Darwin's evolutionary account of creation, and they answered with new laws, like the Butler Act in Tennessee, which outlawed the teaching of human evolution in public schools within the state. The Butler Act led to the famous Scopes Trial, in which teacher John Scopes was tried for having lectured on evolution in a biology class. The trial attracted major media attention to the small town of Dayton, Tennessee, in part because both sides secured celebrity attorneys: former presidential hopeful and Secretary of State William Jennings Bryan argued for the prosecution, and Clarence Darrow joined the defense (Larson 2006). Members of the media, like journalist H. L. Mencken, ridiculed the fundamentalist camp and, in many historical accounts, played a role in evangelicals demobilizing from politics in the decades after the trial (e.g., Jelen 1991). Again, the Scopes Trial is characteristic of the evangelicals' subcultural political style: they were engaged in mainstream culture but advocated values that conflicted with those of mainstream society.

Between the Scopes Trial and the 1960s, evangelicals focused their efforts internally, creating institutions to help maintain a robust religious tradition in an increasingly secular society (Oldfield 1996). In particular, evangelicalism embraced a number of trends and technologies that allowed it to both achieve its theological mission and strengthen its role in the religious marketplace. For example, evangelical leaders were early adopters of both radio and television as ways of reaching wider audiences with their religious teachings. Evangelicals like Walter Maier, Aimee Semple McPherson, and Charles Fuller dominated religious radio, often with more entertaining programming and sounder business practices than their mainline counterparts (Schultze 1988). Later, televangelist preachers like Billy Graham, Oral Roberts, Jimmy Swaggart, Jim and Tammy Faye Bakker, Jerry Falwell, and Pat Robertson built enormous followings and enormous fortunes through their television ministries (Capps 1994; Hadden 1993; Hadden and Shupe 1988). An added benefit of these institutions in the eyes of many theologically conservative evangelicals was that they could provide the entertainment factor of modern technology while at the same time avoiding exposure to some of the objectionable content found in secular entertainment.

In the second half of the twentieth century, this new, stronger subculture paved the way for evangelicals to reengage in American politics (Oldfield 1996). As modernization and secularization became prevalent throughout American law, politics, entertainment, and culture (e.g., Apter 1967; Hunter 1991), evangelicals and other religious traditionalists increasingly perceived threats to their values. For example, court cases like *Engel v. Vitale* (1962), which ruled teacher-led prayers in public schools unconstitutional, and *Roe v. Wade* (1973), which found a constitutional right to abortion rooted in the privacy protections of the Bill of Rights, were perceived as evidence that the Supreme Court was "attacking" the traditional place of religion in public life (e.g., Castle 2015b; Dierenfield 2007; Hunter 1991; Irons 2007; Lebo 2008; Smith et al. 1998). Evangelicals responded to this growing threat in dual fashion. First, in the period from the 1960s to the present, they continued to strengthen the evangelical subculture. Second, and perhaps more important, they became active participants in American party politics.

Building Up the Subculture

The evangelical effort to strengthen the subculture was driven by a desire to insulate insiders from many of the threats in secular culture. Given the frequent controversy surrounding pop/rock artists, from Elvis to the Rolling Stones, it should come as no surprise that music was one of the most noticeable areas where this buildup occurred. The new genre of contemporary Christian music (CCM) sprang up in the 1960s. CCM artists combined modern guitar- and piano-oriented pop/rock with family-friendly and/

or explicitly Christian lyrical content. In the 1980s and 1990s, evangelical musicians such as Amy Grant, Sandi Patty, Michael W. Smith, and Steven Curtis Chapman had numerous hit albums. At the same time, Christian music expanded into the hard rock and heavy metal genres, with bands like Stryper, dc Talk, and P.O.D. providing evangelical alternatives for heavier rock audiences. In the late 1990s and 2000s, artists like Chris Tomlin, Casting Crowns, Matt Redman, and Third Day defined the next generation of CCM, in part thanks to extensive play on Christian radio networks like K-LOVE (Du Noyer 2003; Howard and Streck 1999; Powell 2002).

More recently, the evangelical subculture has turned toward film and television. Sherwood Pictures, an evangelical film studio, began producing evangelical-flavored features, such as *Facing the Giants* (2006), *Fireproof* (2008), and *Courageous* (2011), that examine cultural issues, including divorce and pornography, through subcultural lenses. One of the most well-known evangelical films in recent years is *God's Not Dead* (2014), produced by the evangelical studio Pure Flix Entertainment. The movie tells the story of an evangelical college student named Josh. His college philosophy professor challenges Josh and his classmates to avow God's death or else fail the class. Josh maintains God's existence throughout the film. The characters engage in a series of academic debates over creation and evolution that address the relationship between Christians and society in a decidedly subcultural fashion. *God's Not Dead* was the highest grossing independent film of 2014 and spawned several other films from the studio, including 2016's *God's Not Dead 2* (Graham 2015).

Children were not left out, either. Early cartoon series like Hanna-Barbera's *Greatest Adventure: Stories from the Bible* paved the way for modern franchises like *Veggie Tales*, which retells both biblical and secular stories in a Christian light, using animated vegetable characters like Bob the Tomato and Larry the Cucumber in a style similar to that of the more secular series *Wishbone*. Such DVDs can sometimes be found in secular stores but more often in Family Christian Stores or one of the many Christian gift store chains.

The evangelical subculture has also grown to include theme parks like the Creation Museum in Petersburg, Kentucky, established in 2001. This museum and theme park, which is operated by the creationism-promoting organization Answers in Genesis, includes exhibits that advocate a young earth creationist worldview, including depictions of man walking together with dinosaurs and Bible-based criticisms of evolution. In 2016, Answers in Genesis opened the Ark Encounter, a second theme park that features a full-scale replica of Noah's Ark. These examples show how, across a variety of industries, evangelicals seek to create a subculture that insulates members from many of the perceived dangers of the dominant secular culture.

A side effect of this buildup of the evangelical subculture was the continued vitality of the evangelical tradition throughout the latter half of the twentieth century. As sociologist Christian Smith and colleagues (1998) explain it, evangelicalism has retained its members better than the mainline or Catholic traditions because its subcultural status gives evangelicals a sense of embattlement. According to Smith and colleagues (1998), the distinctive values of the evangelical tradition and the sense that those values are under attack have created both a strong in-group identity and several important negative reference groups (liberals, secularists, and so on). This fosters unity among evangelicals and provides them with reason to maintain high levels of religious, social, and political activity in the tradition to avoid falling victim to threats from the secular world.

Reaching Out

As part of this buildup of the evangelical subculture, evangelical leaders also designed institutions to reach out and engage the broader culture, including political institutions. While none of these organizations were exclusively evangelical, most of their leadership was made up of evangelicals, and evangelicals were their largest constituents. In 1977, psychologist James Dobson founded Focus on the Family, an advocacy organization that emphasized a conservative perspective on cultural issues, including abortion, pornography, divorce, LGBT rights, and stem cell research. Dobson also founded the Family Research Council, Focus on the Family's lobbying arm, which became a separate entity in 1992. In 1979, Southern Baptist preacher Jerry Falwell founded the Moral Majority, again centered around conservative positions on church and state, abortion, homosexuality, and the Equal Rights Amendment. This first phase of the New Christian Right stalled out in the late 1980s, partially as a result of interdenominational tensions inherent in an effort to unite evangelicals and other religious traditions. In 1989, televangelist and failed presidential candidate Pat Robertson created the Christian Coalition. Led by the ambitious and savvy Ralph Reed, the Christian Coalition was an influential part of American politics in the 1990s (Martin 2005). The Christian Coalition distributed voter guides, led grassroots mobilization efforts, and helped set the agenda among Christian conservatives. These New Christian Right organizations also became breeding grounds for both activists and state- and local-level candidates. By taking over school boards and state legislatures, evangelicals achieved success in local politics throughout much of the country (Oldfield 1996). In light of the previous section, this discussion highlights the fact that while the New Christian Right of the 1980s and 1990s was more politically sophisticated than prior evangelical movements (Wilcox 1988), it fits into a familiar pattern of subcultural engagement when widely accepted ideas in society pose a threat to the core values of the subculture.

Also founded during this period were a number of organizations that promote the teaching of creationism and/or intelligent design. Creationism is a rejection of evolution as the origin of human life and an accompanying belief that a supernatural being created the earth. In contrast, most versions of intelligent design accept at least part of Darwin's account of evolution but hold that evolution has been guided by an intelligent supernatural being (Scott 1997). Like the New Christian Right organizations, the organizations associated with creationism and intelligent design are not exclusively populated by evangelicals. Nevertheless, evangelicals are probably the most important constituency within each group. Answers in Genesis, led by Australian-born fundamentalist Ken Ham, is probably the most famous organization promoting creationism. Besides running the Creation Museum and Ark Encounter, Ham's organization publishes *Answers* magazine, *Answers Research Journal*, vacation Bible school curricula, and a variety of other works defending the creationist perspective. Perhaps the best-known organization defending intelligent design is the Discovery Institute, a Seattle-based think tank. The Discovery Institute runs the Teach the Controversy campaign, which advocates for teaching intelligent design as an alternative to evolution in the classroom. The Discovery Institute also runs the Center for Science and Culture, which funds research into intelligent design–related projects. Like the New Christian Right organizations, the creationism/intelligent design organizations specialize in both engaging with the secular culture and pushing back on areas (like evolution) that conflict with the evangelical subculture's core values.

While politically conservative organizations largely defined evangelical politics during this period, the subculture also saw the rise of more theologically liberal organizations. For example, in 1971, a small intentional community of students at Trinity Evangelical Divinity School began publishing *The Post-American*, which later became the monthly magazine *Sojourners*. Sojourners, the American Christian social justice organization, advocates on both a broader set of issues and takes a far more liberal perspective than the Christian Right. The organization's most emphasized issues include peace, global awareness, health care reform, economic justice, and a consistent ethic of life that encompasses issues ranging from abortion to immigration to capital punishment. Founder Jim Wallis, known for a series of influential books including *God's Politics* (2006), has also served on Barack Obama's Advisory Council on Faith-Based and Neighborhood Partnerships. While the organization's tone is distinctive from that of the Christian Right, Sojourners shares the evangelical subculture's emphasis on both engagement and criticism of secular culture. In short, then, the notion of an evangelical subculture can help explain the social and political behavior of evangelicals. The concept of an evangelical subculture can also help us understand public opinion among evangelicals.

A Subcultural Theory of Public Opinion among Evangelicals

Any effort to understand public opinion among young evangelicals must be rooted in a general theory of public opinion. Early studies of public opinion found that most Americans have relatively low levels of political sophistication. In particular, many Americans do not think about politics in left-right ideological terms (Converse 1964). The mass public also has relatively low levels of factual knowledge about government and current events (Delli Carpini and Keeter 1996). To make up for their lack of knowledge, individuals use a variety of psychological shortcuts, or "heuristics," including partisanship, to make political decisions (Campbell et al. 1960; Popkin 1994; Sniderman, Brody, and Tetlock 1991).

Building on this foundation, political scientist John Zaller's (1992) receive-accept-sample (RAS) model provides a general theory of public opinion, asserting that most people possess more considerations on a given political issue than they can efficiently use to develop and maintain political attitudes (Zaller 1992; Zaller and Feldman 1992). Thus, when answering survey questions or otherwise articulating political attitudes, individuals sample a few ideas from the universe of considerations they have been exposed to. Those considerations that have been accessed more often or more recently are more likely be sampled again the next time a respondent answers a political question (Adkins and Castle 2014; Arceneaux and Kolodny 2009; Mondak 1993; Nelson and Kinder 1996; Zaller 1992; Zaller and Feldman 1992). Thus, understanding public opinion among young evangelicals means understanding the unique combination of messages, sources, and issue salience that they have been exposed to.

The subcultural underpinnings of evangelicalism developed throughout this chapter can help us explain and predict what messages evangelicals may have been exposed to and therefore help us understand public opinion among young evangelicals. In particular, applying subcultural theory to the study of public opinion among evangelicals can help us see the myriad ways in which evangelicalism might impact public opinion by altering the salience of various considerations among adherents.

The evangelical subculture takes part in four processes that together give it the potential to influence the political identities and attitudes of adherents.

The first of these is *generating and maintaining social group identity*. Scholars of religion have long understood the importance of "plausibility structures" and identity building in maintaining participation and belief orthodoxy among members (Berger 1967; Berger and Luckmann 1966; Roberts 2004). However, research suggests that identity building is politically important, too. A crucial step in both the sociological and social-psychological models of political attitudes is the development of a social group identity, in part because such an identity serves as a heuristic in identifying which parties or candidates the voter is most similar to (Berelson, Lazarsfeld, and McPhee 1954; Green, Palmquist, and Schickler 2002; Lewis-Beck et al. 2008). In terms of the RAS model of public opinion, those who identify as evangelicals are more likely to hold an evangelical worldview and draw on evangelical considerations when expressing political identities and attitudes.

The evangelical tradition has a number of mechanisms to build group identity. Churches are one key source of identity-building opportunity. The mere act of gathering together weekly in a community allows for the formation of belief in core doctrines and, subsequently, group identity (e.g., Wald, Owen, and Hill 1990). Many churches offer activities like Bible study groups, Sunday schools, book clubs, prayer breakfasts, and social events that help members build a Christian identity. Various ceremonial institutions also build evangelical social group identity. Baptism ceremonies, especially the adult baptisms favored by many evangelical churches, are a very public way of symbolically declaring one's membership in the evangelical tradition. Many churches, especially in more liturgically traditional religious families, like Lutheranism, recite a doctrinal statement like the Apostles' Creed, which includes an admission of belief. Worship music, an important part of modern evangelical services (Smidt 2007), often includes theological/political proclamations about belonging to and obeying God. During holidays like Christmas and Easter, evangelical families might reinforce their evangelical identity through actions like displaying manger scenes, exchanging presents, and reading the Christmas story from the Bible. Together, these actions help develop evangelical identity and therefore raise the probability that adherents will draw on evangelical considerations when forming and articulating political attitudes.

A second way evangelicalism affects public opinion is by *discrediting certain cultural trends that conflict with the tradition's core values*. Indeed, this process is central to evangelicalism's continued status as a subculture (Gay, Ellison, and Powers 1996; Smith et al. 1998). As previously discussed, at various times, the evangelical tradition has taken issue with both prevailing religious doctrine and social doctrines, such as Darwinian evolution, secularization, cultural modernism, and even ideological liberalism (e.g., Hunter

1991; Wuthnow 1988). Over time, the mechanisms used to discredit culture have varied. As we would expect, the activities and teachings of local congregations have played an important role (Smith et al. 1998). The leaders of the New Christian Right, including Jerry Falwell and Pat Robertson, made effective use of television and other media sources to communicate their criticisms of the larger culture (e.g., Capps 1994). This process relates to the RAS theory of public opinion because it suggests that evangelicalism may serve as a "perceptual screen," discrediting certain secular considerations and thereby reducing the probability that adherents will draw on such considerations in the opinion formation process.

The third way that the evangelical subculture impacts public opinion is through *instilling its own distinctive beliefs/core values* on adherents and otherwise promoting them in society. Sociologists and political scientists have identified numerous distinctive beliefs of the evangelical tradition. Many of these beliefs are drawn from the foundation of evangelical theology, including a belief that the Bible is the authoritative Word of God and an emphasis on personal conversion experiences and evangelism (e.g., Smidt 2007). Although these beliefs are not political in and of themselves, they may become considerations when respondents form attitudes about political issues. For example, when an evangelical values the Bible as authority, he or she is more likely to take biblical principles into account when forming attitudes about an issue like the environment. Thus, we would expect that public opinion among evangelicals would be consistent over time because many of these distinctive beliefs are deeply embedded in evangelicalism's group identity and distinctiveness.

Finally, the evangelical subculture may impact public opinion by *delivering explicitly political messages*. When churches, religious leaders, fellow adherents, or institutions within the evangelical subculture take sides on political issues, evangelicals may incorporate that information into the available considerations.

One mechanism for communicating political messages is generally perceptible norms. As noted earlier, the social identities of both liked and disliked groups can serve as heuristics to help voters sort into parties and issue positions (Green, Palmquist, and Schickler 2002; Kinder and Kam 2009; Popkin 1994; Sniderman, Brody, and Tetlock 1991). For example, the mass public recognizes that evangelicals and very religious people are an important part of the Republican coalition, and voters assume that evangelical or highly religious candidates are more Republican and conservative (Adkins et al. 2013; Castle et al. 2017; Campbell, Green, and Layman 2011; McDermott 2009). This social recognition of a linkage between evangelicalism and conservatism may allow otherwise politically unknowledgeable evangelicals to sort into the "socially correct" positions.

Local churches are a second important source of political cues, in part because that is how most people engage with their religious traditions (e.g., Djupe and Gilbert 2009; McDaniel 2008; Smith 2008). Local churches communicate norms in a variety of ways. Most explicitly, some churches have institutional requirements that would prevent LGBT individuals or openly pro-choice people from becoming full members.[2] Many others express their pro-life stance through supporting pregnancy crisis centers and maintaining funds for expectant mothers. Still others send delegations to March for Life (a national anti-abortion parade) or celebrate anti-abortion events, like Sanctity of Human Life Sunday. However, churches do not just connect their values to politics on cultural issues. For example, many churches host food pantries or thrift stores to help the economically disadvantaged. The social interaction that occurs in local churches creates opportunities for transmitting political attitudes and generating civic skills that translate to political engagement (Djupe and Gilbert 2009; McDaniel 2008; Olson 2009; Putnam 2000; Putnam and Campbell 2010; Verba, Schlozman, and Brady 1995; Wald, Owen, and Hill 1988, 1990).

A third source of explicitly political cues may be religious leaders at both the national and local levels. As previously noted, the media played an important role in communicating the political attitudes of nationally visible evangelical leaders, like Jerry Falwell and Pat Robertson (e.g., Capps 1994; Martin 2005; Williams 2010). While more recent celebrity pastors may have been willing to speak out on issues like the environment, AIDS, and poverty, they have not totally given up on talking about cultural issues. For example, in 2008, Rick Warren famously told the members of his church in a video, "If you believe what the Bible says about marriage, you need to support Proposition 8" (Ford and Strasser 2012). Warren is also staunchly pro-life on abortion. In 2013, he garnered much media attention when he tweeted, "Planned Parenthood is the McDonalds of abortion. It's the #1 baby killing franchise" (Clark 2013).

Religious leaders at the local level are just as influential. Sermons and other interactions with congregants offer religious leaders a chance to communicate political doctrines (Guth et al. 1997; Olson 2009; Smidt 2004). Clergy from evangelical denominations like the Wisconsin Evangelical Lutheran Synod, Independent Baptists, Foursquare Church, and Assembly of God are among the most conservative in the country, according to the study by Eitan Hersh and Gabrielle Malina (2017) on the partisan politics of 130,000 American religious leaders. Furthermore, the data from this study show a strong relationship between the political attitudes of clergy and the political attitudes of laypeople. That conservatism carries over to cultural issues in particular: research has demonstrated that evangelical clergy are more likely to emphasize issues like abortion and homosexuality compared to their mainline counterparts (Guth et al. 1997; Smidt 2004). Thus, those who are immersed in the evangelical subculture may receive explicitly political messages through a variety of mechanisms.

Returning to the RAS theory of public opinion, this suggests that evangelicalism's emphasis on core values makes members more likely to draw on these considerations when forming and expressing political attitudes. Thus, the central claim of my subcultural theory of public opinion among evangelicals is that *by instilling evangelical group identity, discrediting certain ideas within mainstream culture, instilling its own distinctive beliefs/core values among members, and sending explicitly political messages, the evangelical subculture has the potential to affect public opinion among members.*

However, research on public opinion suggests that the evangelical subculture is unlikely to exert an impact on all issues equally. While evangelicalism might influence public opinion among adherents, we would still expect considerations from the dominant (secular) culture to influence evangelicals, too. After all, the subcultural perspective helps us recognize that evangelicals are still engaged in the culture and therefore are likely to be exposed to secular issue considerations in their day-to-day lives. The key to my subcultural theory of public opinion is that, at least in some cases, we would expect to see that evangelicalism insulates members from the full effect of those secular considerations.

My theory can help us generate hypotheses about where we see and where we do not see change in public opinion among evangelicals. Because the average American does not think about politics ideologically (Converse 1964), he or she also does not spend a great deal of independent time applying religious values to political issues (Layman and Green 2005). This means that it is unlikely the average American evangelical has thought through how evangelicalism's distinctive beliefs and core values apply to every individual political issue. A more likely scenario is that evangelicals, like other Americans, rely on both elites and social group images as heuristics to understand both issue positions and issue salience (Gilens and Murakawa 2002; Kinder and Kam 2009; Popkin 1994; Sniderman, Brody, and Tetlock 1991; Zaller 1990, 1994). This leads to what I refer to as my issue hypothesis: *the evangelical subculture should exert a disproportionately large impact on issues that have been historically important to the identity of evangelicalism.* In Chapter 2, I argue that Republicanism and political conservatism, as well as conservative positions on cultural issues like abortion and gay marriage, have become an increasingly important part of evangelicalism's distinctive identity. In contrast, I argue that while evangelicals have historically taken conservative positions on issues such as poverty, the environment, immigration, and foreign policy, these issues have not been all that important to evangelicalism's identity.

In fact, it may even benefit evangelicalism to allow some liberalization on these noncentral issues. In a political version of the classic "pick your battles" strategy, it might not benefit a subculture to be politically distinctive on every issue, or else the subculture risks losing its advantage in the religious marketplace by making the costs of membership too high. Subcultures depend on having some elements in common with the broader culture; after all, they have to be engaged in it on a daily basis. Therefore, subcultures may find that a more successful strategy is to highlight a handful of issues that create political distinctiveness and a sense of embattlement to provide an advantage in the religious marketplace, but not so many issues that recruitment and retention become challenging.

Another factor that might condition evangelicalism's impact on public opinion is the growing importance of religious commitment. As noted in the Introduction, religion is a multidimensional concept, composed of "believing," "behaving," and "belonging" (Kellstedt et al. 1996). For much of American history, belonging was the most politically relevant of these factors (e.g., Wilson 2007). The Whig and Republican parties were made up largely of Protestants, while the Democratic Party was made up of Catholics, Jews, and Southern white evangelicals (Berelson, Lazarsfeld, and McPhee 1954; Kleppner 1970, 1979). However, in the 1970s and 1980s, the United States underwent a period of religious restructuring in which religious beliefs (orthodoxy) and behavior (commitment) became more relevant (Hunter 1991; Wuthnow 1988). During this period, differences between those with high and low levels of commitment within the same denomination became much starker. The end result was a new religious cleavage in which the Republican Party was made up of highly committed and culturally orthodox evangelicals, mainline Protestants, and Catholics—whereas the Democratic Party was made up of Jews, black Protestants, seculars, and less committed and culturally modernist evangelicals, mainliners, and Catholics (Hunter 1991; Layman 2001; Smidt, Kellstedt, and Guth 2009).

The increasing importance of religious commitment suggests that we should not expect the subculture to influence all evangelical identifiers to the same degree. Zaller's RAS theory emphasizes the importance of both (1) the balance of considerations and (2) the recency of considerations in forming political opinions and answering survey questions. Reason suggests that those who are more immersed in the subculture are more likely to be familiar with partisan images of evangelicals, to identify with candidates who use religious language, to be exposed to religious messages that discredit culture, and to hear direct messages from religious leaders about political issues like abortion (e.g., Guth et al. 1997; Smith et al. 1998). Thus, those who are engaged within the subculture are likely to have received more subcultural messages over time, and are also likely to have received subcultural messages more recently than their less engaged counterparts. This leads to my commitment hypothesis: *the evangelical subculture's influence on public opinion will be the strongest among those individuals who are most engaged within the subculture.*

The Subculture and Young Evangelicals

Any subculture has an incentive to socialize young people so that they pass on its core values to the next generation. Political scientists have long understood the importance of early-life political socialization in the formation of political identities and attitudes (Campbell 2002; Campbell et al. 1960; Pearson-Merkowitz and Gimpel 2009; Sears and Levy 2003). Political scientists also recognize that partisan attitudes are generally stable over time, especially once measurement error is accounted for (Campbell et al. 1960; Green, Palmquist, and Schickler 2002). Thus, it is particularly important for evangelicals to socialize their youngest members into the tradition to maintain continuity of public opinion within the tradition. In this section, I argue that in addition to the general mechanisms for opinion transmission already highlighted, the evangelical tradition makes use of a series of institutions, including families and evangelical schools, colleges, and clubs on secular college campuses, specifically to ensure opinion continuity among younger members.

One important mechanism for socialization is the family. Political science suggests that families are effective agents of political socialization, particularly when the parents are highly politicized, as is the case with many evangelicals in the post–New Christian Right era (Beck and Jennings 1991; Jennings, Stoker, and Bowers 1999). Likewise, research suggests that parents' level of religious involvement is an important predictor of adolescents' religious views (Bartkowski 2007). We would expect this to be particularly true among evangelicals, because of the importance of the family and the norm of passing on religious (and perhaps political) values to children (e.g., Oldfield 1996). In short, an expectation exists that evangelical parents take their children to church, pray by their bedsides, and otherwise teach them the values of the faith.

Another important source of socialization for young evangelicals is the evangelical education system. Research has generally found that schools are important agents of political socialization, although local context and other factors create wide variation in outcomes (Hess and Torney 1967; see also Pearson-Merkowitz and Gimpel 2009). The evangelical tradition has created institutions to take advantage of the influence of education starting from a young age. Many evangelical churches offer preschools where students are exposed to Bible stories, songs, and lessons that reinforce the subculture's perspective. While Catholics dominate the private K–12 school market in the United States, many communities also have private evangelical K–12 schools. Many evangelical churches offer summer vacation Bible schools, which have the added benefit of enabling participation from students who ordinarily attend public schools. With themes like wilderness adventures, jungle safaris, and space exploration designed to appeal to the interests of children, they emphasize lessons from both the Old and New Testaments. One new curriculum, *Willie's Redneck Rodeo*, uses characters from the A&E television show *Duck Dynasty* to reenact parables from the Bible.

The evangelical tradition's interest in youth also extends to the college-age population. As the United States expanded westward, founding new colleges was essential to training the next generation of clergy. During the Second Great Awakening (1800–1830), hundreds of colleges were founded by denominations like the Methodists, Presbyterians, and Congregationalists. Many of the best-known evangelical colleges followed in a second wave that lasted from the mid-1800s until about 1890. Among the colleges founded during this period were Baylor University (Waco, TX, 1845), Wheaton College (Wheaton, IL, 1860), Hope College (Holland, MI, 1866), Calvin College (Grand Rapids, MI, 1876), Grove City College (Grove City, PA, 1876), Houghton College (Houghton, NY, 1883), Huntington University (Huntington, IN, 1889), Gordon College (Wenham, MA, 1889), and Belmont University (Nashville, TN, 1890). While today these colleges are quite diverse in terms of theology and market, they all share a common history of a desire among evangelicals to train the faithful for positions as clergy, teachers, and professionals.

As the evangelical-mainline split became clearer, a new wave of fundamentalist-leaning evangelical colleges was founded starting in the 1920s, including Bob Jones College (founded by Bob Jones Sr. in 1927, later renamed Bob Jones University), Oral Roberts University (founded by televangelist Oral Roberts in 1965), Liberty University (founded by Jerry Falwell in 1971), and Christian Broadcasting Network University (founded by Pat Robertson in 1978, renamed Regent University in 1989). One motivation behind founding such universities was the feeling that secular forces had corrupted both public and previously existing private universities, and thus a new breed of evangelical college was required to train evangelicals for the cultural environment they faced.

Evangelical colleges have a number of formal institutions designed to build evangelical identity and transmit the core values of the faith. Almost all are residential colleges where students can live in a Christian community with fellow believers. Most require students to take one or more theology classes as part of the general curriculum, thereby ensuring that students are exposed to the key doctrines espoused by the university, and many require their faculty and staff to sign a statement of faith adhering to the college's principles. Some evangelical colleges require students to attend chapel services in which they teach the foundations of the evangelical faith and discuss topics of key relevance to the college age group. Finally, many of these evangelical colleges use their student codes of conduct to make expectations clear to students.

An equally important task for the evangelical subculture is engaging with students in the public school system. In 1844, George Williams founded the Young Men's Christian Association (YMCA) to provide alternatives to bars and brothels for young men living in London. Today, the YMCA (and its sister organization, the YWCA) has moved away from its evangelical heritage and deemphasized its Christian roots, even rebranding itself as simply "the Y" (Krohe 2010). Other organizations, like Youth for Christ and Young Life, followed in the YMCA's footsteps, reaching out to students in middle school and high school with after-school programming, summer camps, and other engagement opportunities. These organizations also have a variety of programs that target special audiences. For example, Youth for Christ has special ministries for urban youth, parents, students in the juvenile justice system, deaf and hard-of-hearing teens, and teens with parents in the armed services. Likewise, Young Life offers programming for urban youth, rural youth, teens who are pregnant and/or have children, teens with mental or physical handicaps, and those with parents in the military. Speaking of targeted ministries, another important organization is the Fellowship of Christian Athletes (FCA), which was founded in 1954 to spread the Christian message to athletes and coaches through sports camps, meetings, and devotionals. The FCA is now in sixty countries and has more than one thousand paid staff members (Fellowship of Christian Athletes 2016). Youth for Christ, Young Life, FCA, and other similar organizations collectively help the evangelical subculture reach millions of students in the public school system.

Likewise, the evangelical subculture has spawned several institutions designed to reach college students, including those at both evangelical and nonevangelical colleges and universities. During the twentieth century, a number of organizations were founded with the express goal of bringing the evangelical faith to nonevangelical colleges. Perhaps the largest and most influential of these organizations is Cru (formerly known as Campus Crusade for Christ). Founded on the University of California, Los Angeles campus in 1951, the organization now holds events in 191 countries (Cru, n.d.). Another important group is InterVarsity, which founded its first American chapter at the University of Michigan in 1938. InterVarsity reports 949 chapters on 616 campuses, and a total involvement of 1,197 field staff and 40,299 students (InterVarsity, n.d.). A third evangelical college group is the Navigators, which was founded by Dawson Trotman as a ministry to the Navy in 1933. In 1951, the first college chapter was started at the University of Nebraska–Lincoln.[3] The activities that these groups facilitate vary from campus to campus, but often include weekly worship meetings, Bible study groups, alternative spring break mission trips, and special outreach events. Scholars have found that evangelical campus organizations such as these help build evangelical identity by creating a safe space where students can talk about their faith in secular universities where faith-sharing might not be accepted (Magolda and Ebben Gross 2009).

The role of these parachurch student groups is not limited to recruitment and identity-building, however. One important ethnographic study of evangelical campus organizations found that they create a shared sense of marginalization consistent with expectations for a subculture (Magolda and Ebben Gross 2009). Furthermore, studies have found that the political views of organizations like Cru are known to campus communities and generate tension within the wider campus population during evangelism and outreach (Magolda and Ebben Gross 2009; McMurtrie 2001). Thus, like the other organizations discussed in this section, evangelical campus groups appear to build evangelical identity, discredit the larger culture, and teach subcultural values.

Given the large number of institutions dedicated to socializing young evangelicals into the tradition's viewpoint, we would expect the issue hypothesis and the commitment hypothesis to apply to young evangelicals as well. Together, then, my subcultural theory of public opinion among young evangelicals should go a long way toward explaining both patterns of continuity and patterns of change in public opinion among young evangelicals.

Overview of the Chapters

The first step in testing my theory is to examine public opinion among young evangelicals. In Chapter 2, I attempt to answer the question of whether young evangelicals are becoming more liberal. In doing so, I test my issue hypothesis, which holds that the subculture should exert a larger impact on measures of behavior that have been historically important to the subcultural identity of evangelicals, such as partisanship, ideology, vote choice, abortion, and gay marriage. To answer this question and test my hypothesis, I rely on a diverse combination of data from the 2007 and 2014 Pew Religious Landscape Studies, the 2012 and 2016 Cooperative Congressional Election Study Panel Survey, the Public Religion Research Institute's 2012 Millennial Values Survey, and the General Social Survey.

In Chapter 3, I attempt to determine whether any changes are caused by forces within or forces outside of evangelicalism. Drawing on my commitment hypothesis, I predict that most change is concentrated at the periphery of the evangelical tradition, among those who are the least committed to the faith. The issue hypothesis suggests that this should hold especially true for measures of political behavior that have become important parts of the evangelical subcultural identity.

In Chapter 4, I test many of the mechanisms behind my theory. In particular, I test whether the evangelical subculture actually undergoes the processes of building identity, teaching core values, discrediting secular culture, and giving direct political cues. These mechanisms are tremendously important for understanding how evangelicalism impacts adherents' views and yet are extremely difficult to test. Therefore, I use a multimethod approach, consisting of both survey data and a series of original interviews with forty-two college-age evangelicals at five colleges.

In Chapter 5, I address the causal claim that it is evangelicalism, specifically, that impacts attitudes among adherents. I use tools including regression analysis to account for a variety of alternative explanations of individual-level attitudes. In addition, I test my theory against an important alternative explanation. For most of the behavioral era of political science, survey researchers assumed that the causal direction of the relationship was from religion to political attitudes. For example, Bernard Berelson, Paul Lazarsfeld, and William McPhee (1954) argued that the social context of religion helped individuals sort into political parties in the months before an election. This assumption of a unidirectional causal influence of religion on politics remained until the groundbreaking work of Michael Hout and Claude Fischer (2002) showed that liberals and moderates are increasingly "sorting out" of religion, in part because of the growing conflation of religion and political conservatism during the "culture wars" era. Subsequent work by Stratos Patrikios (2008) and Robert Putnam and David Campbell (2010) reinforced this finding with additional evidence. Furthermore, this research is supported by more general scholarship suggesting that sorting is an important reason for the polarization we see in American politics (Fiorina with Abrams and Pope 2010; Levendusky 2009). Thus, an important alternate explanation is that conservatives are sorting into the various institutions I have identified as important, including evangelical churches, colleges, and groups. To test my theory against this alternate explanation, I rely on panel data from the 2010–2014 Cooperative Congressional Election Study. While I expect to find some evidence of sorting, my theory predicts that, holding sorting constant, those who are immersed in the evangelical subculture become more conservative over time.

In Chapter 6, I turn my focus to the liberal, highly committed young evangelicals that have fascinated political observers. Again drawing on my subcultural theory, I suggest that these liberal, committed evangelicals represent a smaller subculture within the broader evangelical subculture. While they differ from the dominant (conservative) subculture in some ways, they remain bound by the tradition's norms, including conservatism on cultural issues. I expect to find that liberal evangelicals remain distinctively conservative on cultural issues compared to other liberals. However, I also hypothesize that the liberal evangelical subculture tends to emphasize noncultural issues, like the environment and social welfare, in part because doing so helps reduce the tension between individuals' social identities as liberals and evangelicals.

In the Conclusion, I briefly summarize my findings, discuss their place in both the religion and political science literature, and suggest a number of avenues for future research. I argue that stories of liberalism among young evangelicals have vastly overstated the actual change we see. While young evangelicals have become more liberal on a few issues, they are essentially as conservative as ever in terms of their party identification, ideology, and views on issues like abortion. Moreover, any change on most issues appears to be driven by forces outside the evangelical tradition. In terms of their implications, my findings suggest it is unlikely the present generation of young evangelicals will leave the Republican Party. A more likely scenario is young evangelicals will push the GOP toward the center on a few issues but will continue to be an important part of the Republican coalition for years to come.

2

Winds of Change or Still the Same?

*Political Identities and Issue Attitudes
among Young Evangelicals*

Are young evangelicals becoming more liberal? This simple question seems to be on the minds of campaign managers, journalists, and religious leaders. Since the mid-2000s, a variety of commentators have suggested that young evangelicals hold more liberal positions on a host of political issues, including LGBT rights, poverty, the environment, and immigration (Dokoupil 2009; Wehner 2007). Others have suggested that young evangelicals are increasingly concerned with the environment and poverty, and are therefore ignoring cultural issues like abortion (Banerjee 2008; Harris 2008; Lee 2015; Murashko 2014). Still others have suggested that young evangelicals are leaving the Republican Party and giving their votes to Democratic candidates (Edwards 2008; Zogoby 2009). There is another side of the debate, too: observers ranging from SBC's Russell Moore to former George W. Bush speechwriter Colleen Carroll argue that young evangelicals are essentially as conservative as ever (Carroll 2002; Nazworth 2014). Despite all of the interest in this subject, to date, there have been only a handful of academic attempts to examine trends in public opinion among young evangelicals.

In this chapter, I attempt to provide the most complete examination of public opinion among young evangelicals to date. I draw on my issue hypothesis, introduced in Chapter 1, which holds that we should see evidence of consistency among young evangelicals on partisanship, ideology, and cultural issues. Using data from a variety of sources, I compare evangelicals to nonevangelical Millennials on political identity, voting behavior, and issues including abortion, gay marriage, the environment, welfare, immigration, and foreign policy. I also examine issue salience among young evangelicals, including comparisons to young nonevangelicals. I find that in terms of partisanship, ideology, and abortion, young evangelicals appear essentially as conservative as ever. However, we also see some evidence that young evangelicals may be changing on other issues, such as gay marriage, welfare, and immigration. Overall, the evidence suggests that while young evangelicals may be more liberal on a few issues, on many others they are quite similar to their parents and past generations of young evangelicals. This, in turn, suggests that any accounts of a larger liberal movement among young evangelicals are probably overstating what is, in reality, a nuanced and piecemeal shift.

Public Opinion among Young Evangelicals

In the Introduction, I note that one of the key goals of this book is to generate a complete, theoretically driven account of public opinion among evangelicals. Therefore, it is important to be systematic in looking at public opinion across multiple political issues. In this chapter, I test my issue hypothesis against three broad categories of dependent variables.

First, I consider three of the most important variables in the study of political behavior: partisanship, ideology, and presidential vote choice. Party identification is possibly the single most important variable in the study of political behavior. Research suggests that party identification is a social-psychological identity that deeply affects the way respondents perceive the political world (Campbell et al. 1960; Green, Palmquist, and Schickler 2002). Party identification strongly affects perceptions of both candidates and issues, and it is the single best predictor of voting behavior in American politics (Campbell et al. 1960; Lewis-Beck et al. 2008). Research suggests that left-right ideological identification is also an important social identity (Conover and Feldman 1981). Like partisanship, ideological identification is an important predictor of attitudes toward candidates, issues, and vote choice (Campbell et al. 1960; Lewis-Beck et al. 2008). I also examine voting behavior directly. Voting is one of the most fundamental political behaviors in our democracy, and the presidential vote has massive implications for Americans' everyday lives. While voting is closely related to both party identification and ideology, it is important to study voting in order to account for the possibility that partisans are defecting (that is, voting for a candidate from a party other than the one people identify with).

There are reasons to believe that each of these variables has become central to evangelicalism's political identity over the past half-century. Since the 1970s, the evangelical subculture has become increasingly associated with both the Republican Party and political conservatism (e.g., Oldfield 1996). Prominent evangelical elites, including Jerry Falwell and Pat Robertson, fervently endorsed the GOP, and evangelical organizations like the Moral Majority, the Christian Coalition, and Focus on the Family further linked evangelicalism to conservative politics (Capps 1994; Martin 2005; Wilcox and Robinson 2010; Williams 2010). On the partisan side of the equation, prominent Republican candidates, like Ronald Reagan and George W. Bush, spoke the language of evangelical Protestantism and made a point of reaching out to evangelical voters (Campbell 2007; Domke and Coe 2008). Occasionally, the religious and political spheres even fused, including during Pat Robertson's failed challenge to George H. W. Bush in the 1988 Republican Party primaries. Given the important role that Republicanism and conservatism has played in the evangelical subculture over the past fifty years, *my issue hypothesis predicts that we should find little evidence of change among evangelicals on these three all-important measures of political behavior (partisanship, ideology, and cultural issues).*

Second, I examine attitudes on cultural issues such as abortion and gay marriage. Abortion was a key factor in mobilizing evangelicals into American politics after the period of relative political withdrawal in the 1950s (Hunter 1991; Layman 2001; Williams 2010). Evangelical leaders like Jerry Falwell, Pat Robertson, James Dobson, Phyllis Schlafly, Francis Schaeffer, and others worked hard to connect abortion to the core values of the evangelical tradition (Capps 1994). They often discussed abortion as a sign of cultural decadence and moral decay, and they emphasized the importance of voting for anti-abortion, or "pro-life," candidates as a way of fighting back. Those efforts were quite effective: scholarship shows that cultural issues like abortion led many evangelicals to switch their party identification between the 1970s and the 2000s (Adams 1997; Killian and Wilcox 2008; Layman 2001).

More recently, homosexuality (as a sexual preference) and LGBT rights joined abortion as a signature issue of concern among evangelicals. Evangelical Protestantism (and, prior to the 2000s, much of the rest of society) has historically opposed homosexuality and LGBT rights, but this issue did not become particularly salient until the controversies over Don't Ask, Don't Tell and the Defense of Marriage Act in the mid-1990s. In fact, one could argue that gay marriage did not really become a salient issue for most people until the 2004 election cycle, when the Republican Party used a series of ballot initiatives on gay marriage to attempt to increase turnout among evangelicals and other religious traditionalists (Campbell and Monson 2007). Given the important role that cultural issues have played in the evangelical subculture over time, *my issue hypothesis predicts that we should find little evidence of change among evangelicals on abortion and gay marriage.*

By contrast, the literature suggests that attitudes on poverty and welfare have not been central to the evangelical subculture. While some scholars have suggested that the "Protestant ethic" predisposes evangelicals to conservative attitudes on economic policy (Barker and Carman 2000; Guth et al. 2006; Hargrove 1989; Jelen, Smidt, and Wilcox 1993; Weber 1930), other scholars have found that evangelicals may support antipoverty efforts, especially when directed toward the "deserving poor" or hosted by local congregations (Pyle 1993; Will and Cochran 1995; Wilson 1999; Wuthnow 1994). Furthermore, at the elite level, evangelical clergy have tended to downplay economic and social justice issues in favor of moral issues (Guth et al. 1997; Hadden 1969; Jelen 1993; Quinley 1974). This ambiguity in evangelical attitudes toward social welfare programs led one recent reviewer of the literature to conclude that the religious influence on economic attitudes is "contested and complicated," which is certainly not the type of conclusion that would itself label economic conservatism a central issue concern within the evangelical subculture (Wilson 2009, 195).

Likewise, studies suggest that environmental protection (or the lack thereof) has not been a defining issue commitment of the evangelical subculture. Traditionally, scholarship has suggested that important evangelical theological commitments, including biblical literalism and premillennial dispensationalism, predispose evangelicals to environmental conservatism (Guth et al. 1995; Wilcox and Robinson 2010).[1] However, evangelical leaders, including Billy Graham and Rick Warren, have spoken in favor of preserving the environment, and a recent analysis of evangelical periodicals suggests that opinions on the issue among elites are becoming increasingly polarized and controversial (Danielsen 2013). Furthermore, anecdotal evidence suggests that some evangelicals are willing to change their attitudes on the environment when faced with evidence suggesting that environmental conservatism conflicts with the core values of the subculture. As Clyde Wilcox and Carin Robinson (2010) report, Richard Cizik, a former vice president of Governmental Affairs for the National Association of Evangelicals, came out in favor of greater environmental protection because it could reduce mercury poisoning in the unborn. The ambiguity of opinions on the environment, and the willingness of elites to adjust their positions on the environment to maintain consistency with more salient subcultural commitments, lends substantial evidence to the contention that the environment is not a defining part of evangelicalism's political identity.

Immigration is another issue that currently does not seem to be an important part of evangelicalism's subcultural identity. Of course, that has not always been the case: in the mid-1800s, Protestants were heavily nativist, largely in response to the perceived threat of Catholic and Jewish immigrants.

That nativism made its way into politics through the Know-Nothing Party and later Republican Party. As Catholicism moved from a religious subculture to become part of mainstream American life (Prendergast 1999), and as religious restructuring forged new bonds between Catholics and evangelicals, immigration largely fell off the radar of evangelicals. Recently, given the increasing racial diversity of evangelical congregations, some evangelical pastors are even taking a strongly pro-immigration stance (Campbell 2014). Pro-immigration evangelicals stress how Jesus showed compassion to immigrants and the socially disadvantaged, and they note that support for immigration may even by interpreted as a pro-life issue. While the elites' momentum on immigration appears to be trending in a liberal direction, the literature on evangelicals generally suggests that immigration has not been a defining part of the evangelical subculture's identity in recent times.

Finally, there is considerable debate as to how important a role foreign policy plays in the political attitudes of evangelicals. Some of this debate may have to do with the relative lack of major studies on religion's impact on foreign policy in the United States (Guth 2009). Nevertheless, there are some clear areas where evangelicalism might influence foreign policy attitudes, such as attitudes on Israel (Guth et al. 1996). On other questions, such as the tradeoff between military and diplomacy and the choice between isolationism and internationalism, the influence of religion is less clear. Certainly, we would expect evangelicals to take the more conservative position on each of these issues, but it is unclear whether their religion is actually the driving factor (as opposed to other traits correlated with religion, such as party, ideology, and region). For example, James Guth (2009) finds that once we control for party and ideology, evangelicals are not significantly different from other groups in terms of their support for preemptive attacks in the name of national security (i.e., the Bush doctrine). Furthermore, there are signs of recent evangelical leaders taking steps to move away from the militarism that sometimes characterized New Christian Right leaders. For example, Rick Warren has engaged on global issues, including poverty and AIDS, perhaps signaling support for both diplomacy and interventionism along the way (Pew Research Center 2009). All of this suggests that foreign policy (with the exception of Israel) has not been a major issue for evangelicalism, and it may be an issue on which change is possible.

In summary, my issue hypothesis predicts that we would expect to see the subculture exerting the largest effects on identities and issues that have been an important part of the evangelical subculture's distinctiveness over many decades, including party identification, ideology, abortion, and gay marriage. In contrast, we would expect the subculture to exert a lesser impact on issues like welfare, the environment, immigration, and foreign policy that have not been a central part of the subculture's identity. As such, my issue hypothesis suggests that if young evangelicals are becoming more liberal, it is most likely on these issues.

Data and Methods

To examine the state of public opinion among young evangelicals, and provide an initial test of my subcultural theory of evangelical public opinion, I turn to survey data. I rely on my own analysis of several data sources, including the 2014 Pew Religious Landscape Study, a nationally representative telephone survey of 35,071 respondents (Pew Research Center 2014). The Pew survey is ideal because it contains high-quality questions about a number of religious and political beliefs, and the large sample size facilitates precise comparisons, even when the data are limited to young evangelicals. I also employ the 2007 Pew Religious Landscape Study (N = 35,556), which contains several questions about foreign policy that were not available in the more recent version (Pew Research Center 2007).

For data on electoral behavior, I employ the 2012 and 2016 Cooperative Congressional Election Study (CCES), a national internet-based sample (Ansolabehere and Schaffner 2013, 2017). Research comparing previous CCES studies to other national samples shows that the CCES is a reasonably close approximation of the American electorate, although perhaps slightly more politically knowledgeable (Ansolabehere 2006, 2010b; Rivers 2006; Vavreck and Rivers 2008). Like the Pew Religious Landscape Study, the CCES data reflect much larger sample sizes than most surveys (64,000 for 2016 and 54,000 for 2012).

To obtain as complete an understanding of public opinion among young evangelicals as possible, for each issue or identity covered, I pay attention to three key comparisons. First, for each identity or issue discussed, I compare young evangelicals, defined as those ages eighteen to twenty-nine, with non-evangelicals of the same age.[2] This comparison is useful for getting a sense of whether evangelicals remain politically distinctive from other members of the younger generation. Of course, my subcultural theory would lead us to expect to find evidence that young evangelicals remain distinctive compared to their nonevangelical counterparts.

Second, and perhaps more importantly, I compare young evangelicals to their older counterparts in order to examine the possibility of age-based effects. I have divided respondents into four age groups: ages eighteen to twenty-nine, thirty to forty-nine, fifty to sixty-four, and sixty-five and older. Age-based effects would not, in and of themselves, provide evidence against my subcultural theory, as my theory is primarily concerned with variation over time. Nevertheless, my theory leads us to expect to see evidence of continuity, particularly in terms of partisanship, ideology, and attitudes on cultural issues.

A third relevant question is how young evangelicals today compare to previous generations of young evangelicals. Taking on this question represents an important improvement from previous studies, including Buster Smith and Byron Johnson (2010) and Mikael Pelz and Corwin Smidt (2015), both of which rely entirely on cross-sectional data (e.g., data from one particular point in time, thus precluding the examination of generational change). If my subcultural theory is accurate, we would expect to see continuity over time on partisanship, ideology, and cultural issues. To see how young evangelicals today compare to previous generations of young evangelicals, I turn to time-series analysis of data from the General Social Survey (GSS). Unfortunately, there is not a time-series data set with as many responses as the CCES that has adequate religious and political measures and dates back to at least the 1990s. The GSS is preferable to the American National Election Study (ANES) because in most years the GSS had a slightly greater number of respondents, thereby enabling a somewhat more precise look at the data.

Partisanship and Ideology

Perhaps the single most important arbiter of whether young evangelicals have become more liberal is their party identification, because party is linked to electoral participation, candidate preference, issue attitudes, vote choice, and a host of other important measures of political behavior (Campbell et al. 1960; Lewis-Beck et al. 2008). In the top panel of Figure 2.1, I show mean party identification, which has been recoded to range from 0 (strong Democrat) to 1 (strong Republican), as well as a 95 percent confidence interval. We see that the mean partisanship among eighteen- to twenty-nine-year-old evangelicals is .63, equivalent to an independent-leaning Republican. The figure plainly shows that young evangelicals are not statistically different from older evangelicals, even with the large sample size in the Pew data. Perhaps equally important, young evangelicals are noticeably more Republican than nonevangelicals in every age category. In particular, young evangelicals remain distinctly more Republican compared to their nonevangelical counterparts, whose mean partisanship averages .40.

The second panel of Figure 2.1, drawn from the General Social Survey (GSS), shows the mean partisanship of eighteen- to twenty-nine-year-old evangelicals over time, again recoded to range from 0 (strong Democrat) to 1 (strong Republican). The error bars represent a 95 percent confidence interval for the mean partisanship of young evangelicals. The dotted line shows mean

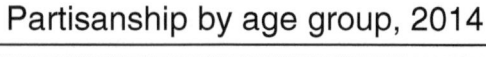

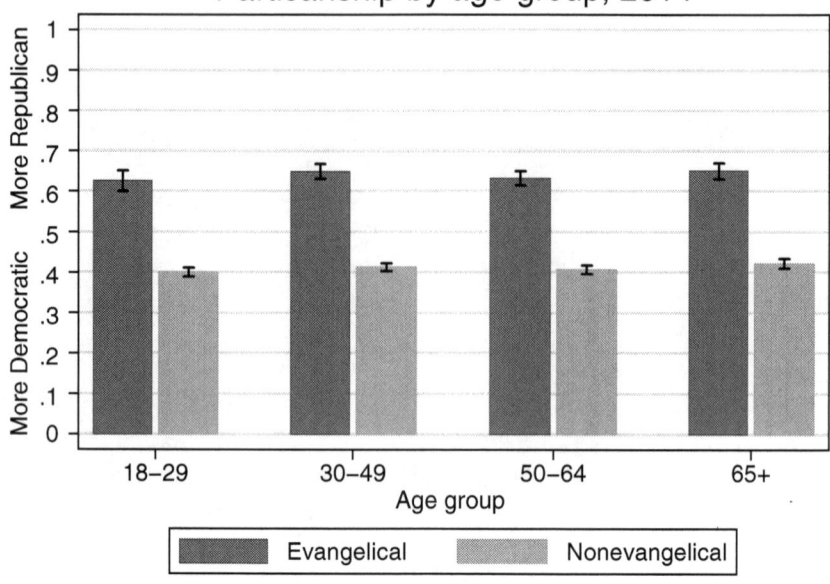

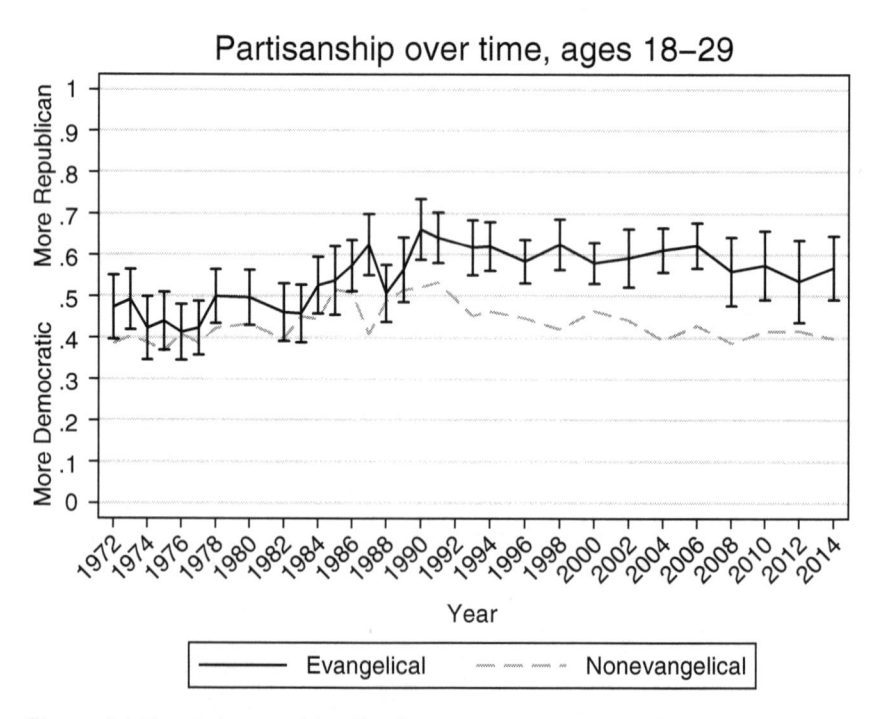

Figure 2.1. Trends in party identification among young evangelicals.

Source: Weighted 2014 Pew Religious Landscape Study; 1972–2014 General Social Survey.
Note: Error bars represent 95 percent confidence intervals.

partisanship among eighteen- to twenty-nine-year-old nonevangelicals for reference (no confidence interval is shown here to maintain the clarity of the graph). Here we clearly see how young evangelicals became more Republican in the 1980s, likely in response to the Republican Party's embrace of cultural conservatism (Layman 2001). We also see that young evangelicals seem to have become slightly more Democratic since the peak in the 1990s, although this trend is not statistically significant. We also see that the gap between young evangelicals and other young people appears to have grown since the 1980s, suggesting that young evangelicals are increasingly distinctive from their nonevangelical counterparts.

Figure 2.2 follows the same methodology, but this time the dependent variable is left-right political ideology. The data have been recoded to range from 0 (very liberal) to 1 (very conservative). As we would expect, the data reveal young evangelicals to be quite conservative on average. Young evangelicals are slightly more liberal than older evangelicals, with a mean ideology of .58, compared to .64 among thirty- to forty-nine-year-olds and .65 among fifty- to sixty-four-year-old evangelicals. This substantively small difference is again overshadowed by a large gap between young evangelicals and the nonevangelical members of their age cohort (where the mean ideology is .45). The bottom panel of Figure 2.2, drawn from the General Social Survey, shows mean ideology over time, again ranging from 0 (very liberal) to 1 (very conservative). The figure indicates that young evangelicals have been trending ever so slightly *conservative* since the 1970s, although the effect is not statistically significant. This suggests that the small differences in ideology between young and older evangelicals that we see in the Pew data are probably due to an age effect in which young evangelicals tend to be more liberal and grow more conservative over time.

The 2012 and 2016 Presidential Vote

The presidential elections of 2012 and 2016 both fostered speculation among those who believe that young evangelicals are becoming more liberal. Indeed, both elections were highly unusual, creating a general sense that the electoral environment was ripe for change. Beginning with the election of 2012, the Republican Party nominated former Massachusetts Governor Mitt Romney. Romney was a controversial candidate in some evangelical circles because of his moderate politics, his equivocation on abortion, and his Mormon faith (Bruns 2012). During the 2012 Republican primaries, many evangelicals preferred candidates such as Rick Santorum and Newt Gingrich who were more ideologically conservative and more reliably pro-life (Hirschkorn and Pinto 2012). The Democratic Party's candidate was Barack Obama, who had

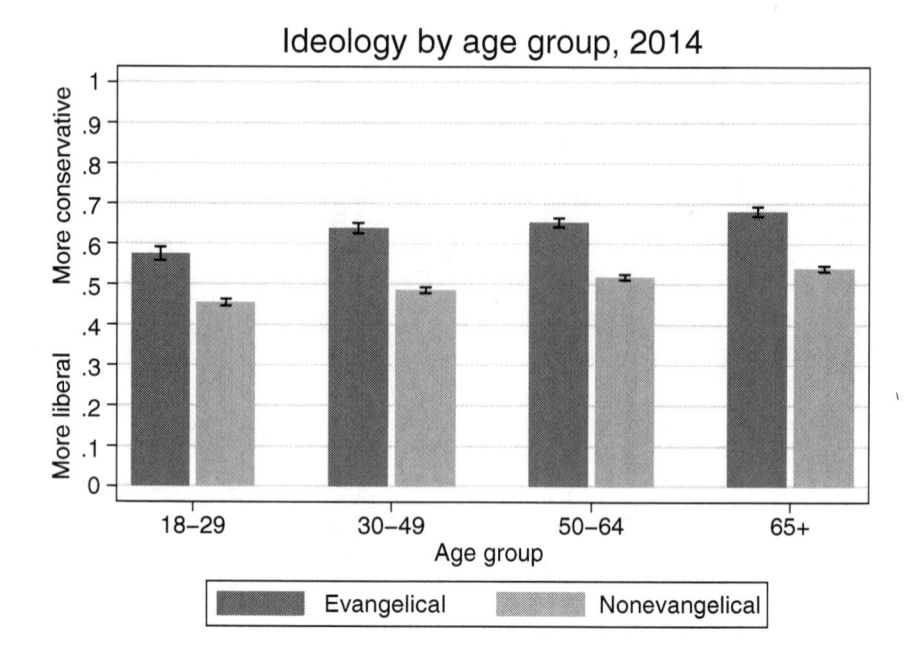

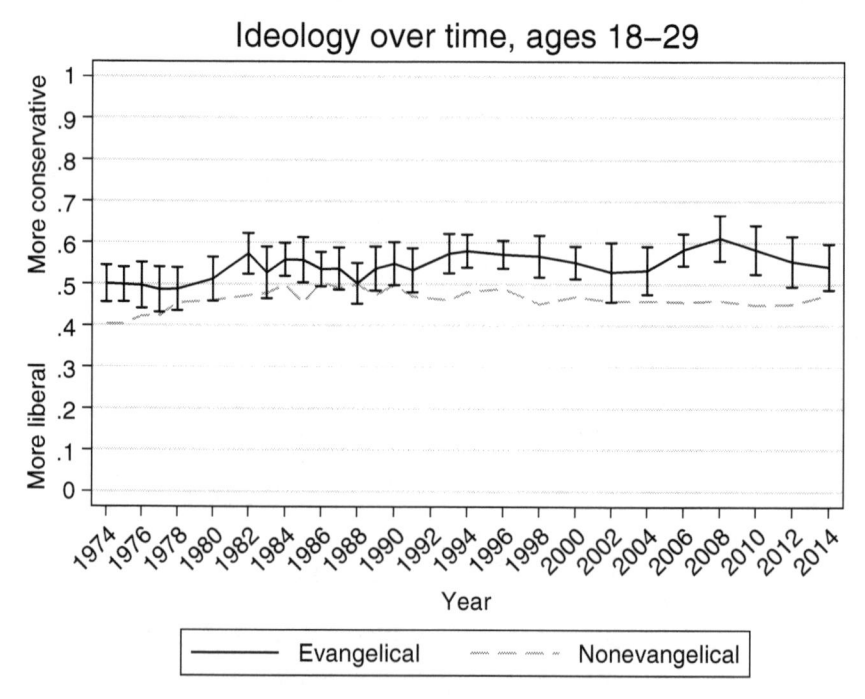

Figure 2.2. Trends in ideology among young evangelicals.

Source: Weighted 2014 Pew Religious Landscape Study; 1972–2014 General Social Survey.
Note: Error bars represent 95 percent confidence intervals.

spoken more powerfully about his religious faith than most Democrats and who had spoken eloquently about abortion (even while taking a pro-choice stance). In short, the 2012 election represented an opportunity for young evangelicals to break from their older counterparts and support the Democratic Party's candidate.

Figure 2.3 shows self-reported 2012 presidential vote results by age for both evangelicals and nonevangelicals, as taken from the 2012 CCES.[3] The figure makes it plain that young evangelicals had much in common with their older counterparts: 71 percent of eighteen- to twenty-nine-year-old evangelicals voted for Romney, compared to 74 percent of fifty- to sixty-four-year-olds and 79 percent of those older than sixty-five (these differences are not statistically significant). More noticeably, in every age category, evangelicals were more likely to support Mitt Romney compared to similarly-aged nonevangelicals. This gap persisted among young people: while 70 percent of eighteen- to twenty-nine-year-old nonevangelicals voted for Obama, just 25 percent of evangelicals did so. Finally, it is apparent that the age gap was much smaller among evangelicals compared to nonevangelicals: eighteen- to twenty-nine-year-old evangelicals were about 5 points more likely to vote for Obama compared to evangelicals ages sixty-five and older. However, eighteen- to twenty-nine-year-old nonevangelicals were about nineteen points more likely to vote for Obama compared to nonevangelicals ages sixty-five and older. Clearly, then, young evangelicals held tightly to the Republican coalition in the 2012 presidential election.

The 2016 presidential election represented an even greater departure from normalcy in American politics. The Democratic Party nominated former Senator and Secretary of State Hillary Clinton, a United Methodist who sometimes seemed uncomfortable discussing the impact of her faith on her political views. In contrast, Republican nominee Donald Trump aggressively courted evangelicals throughout the election, including making high-profile stops at Liberty University (Ambrosino 2016). Trump also took an unequivocal pro-life position while campaigning, including a passionate condemnation of partial birth abortion during the third presidential debate. In other ways, though, Trump was far from the ideal nominee of many evangelicals: by many accounts he was not personally very religious prior to the campaign (Lee 2017), and the leaked *Access Hollywood* video revealed beliefs about personal morality that differed wildly from evangelicals' ideals. On this basis, the 2016 election was interpreted by many as an opportunity for young evangelicals to break with their older counterparts.

The data for 2016, shown in cross-tabulation form in Table 2.1 to provide closer detail for the third-party candidates, indicate a much different pattern than the results from 2012. While a majority of young evangelicals did vote

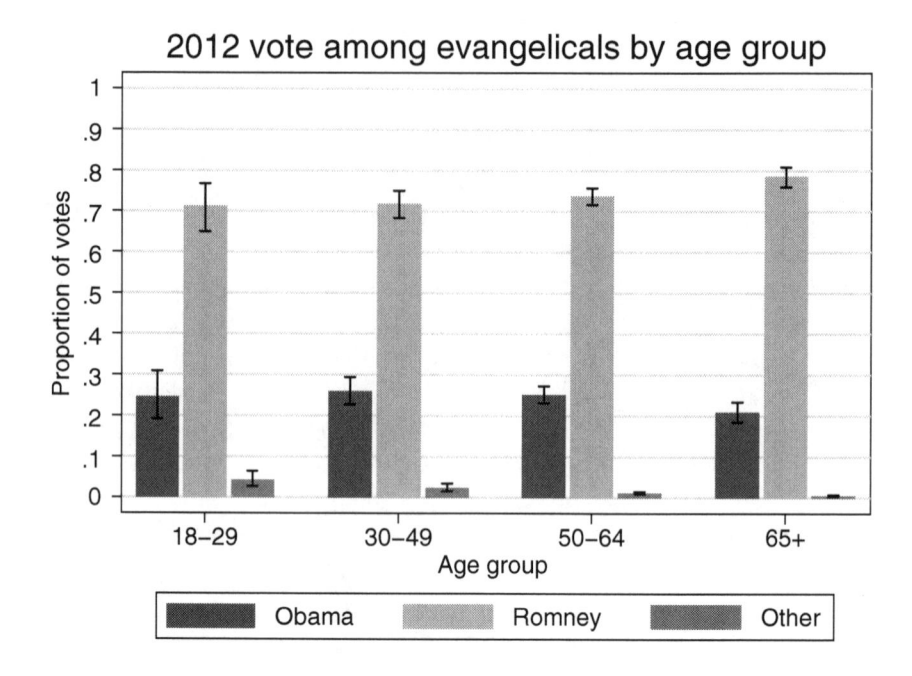

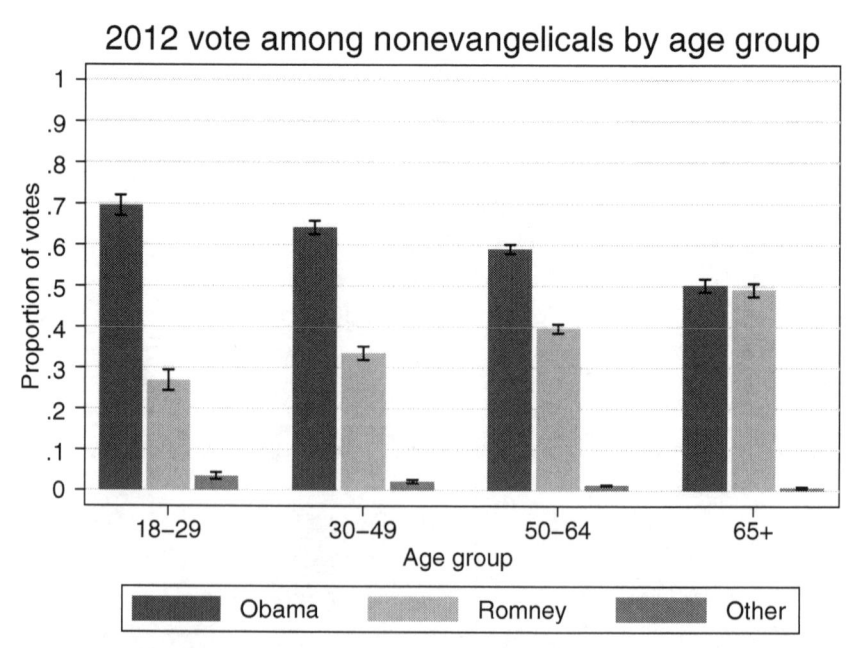

Figure 2.3. 2012 presidential vote among evangelicals.
Source: Weighted 2012 Cooperative Congressional Election Study.
Note: Error bars represent 95 percent confidence intervals.

TABLE 2.1. 2016 PRESIDENTIAL VOTE BY AGE (PERCENTAGE)

	Evangelicals					Nonevangelicals				
	18–29	30–49	59–64	65+	Total	18–29	30–49	50–64	65+	Total
Clinton	25.0	21.1	20.3	16.0	19.9	66.4	59.3	52.3	50.1	55.9
Trump	60.5	70.4	75.9	81.9	74.4	23.1	32.8	43.2	46.9	38.1
Johnson	7.5	4.6	1.4	0.9	2.7	5.0	3.8	1.8	1.0	2.7
Stein	1.0	0.6	0.2	0.2	0.4	2.8	1.6	0.9	0.6	1.3
McMullin	1.3	0.5	0.0	0.0	0.3	0.6	0.6	0.2	0.1	0.4
Other	4.7	2.8	2.1	1.0	2.3	2.1	1.9	1.6	1.3	1.7

Source: Weighted 2016 Cooperative Congressional Election Study.

for Trump (61 percent), older evangelicals showed the Republican nominee an even greater level of support (82 percent among evangelicals ages sixty-five and older). The size of the age gap among evangelicals (21 points) is slightly smaller than the age gap among nonevangelicals (24 points), indicating that the strong age-based effects in 2016 were not confined to evangelicals.

While this age gap might initially be taken as evidence of liberalization among young evangelicals, the data provide reason to be cautious with that conclusion. While young evangelicals did not fully embrace Donald Trump, neither did they fully embrace Hillary Clinton and the Democratic Party. While about 25 percent of young evangelicals voted for Hillary Clinton, about 14 percent of young evangelicals voted for third-party candidates. In contrast, only about 10 percent of young nonevangelicals chose a third-party candidate.

Patterns in voting behavior outside of the major party candidates suggest that many young evangelicals were seeking a more socially and politically orthodox conservative candidate. The most commonly preferred third-party candidate among young evangelicals was Libertarian candidate Gary Johnson, who received 7.5 percent of their votes. Another interesting trend is that 4.7 percent of young evangelicals voted for someone else. A brief examination of young evangelicals' write-in preferences adds evidence to the contention that young evangelicals were looking for conservative alternatives to Trump. Table 2.2 shows all substantive write-in votes by young evangelicals in the 2016 CCES sample (i.e., responses such as "private" and "wrote in" are not included in the table). By far the most common choice was Evan McMullin, a former CIA officer and chief policy director for the House Republican Conference running on an independent conservative platform. While the sample size of young evangelicals' write-in votes is small, it is worth noting that all of the serious candidates written in are cultural conservatives, and

TABLE 2.2. EIGHTEEN- TO TWENTY-NINE-YEAR-OLD EVANGELICALS' WRITE-IN VOTES

Candidate	Number of write-in votes
Evan McMullin	18
Darrell Castle	5
Marco Rubio	3
Paul Ryan	3
Batman	1
Jeb Bush	1
Ben Carson	1
Ted Cruz	1
Mike Maturen	1
Ron Paul	1

Source: 2016 Cooperative Congressional Election Study.
Note: Alternative spellings have been combined into the appropriate category. Responses such as "Private" and "Wrote in" not included.

all but Darrell Castle (of the Constitution Party) and Mike Maturen (of the American Solidarity Party) are Republicans.

Because of the extraordinary nature of the 2016 presidential election, it is difficult to evaluate these results in light of my subcultural theory. While the 2016 election seems to have been a break from the consistent support for Republican candidates that we expect among young evangelicals, the data suggest that young evangelicals are not yet ready to wholeheartedly embrace the Democratic Party. Furthermore, the evidence of young evangelicals' reluctance to support Trump might actually be interpreted as supporting my hypothesis: if evangelicals rejected Trump because he was not "Republican enough" or conservative enough, then they were behaving in a way that is consistent with the importance of Republicanism and conservatism to the evangelical subculture's identity and distinctiveness. While the continued Republican and conservative identification of young evangelicals shown in Figures 2.1 and 2.2 suggests that a return to the Republican fold in 2020 is the most likely outcome, we may have to wait for the results from the 2020 presidential election before we can truly understand the dynamics behind the 2016 contest.

Public Opinion on Cultural Issues: Abortion, Homosexuality, and Gay Marriage

Of all the cultural issues that have driven the evangelical resurgence in American politics, abortion is probably the one that has become the most entrenched within the evangelical subculture. Therefore, it is only natural to study young evangelicals' attitudes toward abortion. In the 2014 Pew Religious Landscape Study, respondents were asked to choose from among four response categories on abortion: "Legal in all cases," "Legal in most cases," "Illegal in most cases," or "Illegal in all cases." The top panel of Figure 2.4 shows the percentage of each group that said abortion should be illegal in most or all cases. The data indicate that, if anything, young evangelicals are actually slightly *more* pro-life than older evangelicals: sixty-nine percent of eighteen- to twenty-nine-year-old evangelicals said that abortion should be illegal in most or all cases, compared to 66 percent of fifty- to sixty-four-year-old evangelicals (this difference is not statistically significant, however). In addition, there is a large gap between evangelicals and nonevangelicals in every age category, suggesting that evangelicals remain highly distinctive in terms of their attitudes on abortion.

The bottom panel of Figure 2.4 shows mean attitudes on abortion over time. Respondents answered the question, "Please tell me if you think it should be possible for a pregnant woman to obtain a legal abortion if the woman wants it for any reason?" Data were recoded to range from 0 (yes) to 1 (no). The graph shows that while young evangelicals have been consistently pro-life over time, they became even more pro-life in the mid 2000s. This finding echoes others, including Ted Jelen (2009) and Robert Putnam and David Campbell (2010), who have argued that abortion attitudes in general are becoming more conservative. Jelen (2009) suggests that the rising salience of "partial-birth" abortions may have changed the frame of abortion generally by causing the public to associate it with this extremely rare procedure. Whatever the cause, my findings suggest that young evangelicals are at least as pro-life as previous generations of young evangelicals.

Next, I consider attitudes toward homosexuality and gay marriage. The Pew Religious Landscape Study contains two questions about the LGBT community. The first question asks respondents to indicate whether they believe homosexuality should be "accepted" or "discouraged" by society. Figure 2.5 shows the percentage of respondents who say that society should discourage homosexuality. Two things are apparent from the figure. First, young evangelicals are considerably less likely than older evangelicals to say that homosexuality should be discouraged: forty-four percent said so, compared to 73 percent of evangelicals ages 65 and older. Second, in all age groups, evangelicals remain considerably more likely than nonevangelicals to say that homosexuality should be discouraged. Among young people, evangelicals remain about 29 percentage points more likely than nonevangelicals to say that society should discourage homosexuality.

The second item asked respondents whether they would "strongly favor," "favor," "oppose," or "strongly oppose" gay marriage. Figure 2.5 shows the

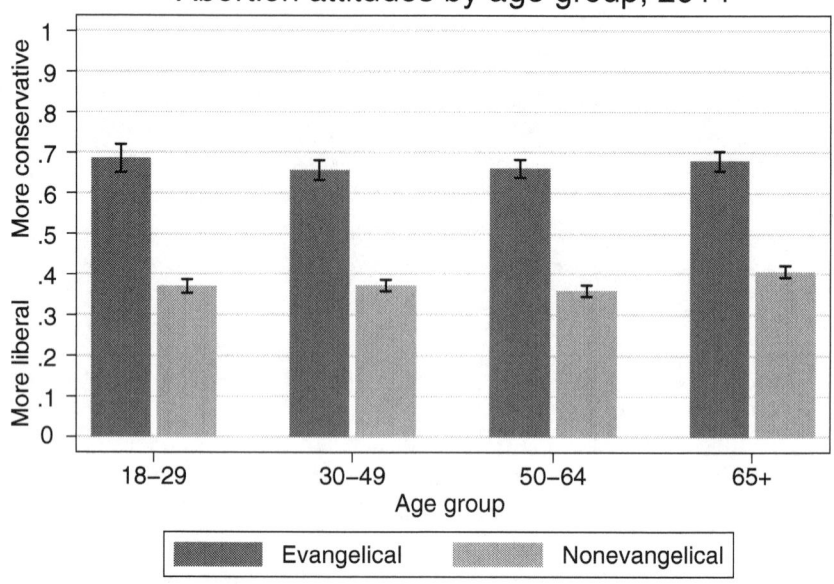

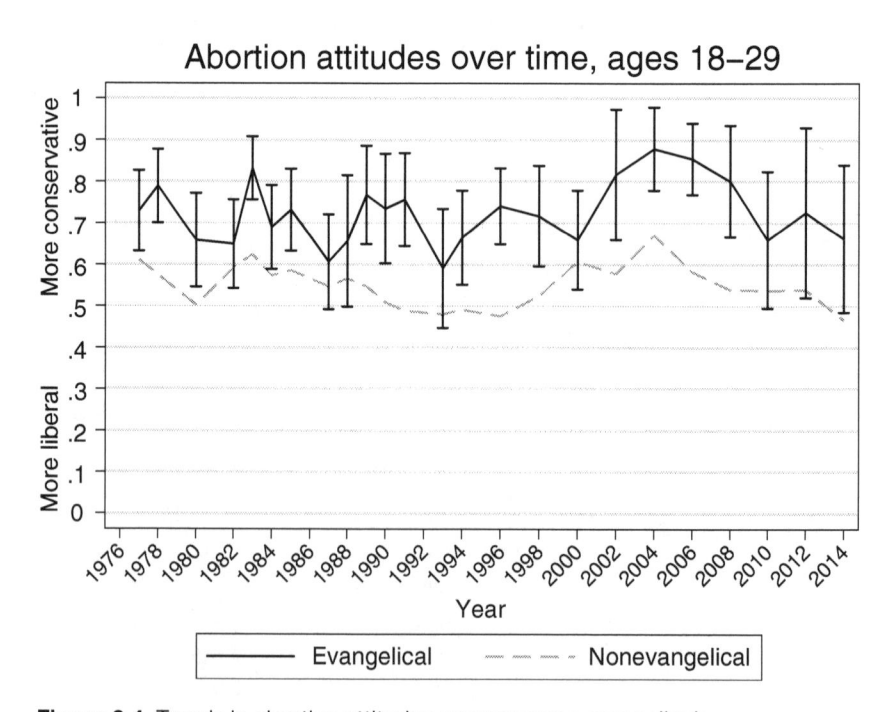

Figure 2.4. Trends in abortion attitudes among young evangelicals.

Source: Weighted 2014 Pew Religious Landscape Study; 1972–2014 General Social Survey.
Note: Error bars represent 95 percent confidence intervals.

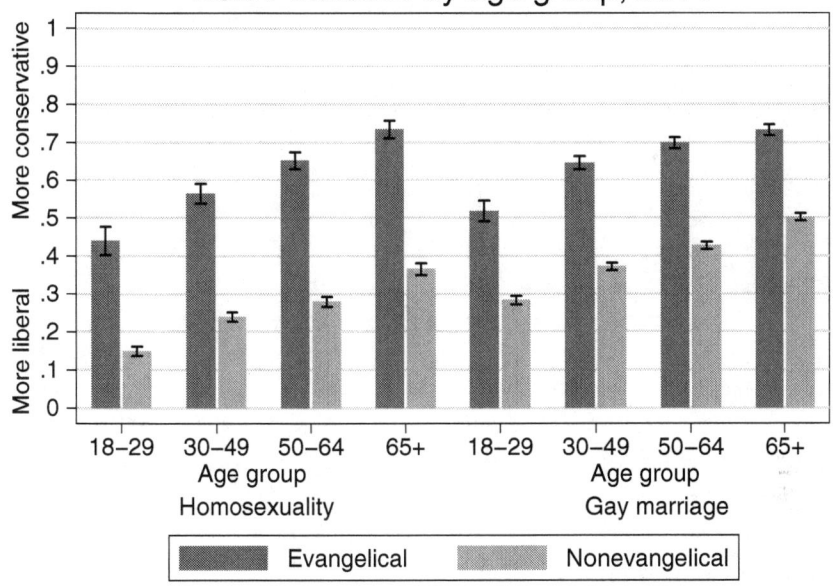

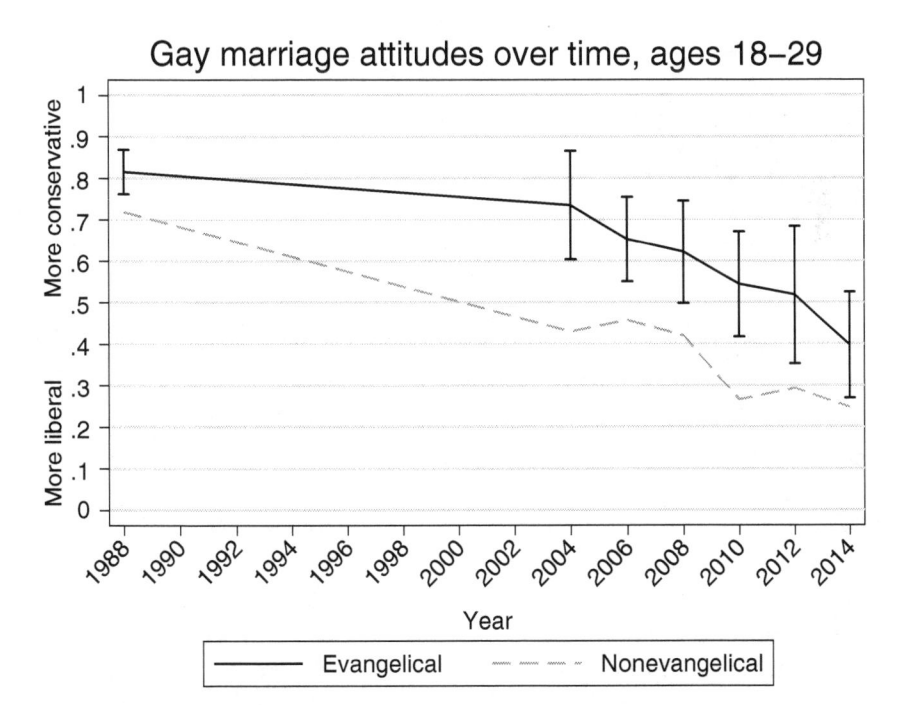

Figure 2.5. Trends in attitudes on homosexuality and gay marriage among young evangelicals.

Source: Weighted 2014 Pew Religious Landscape Study; 1972–2014 General Social Survey.
Note: Error bars represent 95 percent confidence intervals.

percentage who say they oppose or strongly oppose gay marriage. Again, there is a substantial age gap among evangelicals: about 51 percent of young evangelicals oppose gay marriage, compared to 73 percent of evangelicals ages 65 and older. The gap between evangelicals and nonevangelicals in terms of acceptance of gay marriage is again quite wide. Among young people, evangelicals are about 31 percentage points more likely than nonevangelicals to oppose gay marriage.

Although the time series is much shorter on gay marriage because the GSS asked about it only in 1988 and from 2004 on, we can still see that young evangelicals have become significantly more liberal over time. Here, respondents were asked, "Do you agree or disagree? Homosexual couples should have the right to marry one another." Responses have been recoded to range from 0 (strongly agree) to 1 (strongly disagree). Opposition to gay marriage fell dramatically, from a mean of .82 in 1988 to .40 in 2014. This liberal trend is not surprising, as the pro-gay marriage trend in public opinion has been well documented (e.g., Avery et al. 2007; Jelen 2009; Gelman, Lax, and Phillips 2010; Putnam and Campbell 2010). Indeed, it would have been quite remarkable if evangelicals had not changed, given how much society around them was changing.

Public Opinion on Noncultural Issues

In this section, I profile evangelicals' attitudes on a variety of noncultural issues. Beginning with the environment, the 2014 Pew Religious Landscape Study attempted to highlight the trade-off between greater environmental protections and short-term standard of living to generate a more accurate picture of the degree to which the public values the environment. Specifically, the question asked respondents to indicate which of two statements most accurately reflected their beliefs: "Stricter environmental laws and regulations cost too many jobs" or "Stricter environmental laws and regulations are worth the cost." The results, shown in Figure 2.6, indicate that about 44 percent of eighteen- to twenty-nine-year-old evangelicals take the antienvironment position. While young evangelicals are not significantly different from the thirty- to forty-nine-year-old category, they are more pro-environment than evangelicals ages fifty and older. As has often been the case, it is also clear that evangelicals are considerably more conservative than nonevangelicals in every age group. The size of the gap, though, is somewhat smaller than we saw on the cultural issues: among young people, evangelicals are about 12 percentage points more likely to take a conservative position on the environment.

The bottom panel of Figure 2.6 shows the time-series results from the General Social Survey. The question asked, "Are we spending too much, too

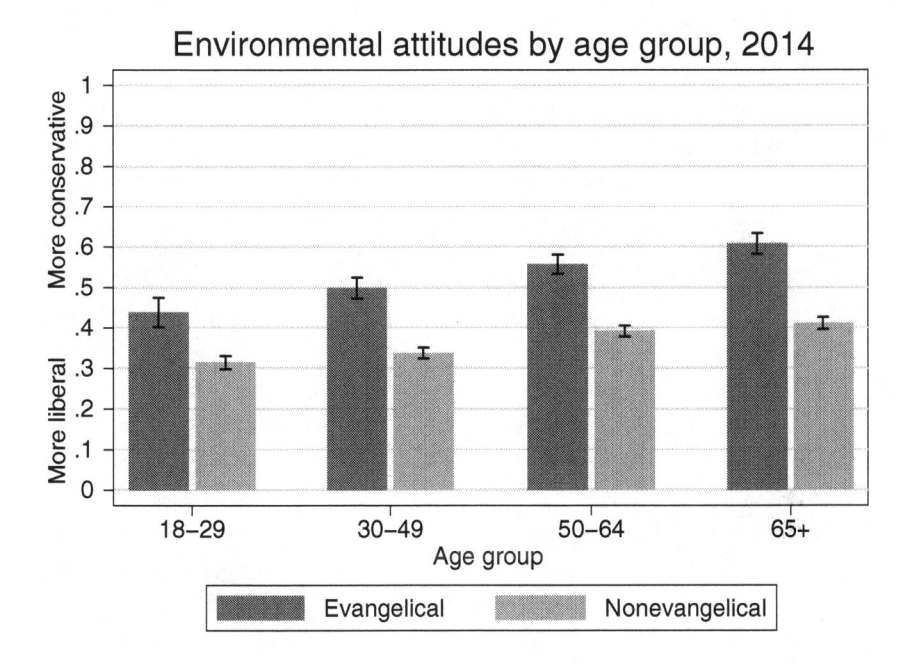

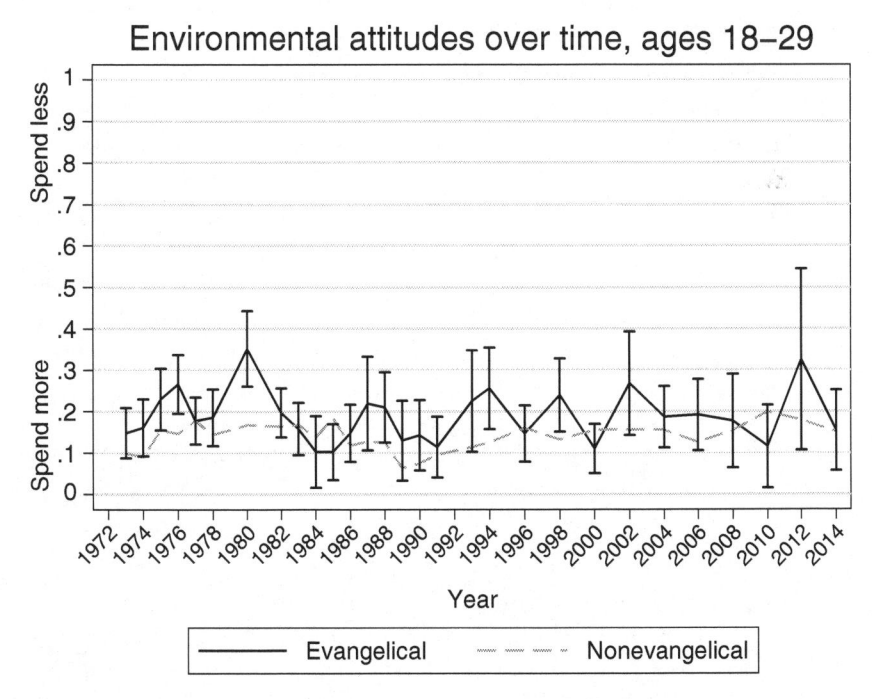

Figure 2.6. Trends in environmental attitudes among young evangelicals.
Source: Weighted 2014 Pew Religious Landscape Study; 1972–2014 General Social Survey.
Note: Error bars represent 95 percent confidence intervals.

little, or about the right amount on improving and protecting the environment?" The data have been recoded to range from 0 (too little) to .5 (the right amount) to 1 (too much). The overall trend in the data is that young people clearly feel the United States is spending too little on the environment. However, it is also clear that young evangelicals have been fairly consistent in their attitudes on this issue since the mid-1990s. In short, while young evangelicals appear more liberal than older generations on this issue, it looks like they probably are not becoming more liberal over time. This suggests that the liberalization of young evangelicals with regard to the environment is an age effect.

Welfare and aid to the poor is another area in which the attitudes of young evangelicals may be changing. In the 2014 Pew study, respondents were asked to choose from between two options: "Government aid to the poor does more harm than good, by making people too dependent on government assistance" or "Government aid to the poor does more good than harm, because people can't get out of poverty until their basic needs are met." The top panel of Figure 2.7 shows the percentage of young evangelicals who took the conservative position on this issue. Young evangelicals tend to hold more liberal views on welfare than their older counterparts, but substantively, the difference is not that large: about 54 percent of young evangelicals said that welfare does more harm than good, compared to about 62 percent for the thirty to forty-nine and fifty to sixty-four age groups. Again, evangelicals are distinctively conservative compared to nonevangelicals in every age category. Among young people, evangelicals were about 14 percentage points more likely than nonevangelicals to take a conservative position on welfare.

In the General Social Survey, respondents were asked, "Are we spending too much, too little, or about the right amount on welfare?" The data have been recoded to range from 0 (too little) to .5 (the right amount) to 1 (too much). From the data in the bottom panel of Figure 2.7, it is clear that most young people think the government is spending too much on welfare. Young evangelicals had been trending in a liberal direction since 1994, although in 2014 they bounced back to a more conservative view. Given the fairly wide confidence interval, we cannot say that this trend is statistically significant, but it bears watching in the future.

One final domestic issue where observers have speculated that young evangelicals may be more liberal is immigration. Here, the 2014 Pew survey asked whether "A growing population of immigrants" has been a "Change for the better," a "Change for the worse," or "Hasn't made much of a difference." The results, shown in Figure 2.8, reveal large age gaps among both evangelicals and nonevangelicals. The data indicate that young evangelicals are considerably more liberal than older evangelicals on this issue. About

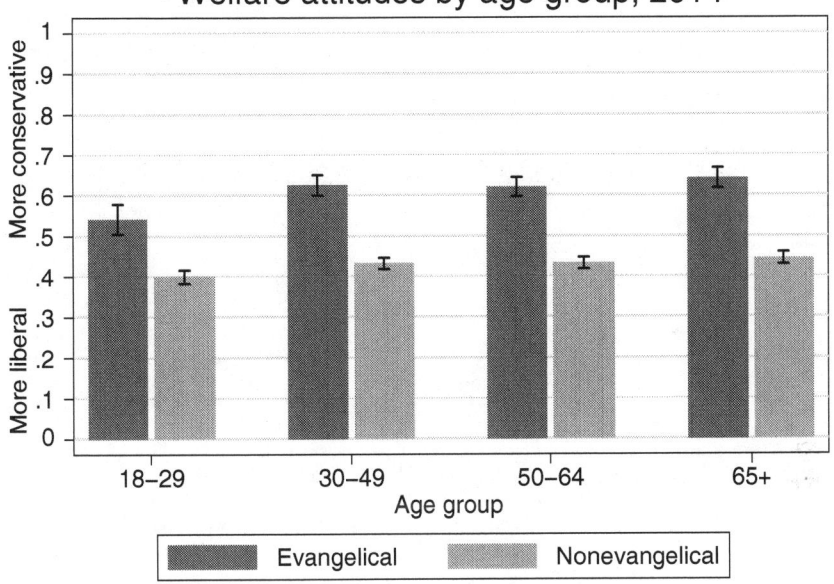

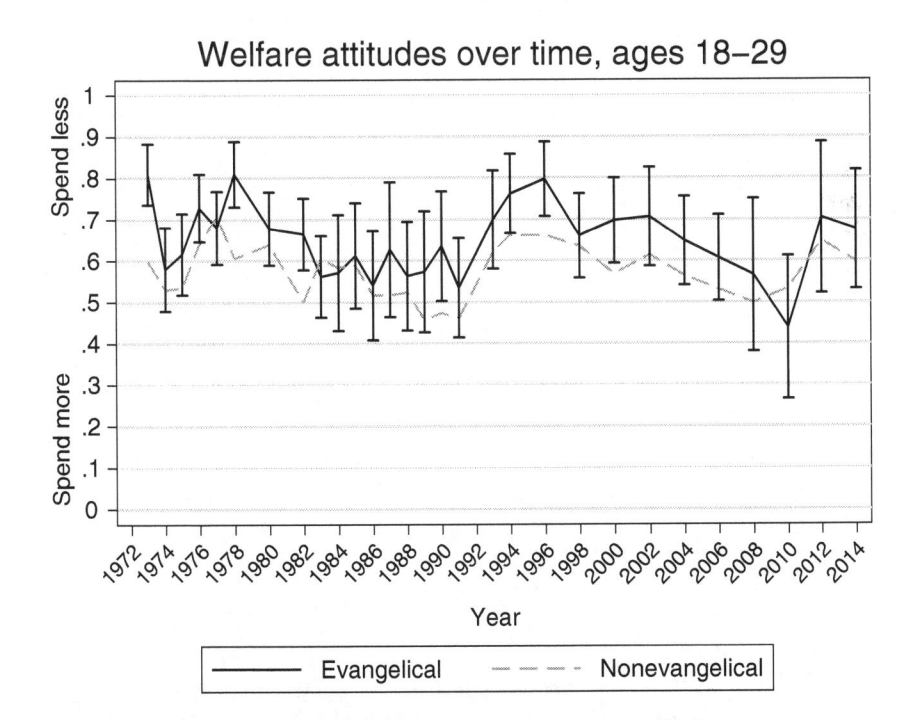

Figure 2.7. Trends in welfare attitudes among young evangelicals.

Source: Weighted 2014 Pew Religious Landscape Study; 1972–2014 General Social Survey.
Note: Error bars represent 95 percent confidence intervals.

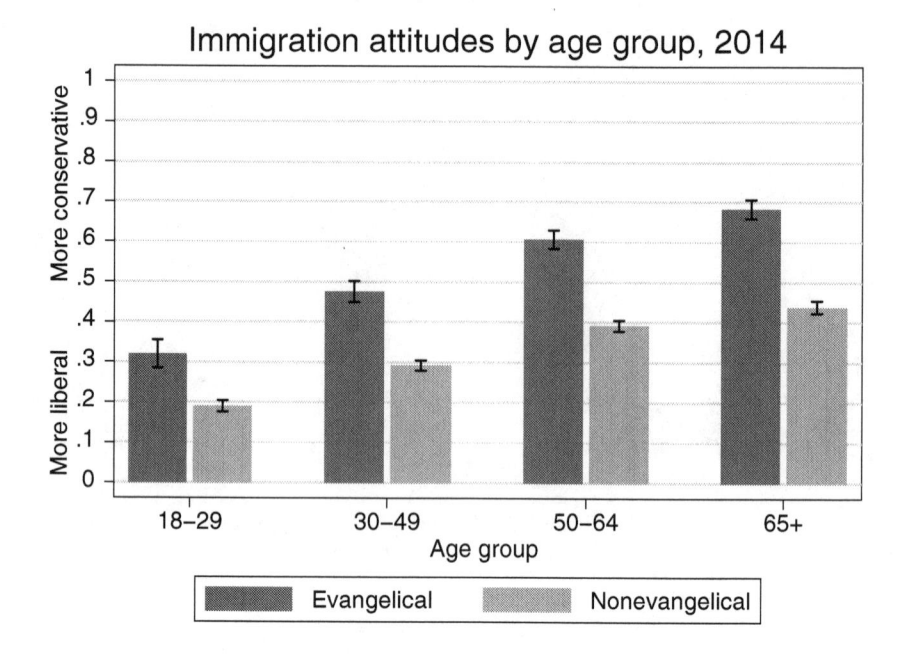

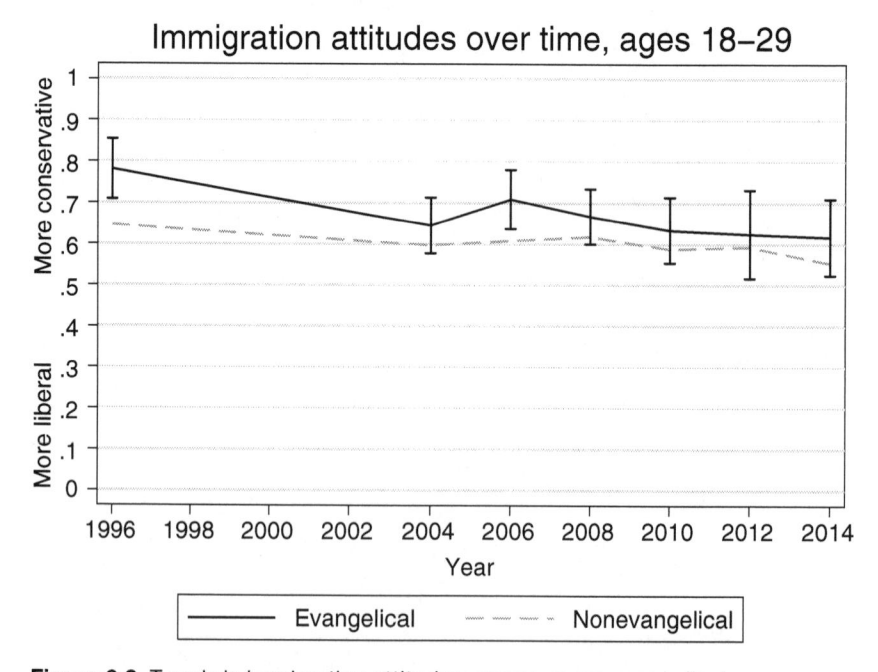

Figure 2.8. Trends in immigration attitudes among young evangelicals.
Source: Weighted 2014 Pew Religious Landscape Study; 1972–2014 General Social Survey.
Note: Error bars represent 95 percent confidence intervals.

32 percent of young evangelicals say that immigrants have been a change for the worse, compared to a whopping 68 percent of evangelicals ages sixty-five and older. Following the now-familiar pattern, in all age groups, evangelicals are distinctive compared to nonevangelicals. In the eighteen to twenty-nine age group, evangelicals were about 13 percentage points more likely than nonevangelicals to take the conservative position.

For time-series data, I employ a GSS question which asked, "Do you think the number of immigrants to America nowadays should be increased a lot, increased a little, remain the same, reduced a little, or reduced a lot." Responses were recoded to range from 0 (increased a lot) to 1 (reduced a lot). Unfortunately, this question was asked only in 1996 and from 2004 to the present, making this time series shorter. The data, shown in the bottom panel of Figure 2.8, reveal that the mean attitude on immigration among young evangelicals has fallen from .78 in 1996 to .62 in 2014 (this effect barely misses statistical significance). The graph also shows that young evangelicals appear to be converging with other young people in their opinions on immigration, and the differences between these groups are now small and not statistically significant.

Foreign Policy Issues

A final area in which young evangelicals may be changing is foreign policy. Unfortunately, more recent surveys like the 2014 Pew Religious Landscape Study and the 2016 CCES did not ask many questions about foreign policy. Therefore, I use data from the 2007 Pew Religious Landscape Study. One issue of interest is attitudes toward the military. The survey asked respondents to choose from between two statements: "The best way to ensure peace is through military strength" or "Good diplomacy is the best way to ensure peace." The data in Figure 2.9 show that about 39 percent of young evangelicals took the pro-military position, compared to 46 percent of the thirty to forty-nine age group and 53 percent of the fifty to sixty-four age group. Evangelicals are again significantly more conservative than nonevangelicals in every age category. Here, young evangelicals are about 16 percentage points more likely to take the pro-military position than young nonevangelicals.

Time-series data again come from the GSS, which asked, "Are we spending too much, too little, or about the right amount on the military, armaments, and defense?" The data have been recoded to range from 0 (too little) to .5 (the right amount) to 1 (too much). Figure 2.9 shows that since the late 1980s, young evangelicals have been fairly consistent in their belief that the United States is spending about the right amount on the military. The figure also shows that young evangelicals tend to favor more military spending

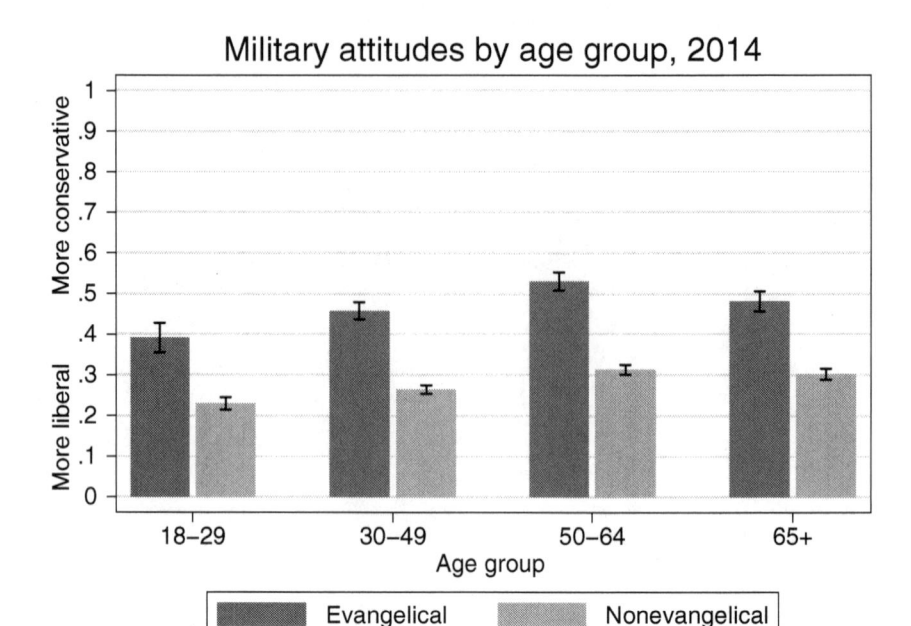

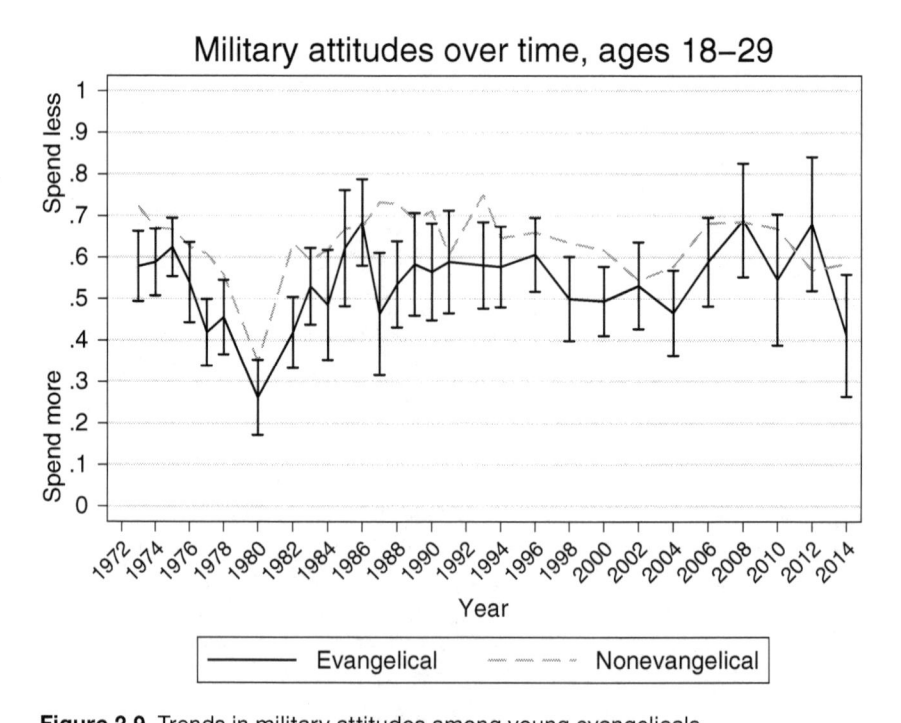

Figure 2.9. Trends in military attitudes among young evangelicals.

Source: Weighted 2007 Pew Religious Landscape Study; 1972–2014 General Social Survey.
Note: Error bars represent 95 percent confidence intervals.

than nonevangelicals, although because of the small sample sizes, the effect is rarely statistically significant.

Another question of interest is how active a role the United States should play abroad. The 2007 Pew Religious Landscape Study asked respondents which of these two statements they most agreed with: "It's best for the future of our country to be active in world affairs" (which I call the internationalist view) or "We should pay less attention to problems overseas and concentrate on problems here at home" (which I call the isolationist view). The data in Figure 2.10 show that about 40 percent of young evangelicals took the isolationist view. In this case, young evangelicals are not statistically different from either older evangelicals or nonevangelicals. Indeed, it appears that evangelicals simply are not that distinctive from other Americans in terms of their views on isolationism.

To measure the internationalist versus isolationist dynamic in the GSS data, I employ a question about spending for foreign aid. The GSS asked, "Are we spending too much, too little, or about the right amount on foreign aid?" The data have been recoded to range from 0 (too little) to .5 (the right amount) to 1 (too much). Figure 2.10 makes it clear that young people tend to believe that the United States spends too much money on foreign aid. Young evangelicals appear to be trending in a liberal direction on this issue since the mid-1990s, although the effect is not statistically significant. Moreover, young evangelicals are more or less indistinguishable from other young people on this question.

The time-series data from the GSS revealed four issues—gay marriage, welfare, immigration, and foreign aid—where young evangelicals have become more liberal over time, suggesting that period/cohort effects may be occurring. To help us distinguish between the period and cohort explanations, Figures 2.11 and 2.12 show additional analyses in which evangelicals have been coded into the Silent (1925–1942), Boomer (1943–1960), Gen X (1961–1981), or Millennial (1982–present) generations based on birth year. If period effects are driving the change, we would see most or all cohorts trending in a liberal direction together (irrespective of any cohort effects). If cohort effects are driving the change, we would see that some cohorts are systematically different from others (irrespective of any period effects). Before proceeding to the analysis, however, a word of caution is in order: in many cases, the per-generation sample of evangelicals in a given year is quite small, sometimes less than one hundred.[4] This means that the confidence intervals on the estimated means are quite broad. Therefore, the results should be taken as suggestive, rather than the final word.

Looking first at gay marriage in the top panel of Figure 2.11, there is obviously a period effect occurring: all four cohorts seem to be becoming more

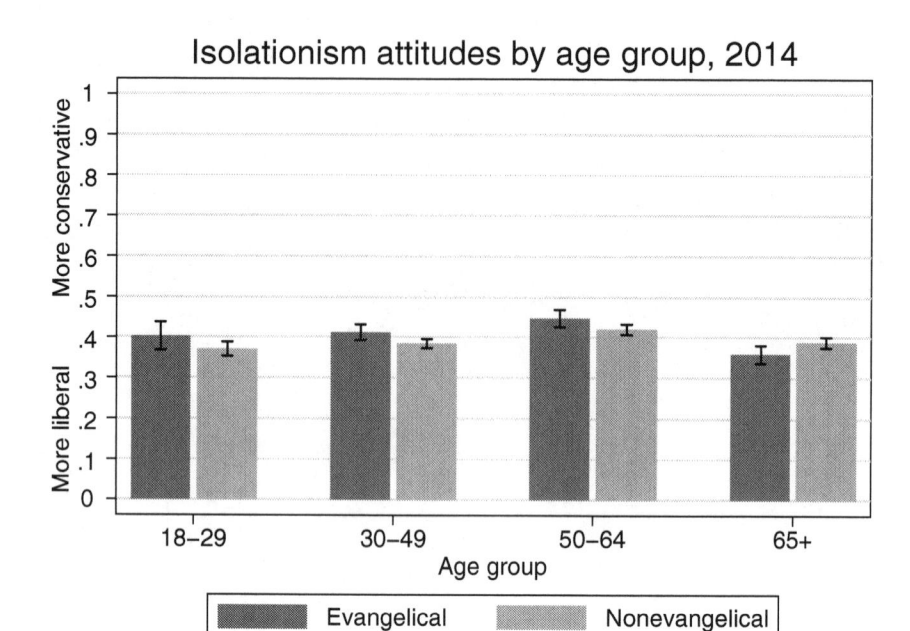

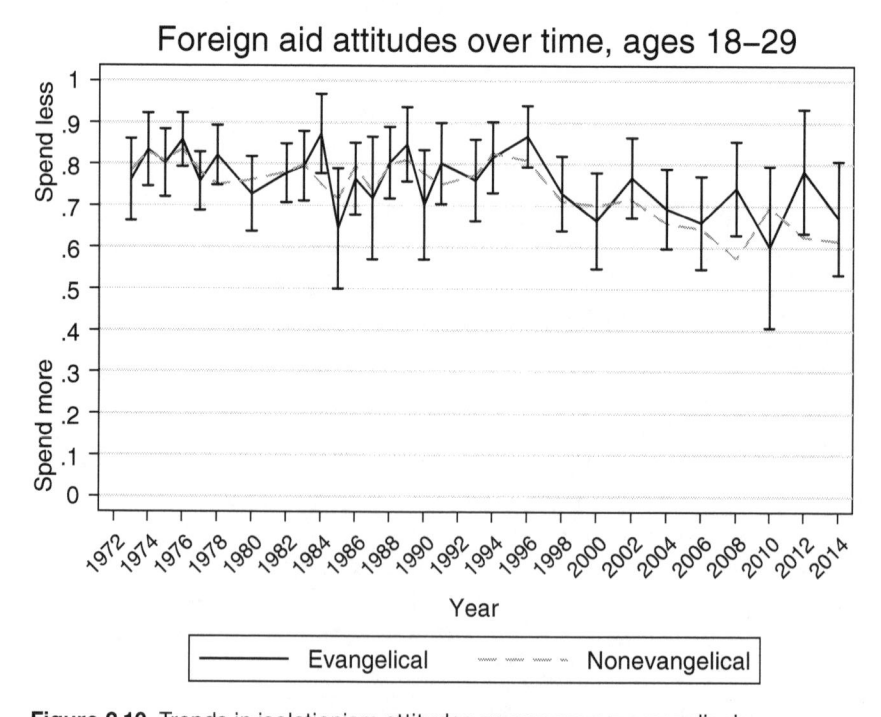

Figure 2.10. Trends in isolationism attitudes among young evangelicals.

Source: Weighted 2014 Pew Religious Landscape Study; 1972–2014 General Social Survey.
Note: Error bars represent 95 percent confidence intervals.

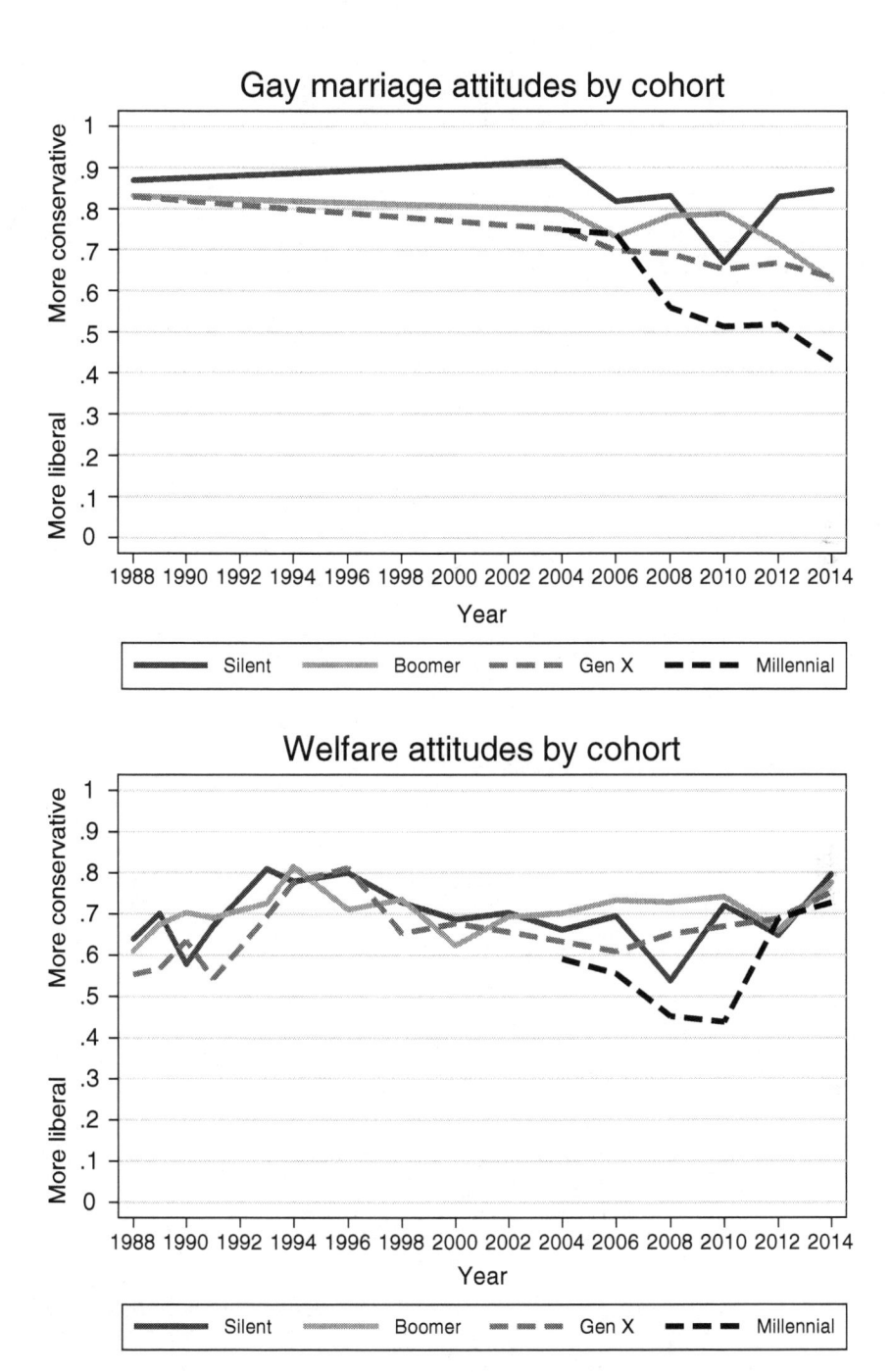

Figure 2.11. Cohort analysis of evangelicals: gay marriage and welfare.
Source: Weighted 1972–2014 General Social Survey.

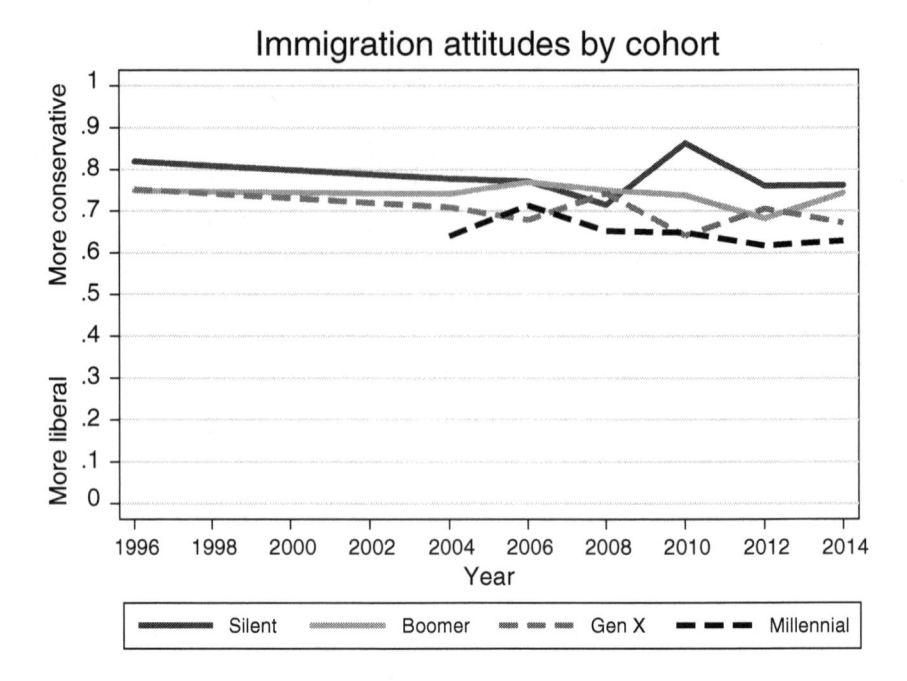

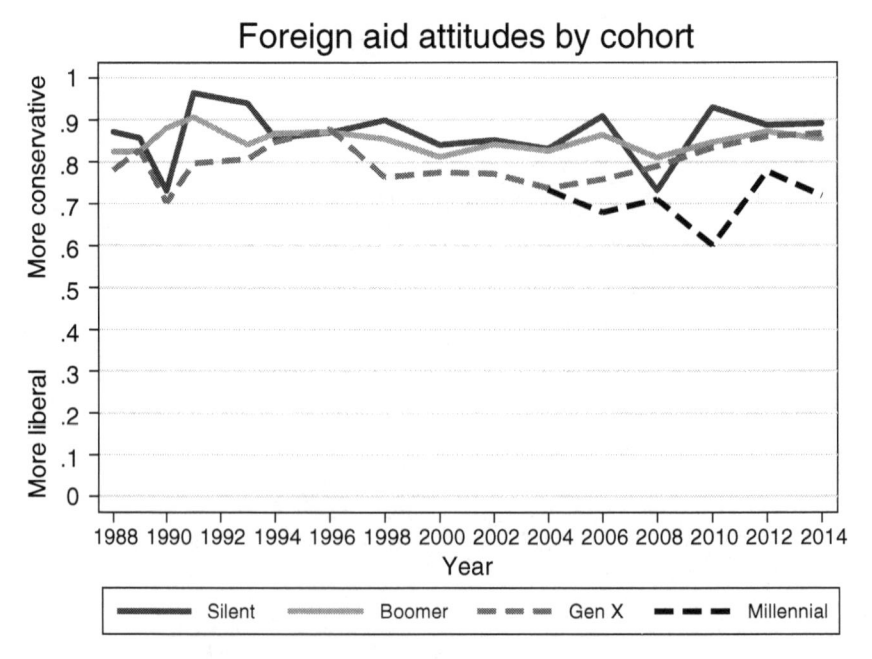

Figure 2.12. Cohort analysis of evangelicals: immigration and foreign aid.
Source: Weighted 1972–2014 General Social Survey.

liberal on gay marriage over time. However, we also see strong evidence of a cohort effect: Millennial evangelicals appear to have a mean that is 0.1 to 0.2 points more liberal than other generations. Turning to welfare in the bottom panel of Figure 2.11, evangelicals seem to have reached a conservative peak during the Republican Revolution in 1994, and have been trending ever so slightly in a liberal direction since. We see some evidence of a cohort effect among Millennials from 2004 to 2010, but by 2012, Millennial evangelicals are quite similar to their older counterparts. Therefore, it is unclear whether there is a cohort effect on welfare or not.

The top panel of Figure 2.12 shows attitudes on immigration. Here, there is evidence of a period effect, as the Silent and Boomer generations appear to be trending in a liberal direction since 2008. However, there is also some evidence of a cohort effect: Millennial evangelicals appear about 0.05 to 0.15 points more liberal compared to the older generations. Finally, as shown in the bottom panel of Figure 2.12, there is some evidence of a cohort effect on foreign aid: Millennial evangelicals appear about 0.2 points more liberal than the older generations on this question, although the size of the cohort effect seems to be shrinking in recent years (possibly in part due to the greater numbers of Millennials in the sample).

My findings in this section suggest that accounts of a new generation of liberal young evangelicals have been accurate in some ways but not others. Observers are correct that there is evidence that young evangelicals are more liberal than older evangelicals on a number of issues, including left-right ideology, 2016 presidential vote, homosexuality, gay marriage, welfare, immigration, and the military. However, the evidence presented here suggests that these differences are probably the result of age effects. When we look at the time-series data, we only see evidence of liberal cohort effects among young evangelicals on the issues of gay marriage, immigration, foreign aid, and (possibly) welfare. On most other issues, young evangelicals seem to be quite comparable to previous generations of young evangelicals. In other words, the lack of change among young evangelicals over time on these issues suggests that young evangelicals tend to be (comparably) liberal and grow more conservative as they get older and spend more time in the evangelical subculture.

How did my issue hypothesis do at explaining trends in public opinion among young evangelicals? Overall, the results are promising. In terms of the party identification, left-right ideology, and their positions on abortion, young evangelicals appear to be remarkably steady over time. I attribute this stability in part to the influence of the evangelical subculture, which for the past several decades has been socializing members into (predominantly) conservative political identities and issue positions. The only area where we saw change that did not fit with my issue hypothesis was gay marriage. However, without any data on whether the change is coming from within evangelicalism or from external sources, drawing lengthy conclusions on the nature of liberalization on these issues would be premature. Therefore, I save a more complete discussion of homosexuality and LGBT rights for Chapter 3, once I have tested the commitment hypothesis.

Issue Salience among Young Evangelicals

The previous analyses help answer some of our questions about public opinion among young evangelicals. However, some observers have also suggested that young evangelicals care less about cultural issues like abortion and gay marriage, and are instead embracing new issues like poverty and the environment (e.g., Harris 2008; Vicari 2014a). My subcultural theory, however, would lead us to expect that cultural issues would still play a major role in the political attitudes of evangelicals.

To examine issue salience among young evangelicals, I analyzed the Public Religion Research Institute's (PRRI's) Millennial Values Survey (2012), an online survey of eighteen- to twenty-four-year-olds conducted by Knowledge Networks (Public Religion Research Institute 2012). The survey gave respondents a list of issues and asked them to indicate whether each was a "critical issue," "one among many," or "not that important." In Figure 2.13, I compare the percentage of young evangelicals labeling each policy a "critical issue" to all nonevangelicals.[5] The data are organized with the most important issues to young evangelicals on the left. Not surprisingly, we see that issues that are closely related to young people's daily lives are rated highest. The most important issue among both groups was jobs and unemployment, which 72 percent of evangelicals and 77 percent of nonevangelicals said was a critical issue.

The data make it clear that young evangelicals are distinct from nonevangelicals in the degree to which they care about cultural issues. About 43 percent of young evangelicals labeled abortion a critical issue, making it their number four priority. In contrast, just 18 percent of nonevangelicals considered abortion a critical issue (this difference is significant at $p < .05$). Likewise, 33 percent of young evangelicals labeled gay marriage a critical issue, compared to just 20 percent of nonevangelicals (this difference is significant at $p < .05$). The figure also shows that young evangelicals care significantly less about education and significantly more about the federal deficit compared to nonevangelicals (both differences are statistically significant at $p < .05$).

Figure 2.13 also speaks to the argument of those observers who suggest that young evangelicals are increasingly concerned with issues like immigration, poverty, and the environment. Of the nine issues that the PRRI survey

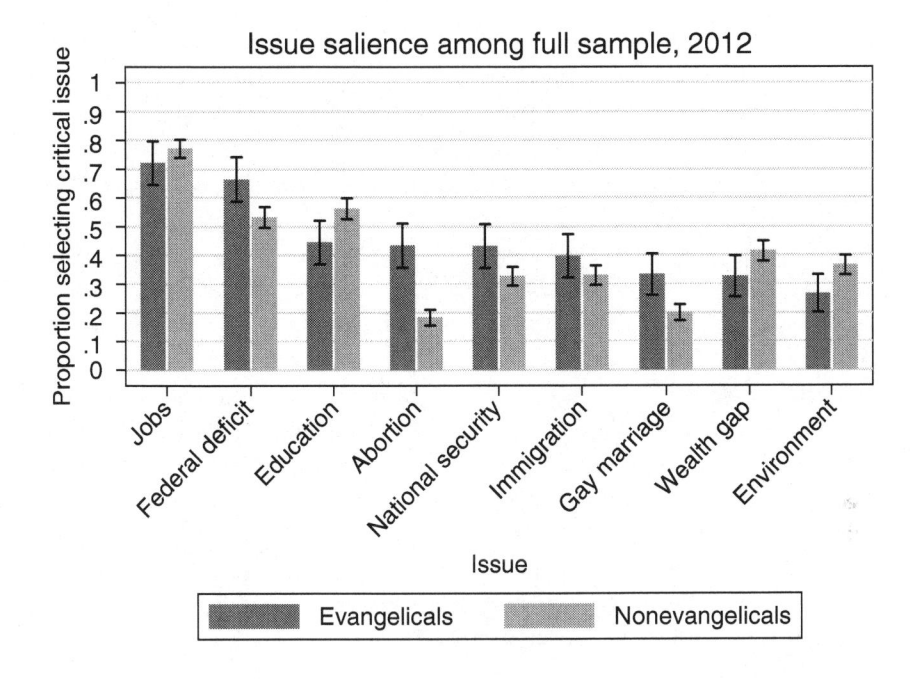

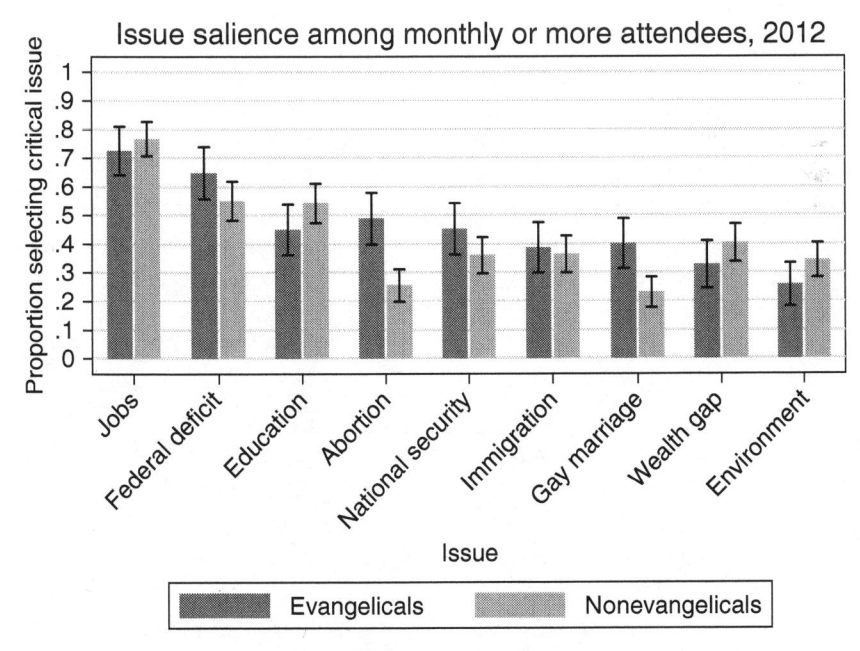

Figure 2.13. Issue salience among young evangelicals.

Source: Weighted Public Religion Research Institute Millennial Values Survey, 2012.
Note: Error bars represent 95 percent confidence intervals.

asked about, young evangelicals ranked immigration sixth, poverty and the wealth gap eighth, and the environment last (ninth). In short, there is little evidence here that young evangelicals are downplaying cultural issues like abortion and instead embracing issues like poverty and the environment.

The bottom panel of Figure 2.13 shows issue salience among "frequent attenders" (those who attend once or twice a month or more), allowing us to test whether the patterns we see hold up among those who are the most engaged in the evangelical subculture. This figure reinforces the findings from the top panel: among frequently attending evangelicals, abortion is the number three issue, behind jobs and the federal deficit, with 49 percent of frequently attending evangelicals labeling it a critical issue. Frequently attending evangelicals are more likely than nonevangelicals to label both abortion and gay marriage critical issues (significant at $p < .05$ in both cases). Finally, we see that frequently attending young evangelicals ranked immigration number seven, the gap between the rich and the poor number eight, and the environment number nine (last) on the list of issues. Once more, there is little support for the notion of young evangelicals moving their issue concerns away from cultural issues like abortion.

Conclusion

This chapter begins with a simple question: Are young evangelicals becoming more liberal? Clearly, the answer depends on which measures of public opinion we focus on. We see that in terms of their partisanship, attitudes on abortion, and isolationism, young evangelicals are about as conservative as ever. On a number of issues, including left-right ideology, homosexuality, gay marriage, welfare, immigration, and the military, young evangelicals are more liberal than older evangelicals. However, in most cases, those differences appear to be primarily age-based effects. Only on gay marriage, welfare, and immigration did we find that young evangelicals today are more liberal than previous generations of young evangelicals. Even here, it is important to note that the continued Republican identity and political conservatism of young evangelicals suggests that any issue changes do not seem to be affecting their overall political affiliations. In short, the results cast serious doubt on general accounts of a new generation of young, liberal evangelicals (e.g., Harris 2008).

The data also suggest that narratives of changing issue priorities among young evangelicals are probably overstated. In the issue salience data, we see that pocketbook issues and cultural issues like abortion appear to remain the most important in the minds of young evangelicals. Equally as important, young evangelicals continue to rank immigration, the wealth gap, and the environment fairly low in terms of their issue concerns.

The findings in this chapter generally support those of the existing literature. For example, while the use of time-series data represents an improvement over the cross-sectional data employed by Buster Smith and Byron Johnson (2010) and Mikael Pelz and Corwin Smidt (2015), the essential finding across these three studies, that young evangelicals are not so different from older generations of evangelicals in terms of their partisanship, ideology, and attitudes on abortion, lends confidence to the suggestion that evangelicals are quite stable on measures of importance to their tradition's identity. At the same time, the present chapter finds greater evidence of age differences on same-sex marriage and a variety of noncultural issues than does Smith and Johnson (2010). In Chapter 3, I examine the source of these differences in greater detail.

What the continued Republican identification and political conservatism of young, highly committed evangelicals means for larger social trends is still unclear. A number of studies have suggested that the growth in the religiously unaffiliated is due in part to moderate and liberal Christians leaving the church for political reasons (Hout and Fischer 2002; Patrikios 2008; Putnam and Campbell 2010). If young, highly committed evangelicals are staying about as Republican and conservative as they have always been, will this continue to fuel religious polarization in American society? Will the mainline and Catholic faiths face an even greater struggle to retain members as these young, conservative evangelicals continue to fuel stereotypes about religious people? Only time will tell. But given the importance of religion in predicting voting behavior and a variety of political attitudes, the answers to these questions are sure to affect the way Americans engage in politics in the coming years. Therefore, continued monitoring of the trends discussed in this chapter is most certainly warranted.

3

Inside Out or Outside In

Explaining Change among Young Evangelicals

Both within the evangelical subculture and in the broader culture, there is a sense that young evangelicals are different. As Chapter 2 reveals, there is some truth to the idea that young evangelicals are more liberal than previous generations of young evangelicals on issues like gay marriage, welfare, and immigration. The question is why? More specifically, are any of the changes we see driven by factors internal to the church or are they driven by factors external to the church? What seems like a relatively straightforward question turns out to provoke wildly varying answers. I divide explanations for change into two basic categories. One school of thought is that changes *external* to evangelicalism, such as modernization, secularization, and the liberalism of the Millennial generation, are pushing young evangelicals toward the left. A second school of thought argues that changes *internal* to evangelicalism, including the collapse of the institutions of the New Christian Right and a new generation of more moderate religious leaders, might be the real cause of the change.

In this chapter, I attempt to use social science to answer this debate. If factors external to evangelicalism are driving the change, we would expect to see change concentrated among infrequent attendees who are more exposed to secular messages and less exposed to the insulating qualities of the evangelical subculture. If factors internal to evangelicalism are driving the change, we would expect to see change concentrated among frequent attendees, who are most embedded in the subculture and who therefore will hear the new messages more frequently.

Answering this debate provides an ideal opportunity to test my commitment hypothesis, which emphasizes that the evangelical subculture's impact should be greatest among those who are immersed in the evangelical subculture. Such individuals are more likely to develop evangelical identities, hold evangelicalism's distinctive beliefs, be exposed to its messages that discredit secular culture, and receive direct political messages from evangelical sources. Thus, the commitment hypothesis leads us to expect to find mostly evidence of changes *external* to evangelicalism, especially on partisanship, ideology, and cultural issues. If we are to find any evidence of changes *internal* to evangelicalism, we are likely to do so on noncultural issues.

Explaining Change among Young Evangelicals

Explanations have suggested two possible sources for any liberalization among young evangelicals, which I label "change from the outside" and "change from the inside." The "change from the outside" narrative focuses on how factors external to evangelical Protestantism (that is, changes to the broader society) are liberalizing evangelicals. One natural starting place is the general assumption that Millennials as a whole are more liberal than the preceding generations. The scholarly literature generally supports this analysis, although the trend is not apparent in every issue and is easily overstated (Abramson, Aldrich, and Rohde 2011; Winograd and Hais 2008, 2011; Zukin et al. 2006). The "change from the outside" narrative assumes that evangelicals, like other members of their cohort, have been affected by these changes.

One important factor that may be making Millennials more liberal is modernization. Key aspects of modernization, including rationalization and the adoption of science, have generally been understood to undermine the credibility of traditional religious worldviews (e.g., Apter 1967; Weber 1930). Modernization is behind many of the most important social changes of the past century, including globalization, the increasing emphasis on science, engineering, technology, and mathematics (STEM) fields, and the increasing reliance on technology to create social change. In addition, modernization's rejection of traditional ways of knowing is naturally connected with an emphasis on accepting diversity. Morley Winograd and Michael Hais (2008) argue that Millennials have been socialized into tolerance and acceptance, and this serves as a foundation for their bourgeoning liberalism. Cohort theory suggests that these common experiences would apply to evangelicals as much as any other group.

Modernization is also frequently accompanied by secularization, which Keith Roberts defines as "the declining scope of religious authority" across various areas and levels of society (2004, 314) (e.g., Bellah 1970; Berger 1967, 1979; Chaves 1993, 1994; Parsons 1964; Tschannen 1991; Weber 1930). Manifestations of secularization may include increasing differentiation between secular and religious spheres, the declining power of organized religion and an accompanying privatization of religion, desacralization, and liberalization of religious doctrine (Berger 1967, 1979; Roberts 2004; Tschannen 1991; Wald and Calhoun-Brown 2014). As organized religion's influence fades because of secularization, we might expect evangelicals to become more liberal simply because they reject the teachings of religious elites.

The Millennial generation has also been disproportionately affected by the politicization of religious affiliation. Robert Putnam and David Campbell (2010) summarize the religious history of the twentieth century in terms of an "earthquake"—the liberalism of the 1960s. This earthquake led to an "aftershock" in the 1970s and 1980s, including the rise of the New Christian Right. However, the New Christian Right's fusion of religion and politics led to a "second aftershock" in the 2000s, in which American interest in organized religion waned and the percentage of Americans with no religious affiliation increased rapidly. While some of that reduction in interest in religion may stem from secularization, the politicization of religion appears to be having its own independent effect (Hout and Fischer 2002, cf. Marwell and Demerath 2003). Another consequence of the politicization of religion may be a growing desire for political civility among Millennials, leading them toward more moderate political views (Howe and Strauss 2000). Naturally, then, this explanation would lead us to expect that the evangelical fervor of the 1980s, especially on cultural issues, may be weakening. In his influential article "The End of Christian America," author Jon Meacham (2009a; see also 2009b) describes two religious trends of the 2000s—the increasing percentage of Americans with no religious affiliation and the collapse of the Christian Right (to be discussed)—as the most important factors in the waning influence of Christianity in the United States. This declining influence has been felt among all generations (Hout and Fischer 2002) but is most apparent among Millennials (e.g., Wuthnow 2007).

In contrast, the "change from the inside" narrative suggests that developments within evangelicalism might be driving changes in public opinion. One potential source of change may be shifts in religious leadership within the tradition. Public opinion theory acknowledges that elites are an important source of opinion leadership (e.g., Carmines and Stimson 1989; Katz and Lazarsfeld 1955; Layman 2001; Lazarsfeld, Berelson, and Gaudet 1944). Religious elites, in particular, can have a powerful influence on the attitudes of mass-level adherents (e.g., Campbell, Green, and Monson 2014,

Ch. 6; Djupe and Gilbert 2002, 2003, 2009; Guth et al. 1997; Kohut et al. 2000; Smidt 2004; Smith 2008). At the national level, a group of charismatic elites, including Jerry Falwell, Pat Robertson, James Dobson, and Phyllis Schlafly, were an important factor in the increasing perception of evangelicals as staunch political conservatives (Capps 1994; Martin 2005; Wilcox and Robinson 2010; Williams 2010). However, several of these leaders of the Christian Right have passed away, including Jerry Falwell in 2007 and Phyllis Schlafly in 2016. Others have faded from the public eye. James Dobson stepped down as president and CEO of Focus on the Family in 2003, although he continues to record his radio show *Family Talk* (not affiliated with Focus on the Family). As of March 2019, Pat Robertson still hosts *The 700 Club*, but his political influence has clearly waned since the 1990s.

Observers have noted that the next generation of evangelical leaders are different in both style and substance. Often grouped together under the label of "the new evangelicals," Rick Warren, Joel Osteen, Joel Hunter, and others have seemingly taken a more moderate tone on divisive cultural issues like abortion and homosexuality (Lyons 2012; Pally 2011; Wear 2014; Wehner 2007). They have also increased the salience of a host of new issues, including poverty, environmental stewardship, AIDS, and immigration (FitzGerald 2017). In addition, Pope Francis is quite popular among evangelicals, and his style has helped create a more general perception that religious leaders are prepared to move beyond the "culture wars" (e.g., Moon 2013; Wehner 2015). Observers suggest that more liberal clergy are translating into a more general movement of young evangelicals toward liberal politics and the Democratic Party (Harris 2008; Mendenhall 2006; Vicari 2014a; Wear 2014).

A second major change is a collapse of many of the subcultural institutions that fueled the mobilization of evangelicals into conservative politics. The Moral Majority, which helped propel Ronald Reagan to the presidency in the 1980s, fell apart because of budget concerns in 1989. Pat Robertson's Christian Coalition picked up where the Moral Majority left off, achieving the height of its influence in the early 1990s (Martin 2005). The organization still exists today, but shrinking budgets and declining grassroots support have reduced its influence to a fraction of what it once was (Cooperman and Edsall 2006). Focus on the Family is probably the strongest of the remaining Christian Right organizations, but it, too, has experienced waning influence, shrinking budgets, and staff layoffs since the peak of the New Christian Right (Draper 2011). Given the role that the Christian Right played in mobilizing evangelicals, it might be the case that once these organizations lost influence, young evangelicals had fewer cues to guide them to conservative politics, thereby making room for liberalization.

The Source of Change: Testing the Commitment Hypothesis

On their face, both "inside out" and "outside in" seem plausible, so determining which is accurate may be difficult. Luckily, the commitment hypothesis introduced in Chapter 1 can help make predictions on the causes of change among young evangelicals. Experts stress that religious commitment is an increasingly important factor in the development of political attitudes (e.g., Kellstedt et al. 1996; Layman and Green 2005; Leege and Kellstedt 1993; Smidt, Kellstedt, and Guth 2009). Those who are in the pews on Sundays, and who are otherwise active in their faith, are more likely to be exposed to political messages from pastors, religious leaders, and their fellow members (e.g., Djupe and Gilbert 2009; Smith 2008). This suggests that if developments internal to evangelicalism are driving any observed change, we would expect to see the evidence of change concentrated at the "center" of the tradition, among the most committed evangelicals. In other words, if changes *internal* to evangelicalism were causing the liberalization, we would expect to see a pattern in which there was a comparatively large age gap among the most religiously committed and a comparatively smaller age gap among the least religiously committed.

In contrast, the commitment hypothesis that I derive from my subcultural theory says that any evidence of change, especially on issues like abortion, gay marriage, party, ideology, and vote choice, that are closely tied to the evangelical subculture's identity, should be concentrated at the periphery of the tradition, among those with the lowest levels of religious commitment. Practically speaking, if change is coming from outside evangelicalism, we would expect to find either (1) the age gap to be roughly the same, no matter the level of religious commitment or (2) the age gap to be small or nonexistent among the most religiously committed, and larger among the least religiously committed.

Methods and Data

I test my hypothesis using the 2007 and 2014 Pew Religious Landscape Studies, as well as the 2012 and 2016 Cooperative Congressional Election Studies.[1] To visualize the difference between high- and low-commitment evangelicals, for each measure of political identity and issue covered in Chapter 2, I ran an appropriate regression model (ordinary least squares [OLS] or logistic regression) on all evangelicals. The independent variables in the model include age, age squared (to account for the possibility of curvilinear age effects), religious commitment, and a religious commitment x age interaction term.[2] I then calculated predicted probabilities by fixing each respondent's religious commitment at 0 (the lowest possible) and 1 (the highest possible), and varying the imputed age (e.g., Rising 2012).

In the top panel of Figure 3.1, we see that the predicted partisanship as an individual ages is remarkably stable for the most committed evangelicals. The predicted partisanship for highly committed eighteen-year-old evangelicals is about .70, essentially identical to the prediction for seventy- to seventy-four-year-old evangelicals. We also see quite a bit of stability among the least-committed evangelicals. There, the predicted partisanship for eighteen-year-olds is .31, compared to .36 for evangelicals in the seventy to seventy-four age range.

The pattern for ideology, shown in the bottom panel of Figure 3.1, is similar. Among the most-committed evangelicals, the predicted ideology for eighteen-year-olds is .65, compared to .73 among the seventy to seventy-four age group. Among the least-committed evangelicals, the predicted ideology for eighteen-year-olds is .27, compared to .45 among seventy- to seventy-four-year-olds. We can also see that while the gap between the eighteen to twenty-four and seventy to seventy-four age groups was about .08 among highly committed evangelicals, it grew to .18 among low-commitment evangelicals. This suggests that any change in ideology among evangelicals is concentrated at the periphery of the tradition.

A similar pattern is visible in Figure 3.2, which shows the predicted probability of voting for Mitt Romney (based on a dichotomous version of the 2012 vote). As the figure indicates, the predicted probability for highly committed eighteen-year-old evangelicals (.84) is only slightly smaller than the predicted probability for seventy-eight-year-olds (.87). Among evangelicals with the minimum level of commitment, the gap is much wider: the probability of voting for Romney is .50 for seventy-eight-year-olds, but just .33 for eighteen-year-olds. This suggests that while political observers are certainly correct that some young evangelicals were breaking for Obama, the change again seems to be concentrated among the least-committed evangelicals.

For 2016, it is clear that the age gap among evangelicals is larger, but the underlying dynamics are similar. The bottom panel of Figure 3.2 shows the probability of voting for Donald Trump in a two-candidate race between Trump and Hillary Clinton. The data indicate that, among highly committed evangelicals, the probability of eighteen-year-olds voting for Trump was about .76, compared to about .90 among seventy-eight-year-olds. Among the least-committed evangelicals, the probability of eighteen-year-olds voting for Trump was .38, compared to .54 among seventy-eight-year-olds. The fact

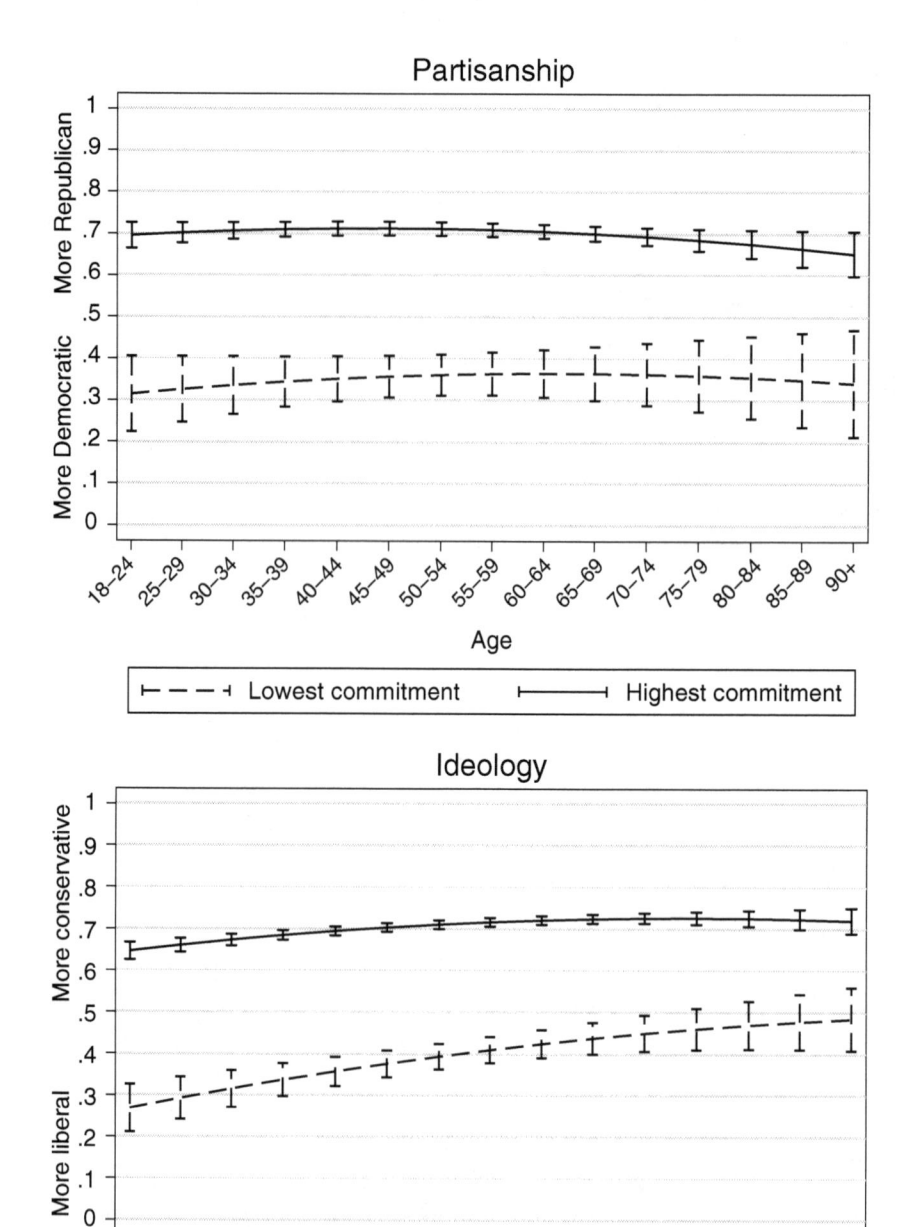

Figure 3.1. Predicted partisanship and ideology among evangelicals by religious commitment.

Source: Weighted 2014 Pew Religious Landscape Study.
Note: Error bars represent 95 percent confidence intervals.

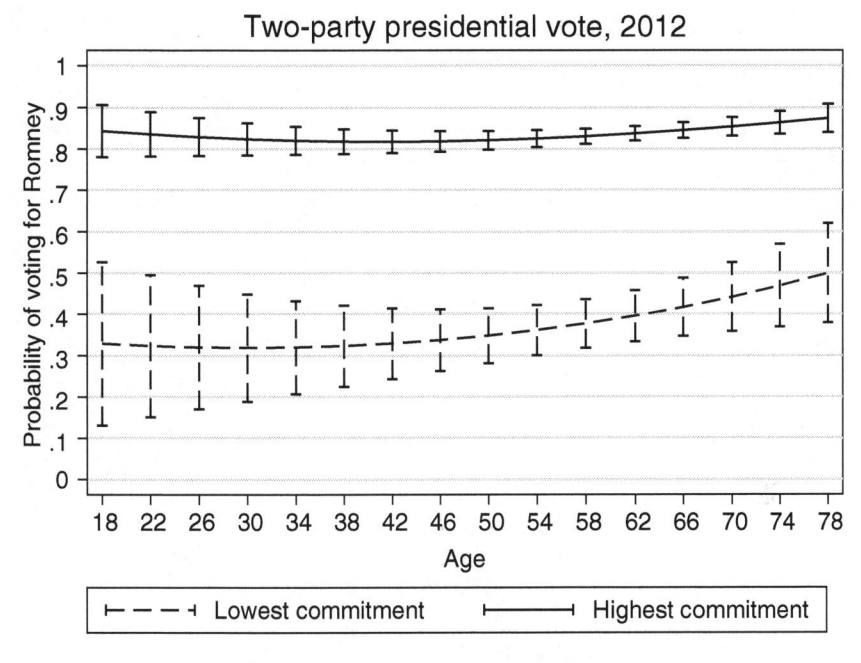

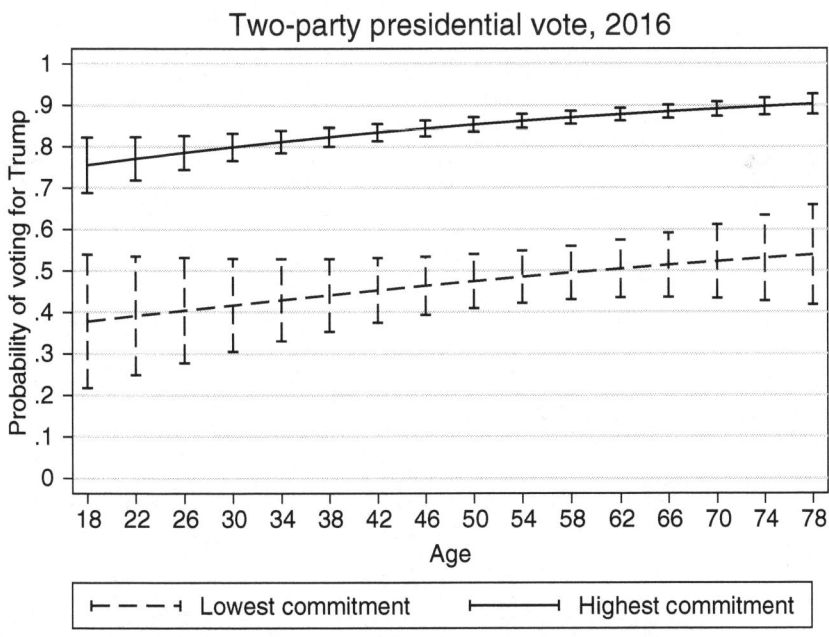

Figure 3.2. Predicted presidential vote among evangelicals by religious commitment, 2012 and 2016.

Source: Weighted 2012 and 2016 Cooperative Congressional Election Study.
Note: Error bars represent 95 percent confidence intervals.

that the age gap among committed evangelicals (.15) is very similar in size to the age gap among low-commitment evangelicals (.16) again suggests that the age gap is probably driven by factors external to evangelicalism, such as Donald Trump's comparatively conservative policies on issues important to younger voters, like student debt and LGBT rights.

Figure 3.3 shows predicted attitudes on abortion. In a familiar theme from the previous chapter, the model indicates that highly committed young evangelicals are actually more conservative on abortion compared to their middle-aged counterparts. The predicted attitude on abortion for highly committed eighteen-year-olds is .78, compared to .70 for their seventy- to seventy-four-year-old counterparts. In contrast, the predicted attitude on abortion for the least-committed eighteen-year-olds is .10, compared to .16 among seventy- to seventy-four-year-olds.

This finding may give reason to question the accuracy of existing explanations of why public opinion on abortion is becoming more conservative. One commonly cited factor for the conservative trend in public opinion on abortion is the debate over partial birth abortion (Jelen 2009). A second com-

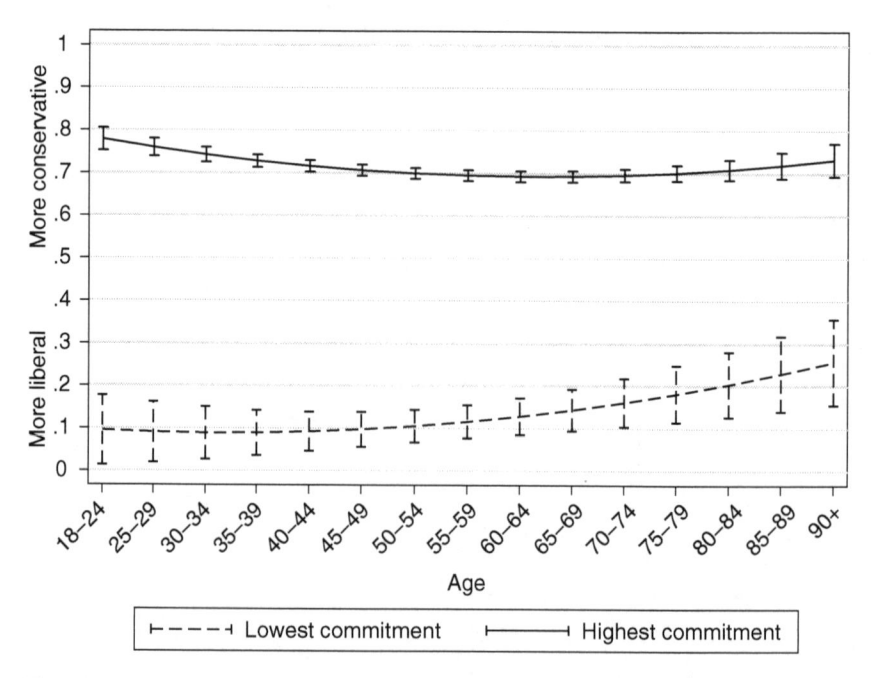

Figure 3.3. Predicted abortion attitudes among evangelicals by religious commitment.

Source: Weighted 2014 Pew Religious Landscape Study.
Note: Error bars represent 95 percent confidence intervals.

monly cited factor is the decoupling of religion and abortion. Robert Putnam and David Campbell label Millennials "the Juno generation" because they are more pro-life than previous generations for secular reasons, which can be seen, for example, in the negative portrayal of abortion in film and media (2010, 412–414). If these two factors were driving the change among evangelicals, we would expect to see the change concentrated among those with the lowest levels of religious commitment. Instead, we see that increasing conservatism on abortion is concentrated among the most committed, suggesting instead that changes internal to evangelicalism are driving the differences. For the sake of speculation, perhaps evangelical leaders are becoming more persuasive in discussing the issue, or perhaps young evangelicals are growing up in an era where the expectations in terms of attitudes on abortion are even more clear than they were in the 1980s. In any case, this is an interesting finding that warrants further research.

How does this subcultural theory help explain those public opinion items where we saw greater evidence of change: gay marriage, welfare, and immigration? Beginning with attitudes toward homosexuality (shown in the top panel of Figure 3.4), the model predicts that highly committed eighteen- to twenty-four-year-old evangelicals would have a .65 probability of saying society should discourage homosexuality, compared to a .88 probability among those ninety and older. Among low-commitment evangelicals, eighteen- to twenty-four-year-olds have a .01 probability of saying society should discourage homosexuality, compared to a .24 probability among those ninety and older. Turning our attention to attitudes on gay marriage (shown in the bottom panel of Figure 3.4), the pattern is familiar. Among highly committed evangelicals, the predicted probability of opposing gay marriage is .71 for eighteen-year-olds, compared to .92 for those ninety and older. Among the least-committed evangelicals, the predicted probability of opposing gay marriage is .02 for eighteen- to twenty-four-year-olds, compared to .33 for their ninety-plus counterparts. The fact that frequent attendees and infrequent attendees seem to be changing at about the same rate on both measures suggests that factors external to evangelicalism are probably driving the liberalization.

Nevertheless, from the perspective of my issue hypothesis, it is surprising that we would find any change among the most committed evangelicals. There are a few possible explanations for this finding. First, given the dramatic age gap among low-commitment evangelicals, the most likely explanation is that the messages on homosexuality and gay marriage in the secular culture, ranging from *Will and Grace* and *Glee* to comic book characters like the Green Lantern, are making their way to highly committed evangelicals as well (Douglas and Clark 2015).

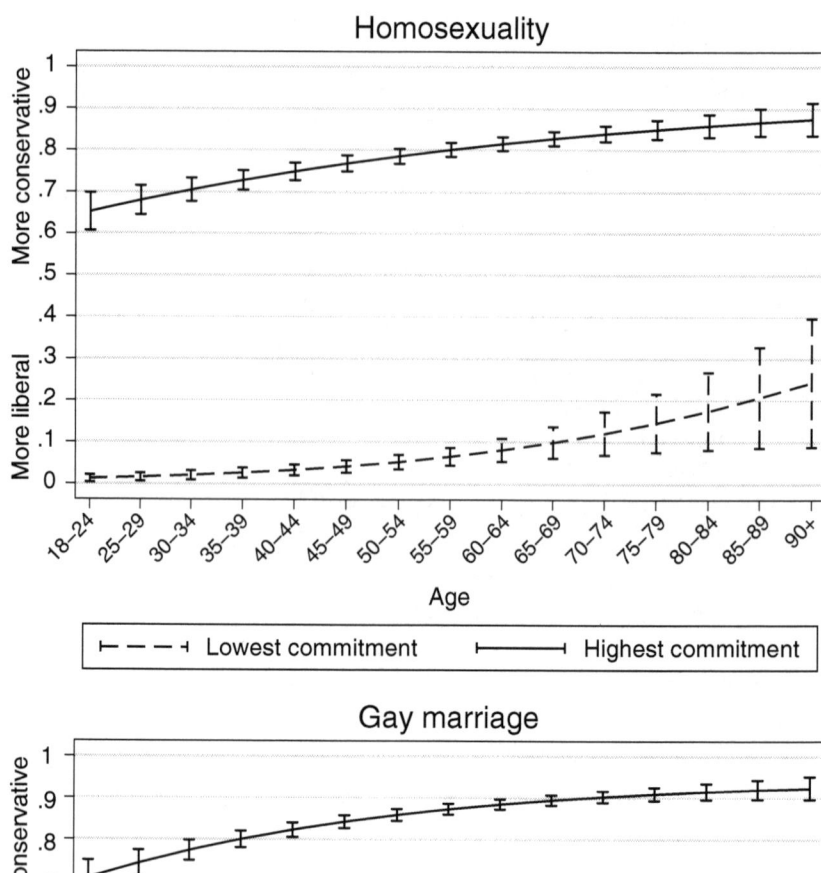

Figure 3.4. Predicted attitudes on homosexuality and gay marriage among evangelicals by religious commitment.

Source: Weighted 2014 Pew Religious Landscape Study.
Note: Error bars represent 95 percent confidence intervals.

However, there are two other possibilities that warrant further discussion. First, as I note in Chapter 1, sometimes subcultures have to give up beliefs that have previously been important to them if those beliefs begin to threaten their continued success in the religious marketplace. An example is the Mormon subculture giving up on polygamy when it became clear that maintaining the practice would lead to continued conflicts with non-Mormons and the United States federal government (Campbell, Green, and Monson 2014). Given the enormous emphasis on gay marriage in the late 2000s and the increasing degree to which opposition to LGBT rights is heavily criticized in secular society, it may be that the evangelical subculture is in the early stages of giving up its commitment to conservative views on homosexuality and gay marriage.

Finally, it may be that opposition to homosexuality and gay marriage were never really as important a part of the evangelical identity as left-right ideological conservatism and pro-life attitudes. As I argue in Chapter 1, while the evangelical subculture was always opposed to homosexuality, homosexuality and gay marriage are only fairly recent additions to the political agenda. The 2004 election was probably the first in which gay marriage "mattered," and even then, it was on the agenda only because of strategic behavior among Republican elites (Campbell and Monson 2007). Adjudicating between these explanations for why we see some change at the core of the evangelical tradition on homosexuality is beyond the scope of this chapter, but it could be an important question for future research.

When it comes to attitudes on the environment (top panel of Figure 3.5), we see a large age gap among both the most and the least committed. The figure shows that the probability of highly committed eighteen- to twenty-four-year-old evangelicals saying that stricter environmental laws cost too many jobs and hurt the economy is .47, compared to .63 among seventy- to seventy-four-year-olds. Likewise, the probability of taking the antienvironment stance among the least religious is .20 among eighteen- to twenty-four-year-olds and increases to .46 among seventy-five- to seventy-nine-year-olds. The relative symmetry of the figure suggests that something external to the church is responsible for the change we see. The strong age-based effects suggest that factors like education or a realization that young people will have to live with the consequences of climate change are more likely behind any shifts among evangelicals on this issue.

The bottom panel of Figure 3.5 shows the probability of a respondent believing that welfare does more harm than good. Here, we see a curvilinear pattern among both the most and the least committed. The figure shows that the probability of highly committed eighteen- to twenty-four-year-old evangelicals responding that welfare does more harm than good is .58, which

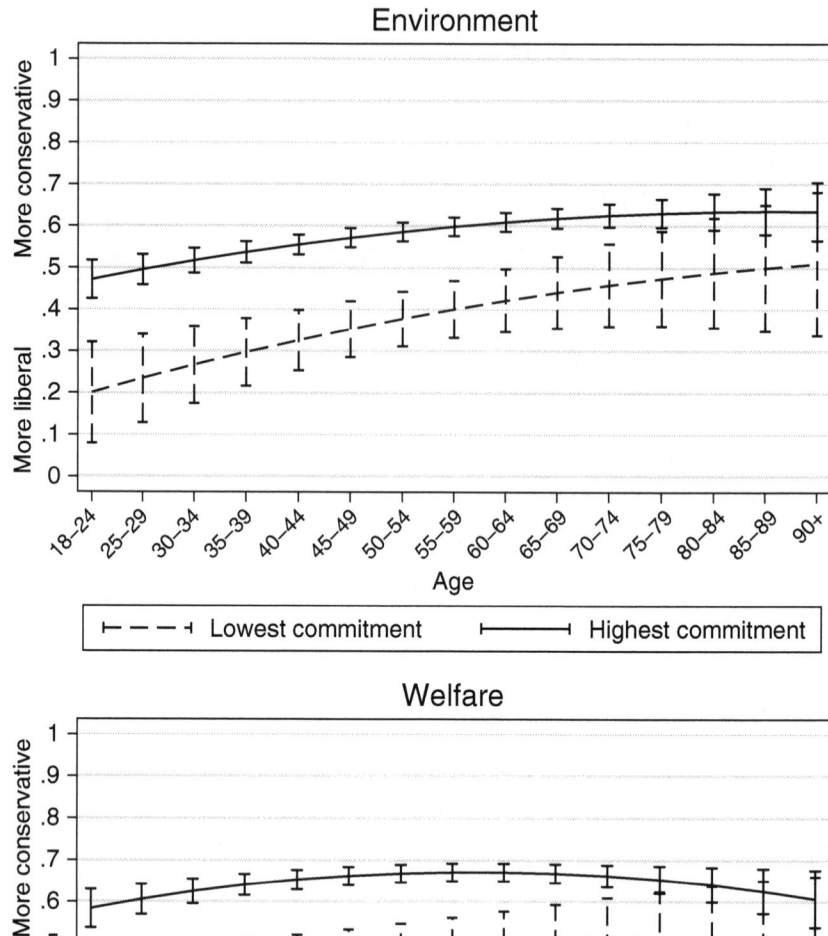

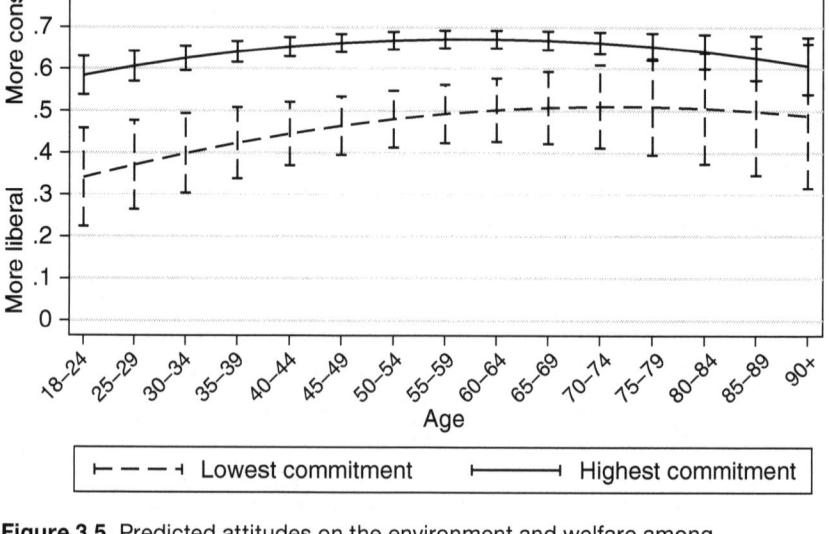

Figure 3.5. Predicted attitudes on the environment and welfare among evangelicals by religious commitment.

Source: Weighted 2014 Pew Religious Landscape Study.
Note: Error bars represent 95 percent confidence intervals.

rises to a peak of about .67 among sixty- to sixty-four-year-olds before declining to about .61 among those 90 and older. It might be tempting to attribute this rise to a cohort effect among those who grew up in the 1980s, during the peak of the Christian Right's influence. However, the pattern is similar among the least committed: the probability of believing that welfare does more harm than good among the eighteen to twenty-four age group is .34, which rises to .51 among fifty to fifty-four-year-olds before dropping slightly to .49 among those 90 and older. The similar patterns among the most and least committed suggest that the curvilinear pattern is probably more likely an age-based effect, in which low earners (the young and the elderly) naturally prefer a larger safety net, while high earners (forty- and fifty-year-olds) prefer a smaller safety net.

On the issue of immigration, a very different pattern is evident. Figure 3.6 shows the probability of responding that immigration has been a change for the worse. Overall, it is clear from the figure that evangelicals are far from progressive on immigration. However, this is the first time that we have seen change concentrated among highly committed evangelicals. The figure shows a .27 probability of highly committed eighteen- to twenty-four-year-old evangelicals saying that increasing immigration has been bad for society, compared to a .72 probability of someone from the ninety and older age group making the same statement. Among low-commitment evangelicals, there was a .40 probability of eighteen- to twenty-four-year-olds saying immigrants have been a change for the worse, which is quite comparable to the .53 probability of those ninety and older saying the same. Thus, while the age gap between young and old evangelicals is about .13 points among the least committed, the age gap rises to about .45 points among the most committed. In short, it appears that the evangelical tradition may be changing its views on immigration from the inside.

To measure respondent attitudes on the trade-off between military and diplomacy, I return to the 2007 Religious Landscape Study. Figure 3.7 shows the probability of agreeing with the statement "The best way to ensure peace is through military strength." We see that the probability of taking the militaristic perspective for high-commitment eighteen-year-old evangelicals is .35, compared to a high of .56 among sixty-two-year-olds. Among low-commitment evangelicals, the probability of taking the militaristic perspective is .30 for eighteen-year-olds, compared to .38 among fifty-year-olds. Although the trend is not as clear as immigration, this appears to be another area where the age gap is greater among young evangelicals than their older counterparts, suggesting that perhaps the evangelical tradition is experiencing (slow) change from the inside on this issue.

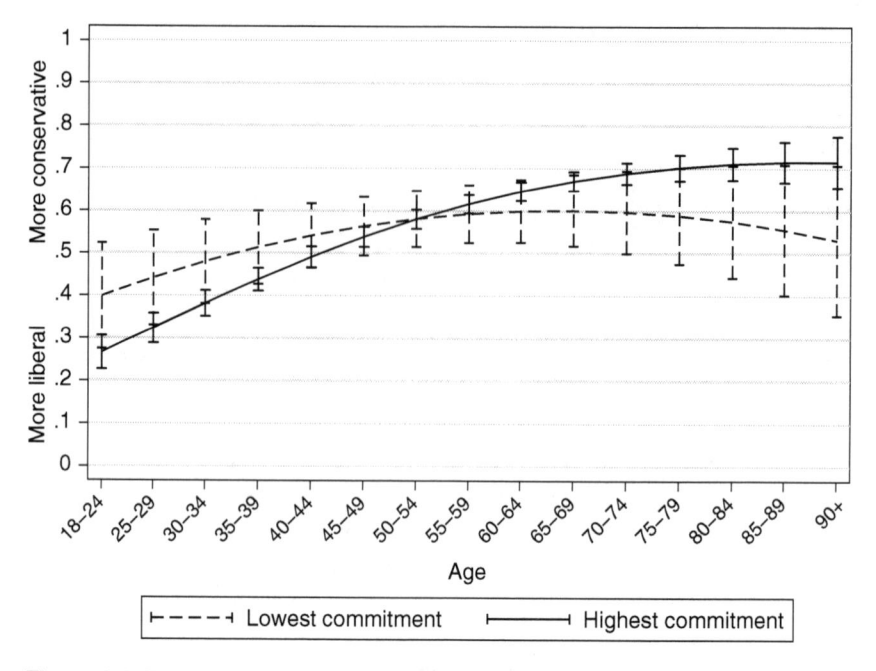

Figure 3.6. Predicted attitudes on immigration among evangelicals by religious commitment.
Source: Weighted 2014 Pew Religious Landscape Study.
Note: Error bars represent 95 percent confidence intervals.

The bottom panel of Figure 3.7 shows the probability of agreeing with the statement, "We should pay less attention to problems overseas and concentrate on problems here at home." The probability of highly committed eighteen-year-old evangelicals taking the isolationist perspective is .53, compared to a maximum of .56 among thirty-eight-year-olds. Given the confidence intervals, we cannot really say that the core of the subculture has changed on this issue. Among low-commitment evangelicals, the probability of holding the isolationist views ranged from .15 among eighteen-year-olds to .19 among fifty-year-olds.

Conclusion

The question that motivated this chapter is "Does any change we see among young evangelicals appear to be internal or external to evangelicalism?" Examining this question represents an important improvement over previous studies of young evangelicals (e.g., Pelz and Smidt 2015; Smith and Johnson 2010), which do not consider the likely causes behind any changes in public opinion among young evangelicals. Overall, the patterns we see in the data

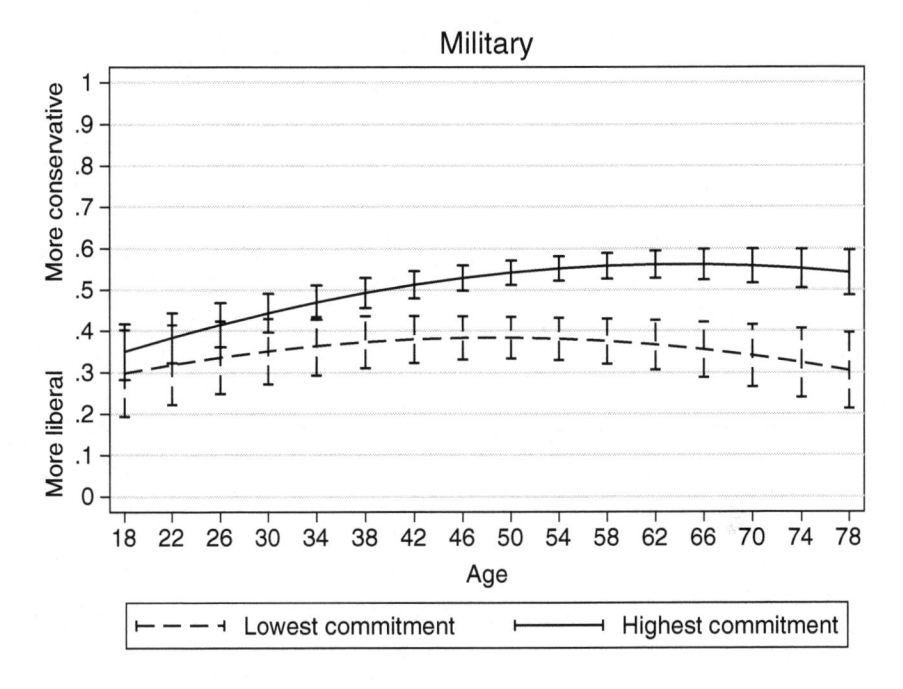

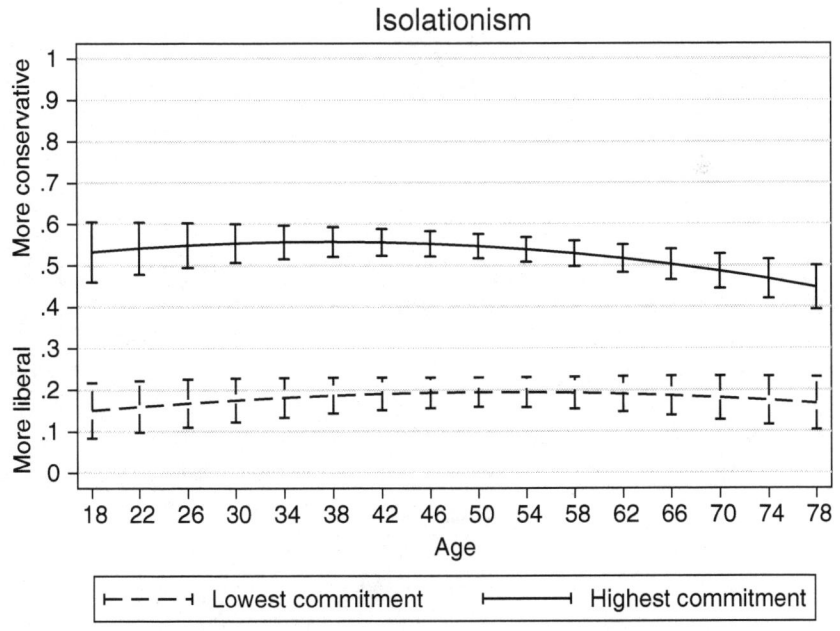

Figure 3.7. Predicted attitudes on the military and isolationism among evangelicals by religious commitment.

Source: Weighted 2007 Pew Religious Landscape Study.
Note: Error bars represent 95 percent confidence intervals.

match up quite well with what we would expect if the subcultural theory of evangelicalism were true. On some identity/issue measures, like party identification and isolationism, we see very little evidence of change among either high- or low-commitment evangelicals. On abortion, we actually notice conservative-leaning change concentrated among high-commitment evangelicals.

For a number of issues, the evidence suggests that forces external to evangelicalism are causing any change we see. On ideology, change is concentrated among infrequent attenders, but highly committed young evangelicals are only slightly more liberal than their parents. On a variety of measures, including the 2016 two-party presidential vote, homosexuality, gay marriage, welfare, and the environment, we observe that change appears to be happening at about the same rate among high- and low-commitment evangelicals, suggesting that factors external to evangelicalism are driving the change. These results generally line up with Justin Farrell's (2011) finding that factors such as higher education, delayed marriage, and shifts in views on moral authority are behind the liberalization in religious and social beliefs discussed in his article.

We should not be surprised that the two issues on which we found that the age gap among evangelicals was larger than the age gap among non-evangelicals, thereby suggesting change coming from inside the evangelical tradition, were immigration and the military-diplomacy trade-off. Neither are cultural issues, and neither have been historically important to the evangelical tradition's identity or distinctiveness.

In Chapter 2, I conclude that speculation about a larger-scale movement of young evangelicals toward the Democratic Party and political liberalism at this point seems unjustified. The results from this chapter indicate that the speculation of large-scale change coming from within evangelicalism is even more unjustified. While we can certainly point to (at least comparatively) liberal evangelical elites like Jim Wallis, Ronald Sider, and Tony Campolo, their message does not yet seem to be causing wholesale change at the mass level. In short, the patterns in the data suggest that forces outside evangelicalism are most likely responsible for the change we see on most issues.

At the end of Part I, then, I conclude that my subcultural theory performs well at explaining trends in public opinion among young evangelicals. It provides a unified account of why we see change on some issues but not others as well as an explanation of where the change is coming from. So far, however, I have not tested the mechanisms behind my theory, including whether the evangelical subculture actually engages in the processes of building evangelical identity, discrediting mainstream culture, teaching core values, and delivering political messages. Furthermore, I do not convincingly show that engagement in the evangelical subculture *causes* adherents to move toward a Republican Party identification, a conservative ideology, or conservative issue attitudes. In Part II, I focus on testing various aspects of my subcultural theory to help us further understand public opinion among young evangelicals.

PART II

Methods of Understanding Public Opinion among Young Evangelicals

The previous two chapters suggest that the claim that a new generation of young liberal evangelicals is entering the political sphere is largely exaggerated. As Chapter 2 reveals, young evangelicals are comparable to previous generations in terms of their partisanship, ideology, and attitudes toward abortion. Chapter 3 shows that in the areas where young evangelicals are becoming more liberal, the change is for the most part concentrated among infrequent attendees, suggesting that forces outside of evangelicalism are the most likely culprits. The patterns of public opinion Chapters 2 and 3 discuss are largely consistent with what we would expect to find if my theoretical account of public opinion among young evangelicals was true.

So far, however, I have not tested the mechanisms behind my theory, including whether the evangelical subculture actually engages in the processes of building evangelical identity, discrediting mainstream culture, teaching evangelicalism's distinctive beliefs, and delivering explicitly political messages. Furthermore, I have not convincingly shown that engagement in the evangelical subculture *causes* adherents to move toward a Republican Party identification, a conservative ideology, or conservative issue attitudes. In Part II, I focus on providing a stronger test of various aspects of my subcultural theory to provide a deeper understanding of public opinion among young evangelicals.

Testing the theoretical mechanisms behind evangelicalism's influence turns out to be a difficult task. While it is relatively easy to show that relationships exist between two variables using survey data thanks to the power of inferential statistics, testing causal claims is much more difficult. First, cross-sectional data often results in a chicken-or-egg problem, where it is difficult to determine which variable influences which. In addition, the usefulness of survey data is limited by the questions asked. Third, even with good questions, survey data can fail to show the richness of the relationships that exist in the natural world.

Therefore, to provide a convincing test of my subcultural theory of public opinion among young evangelicals, throughout Part II, I use a mixed-methods approach, involving the use of both nationally representative survey data as well as a series of semistructured interviews with young evangelicals at five colleges. In this short section, I introduce the interview data that is deployed in Chapter 4.

A Mixed-Methods Approach to Studying Young Evangelicals

Since the behavioral revolution of the 1950s, political scientists have become increasingly reliant on nationally representative survey data. Indeed, nationally representative surveys are the foundation of this book. Without survey data, it would be easy to fall into the trap of making conclusions about public opinion among young evangelicals by watching and listening to small but vocal minorities of activists on either side of the political spectrum. While it is important to acknowledge both the conservative evangelicals who turn out to Donald Trump rallies and the liberal evangelicals who protest Republican action on climate change, neither is very helpful for understanding the distribution of opinion among young evangelicals at the mass level.

While nationally representative survey data are ideal for describing trends and testing certain aspects of theories, survey research is not without its drawbacks. One shortcoming of survey data is that they provide only a limited view of respondent opinion. Question design and response options limit the ability of respondents to express the totality of their feelings (e.g., Johnson, Reynolds, and Mycoff 2008).

Therefore, qualitative data can be a helpful supplement, as they allow respondents to speak for themselves rather than force them to choose from fixed-response options. According to Janet Johnson, H. T. Reynolds, and Jason Mycoff, "An in-depth interview gives the interviewer a chance to probe, to clarify, to search for deeper meanings, to explore unanticipated responses, and to assess intangibles such as mood and opinion intensity" (2008, 388). Although public opinion researchers have traditionally favored survey data over interviews, recent high-profile works, such as Katherine Cramer's (2016) masterful study of rural resentment's impact on political attitudes in Wisconsin, highlight the usefulness of interview data in the field of public opinion.

Qualitative data, including interviews, may be particularly helpful, given my desire to test the mechanisms behind my subcultural theory. A second shortcoming of survey data is that it can be difficult to identify and understand the reasons behind the relationships that we see in survey data. For example, survey data can help us see that young evangelicals are more likely than their nonevangelical peers to hold negative attitudes toward culture. We assume that something about the evangelical subculture has made them that way, but survey data alone might make it difficult to figure out what that "something" is. Interviews and other forms of qualitative data can help fill in the gaps, clarifying the reasons why individuals hold certain opinions and elucidating the mechanisms through which institutions affect behavior.

Therefore, during the spring of 2013, I conducted a series of forty-two semistructured qualitative interviews with evangelical students at five colleges. Most interviews were between forty-five minutes and one hour in length. The interviewees were all traditional college students, ranging in age from eighteen to twenty-four. Participants were asked questions in five general categories: (1) their political attitudes, (2) their perceptions of Millennials, (3) their views of secular culture, (4) their perceptions of evangelicals, and (5) their personal religious backgrounds, churches, and colleges. This order was chosen to avoid priming participants to think about their religious beliefs when discussing their political attitudes, their perceptions of Millennials, and their attitudes about American culture. Therefore, we can be more confident that any religious sentiments expressed in the political section are the respondents' own unprimed feelings. By combining these interviews with survey data throughout the remainder of this book, my hope is to provide both quantitative evidence of national-level trends and personal accounts of how young evangelicals see the evangelical subculture influencing their own lives and attitudes.

Because subcultural engagement is an important part of my theory, a key element of the research design was selecting interviewees with differing levels of subcultural immersion. I defined immersion on the basis of two characteristics: the religious affiliations of colleges they attended (evangelical Protestant or nonevangelical) and whether they were members of evangelical student organizations on their college campuses. Interviewees were located by one of three methods: professors passing around signup sheets in class, professors distributing a recruiting email, and evangelical student organizations distributing a recruiting email to their membership lists.

A key problem was identifying and selecting college-age evangelicals for the interviews. As I discuss in the Introduction, the meaning of evangelical is contentious, and it is entirely reasonable that some college students might not know whether they belonged to an evangelical religious tradition or not. Rather than attempting to provide any one definition of evangelical, I relied on self-identification. Specifically, on the recruiting form I asked two simple questions: "Would you describe yourself as an evangelical Christian?" and "Are you a member of any religious clubs or organizations on campus (not counting your church)?" My reliance on self-identification for the most part led to interviews with exactly the sort of students one might expect: students who belonged to religious traditions that researchers would characterize as evangelical. However, there was a small number of students whose categorization was more controversial. Most notably, there were at least two students who self-identified as evangelicals during recruitment but named mainline Protestant denominations during the interviews. Ultimately, I chose to include these students in the study since they self-identified as evangelical. However, in the analysis, I am also careful to make note of their more unique religious backgrounds when appropriate.

The Colleges

In this section, I provide a brief profile of each of the five colleges where I conducted interviews to give readers a better sense of the culture of each institution. As I frequently rely on examples from the interviews when discussing how the evangelical subculture influences public opinion, understanding the differences among the colleges proves advantageous. To help protect the identity of interviewees, the names of the colleges have been changed to generic code names that reflect their institutional character. In addition, when necessary, potentially identifying details, such as the names of courses and assigned textbooks, have been omitted or replaced with generic details. Also, quotes have also been edited for grammar and flow. To maintain transparency, significant changes and edits are indicated using brackets.

Old Faithful College

Old Faithful College is an evangelical Protestant college affiliated with a comparatively small, regionally concentrated denomination. Founded during the push for evangelical colleges in the middle to late 1800s, the college is well-known for its affiliation with a specific theological perspective within the broader evangelical movement. The student body is disproportionately made up of upper-middle-class and wealthy evangelical Christians, although there is also some diversity in both socioeconomic status and religious background.

As one might expect from an evangelical Christian college, students of Old Faithful College highlighted the important role that religion plays on the campus. In the interviews, I routinely asked students about the religious character of their college. This politically conservative student's explanation is typical:

> I'd say it's quite religious. You definitely have an opportunity to be a part of a religious community. You're going to hear about it. There's no way you're gonna be able to hide from it. It predominates most classes, and you can see there are religious views presented in the classes. But also, there's quite a wide range [in terms of religious beliefs] and even the political spectrum here.

While strongly loyal to both its denomination and the larger evangelical tradition in its teachings, the students often pointed out that compared to more fundamentalist-affiliated evangelical colleges, Old Faithful College is less strict in its treatment of morality. One politically moderate student explained:

> As a Christian school, they seem more on the liberal side. Maybe it's in the middle. It's interesting because both of my sisters went to the same Christian college that isn't [Old Faithful], and compared to there, [Old Faithful] is more [theologically] liberal. . . . Until recently, . . . chapel [was] mandatory for them. It's not mandatory here. I feel like there's more freedom here. They had to sign [a statement that said] they won't drink while they're a student there, except for at weddings. I think it said they won't smoke, too, but I'm not sure about that. . . . I find rules like that odd, but they're definitely more on the conservative side, whereas [Old Faithful College] doesn't seem to care as much.

Another theme across the interviewees at Old Faithful College was that, even within such a highly subcultural institution, not all students are equally committed to their faith. One politically and theologically conservative student put it this way:

> I guess we have a wide range of Christians: people who really speak their opinion, and you can definitely see they're a Christian by the way they act, and others who, maybe they're not even Christian, or they are Christian but they're not so outspoken about it. I guess we have a wide variety on this campus.

Overall, then, Old Faithful College is typical of what we might describe as a "theologically moderate" evangelical College, where faith is an important part of the campus culture, but students still retain a degree of autonomy in how they go about their religious practice.

New Faithful College

New Faithful College is a nondenominational evangelical Protestant college founded in the middle to late 1800s. Compared to Old Faithful College, it is more theologically conservative, and perhaps more politically homogeneous as well. That said, it is far from being as conservative and insular as fundamentalist-affiliated colleges, such as Liberty University or Bob Jones University. Almost all of its students self-identify as evangelicals, and religion plays an extraordinary role in campus life. Students are required to attend chapel services several days a week, and all students must take multiple religion courses to graduate.

One theme that was readily apparent in the interviews was that many of the New Faithful College students take pride in the fact that the college introduces them to both evangelical and secular thought, and puts an emphasis on resolving the tension between their evangelical beliefs and secular ideas. Here is how one politically conservative student answered when I asked him to explain the religious culture of the campus:

> Strong, obviously. . . . I'm a poli-sci major. . . . Definitely, in the classes I've taken, there's an emphasis on understanding intellectually the implications of what you believe. So, for example, I took my senior sem[inar] for poli-sci, and you have to write a big capstone paper at the end that's [about] what is an area of tension between your politics and your faith and kind of trying to work through that. With my philosophy classes, it's not just that we read only Thomas Aquinas and Augustine; you work through all the big philosophers but also people like Spinoza and Hume and Kant and Bertrand Russell and those people who are gonna be . . . kind of more antagonistic, . . . understanding, here's what's out there, and how do we work through this in discussion? What are the ins and outs of this intellectually? Where do you need to be more intellectually modest as opposed to where you can kind of take a more aggressive stance? It's not that it's spoon-fed to you, in that sense, but here's thinkers who have gone against the way I think, present the argument, work through it, and try to handle it.

The faculty and administrators at New Faithful College seem to believe in the importance of teaching the nuances of evangelical doctrine but don't necessarily want to take sides on the finer points of evangelical theology, perhaps out of fear of denominational infighting. In the interviews, I asked the students if New Faithful College emphasized any particular religious doctrines or beliefs. One student answered as follows:

> As a whole campus, I would say no. I think you do have a lot of different professors, a lot of different backgrounds, and I think that does lead to a diversity of opinions about what's really essential about the faith. I can say that because all students [take a course on the Bible], pretty much any idea espoused in there will probably be something that most students take in tow around the campus—ideas like shalom, the political Christian, common elements of doctrine that we share. . . . But as far as "the thing" that we as a campus really emphasize, I don't know that there is one.

Overall, then, New Faithful College provides a nice contrast to Old Faithful College. New Faithful is more theologically conservative and perhaps more coercive in its efforts to instill an evangelical faith among its students, but it is also less likely to emphasize the perspective of a given denomination.

Top 100 College

Top 100 College is a secular liberal arts college that was once affiliated with a mainline Protestant denomination. However, over the years, the college has become increasingly secular. As its pseudonym suggests, it is generally listed from between eighty and one hundred twenty in the *U.S. News and World Report*'s rankings of liberal arts colleges. Its student body is more religiously diverse than either of the evangelical colleges. Recruiting for the interviews was much more difficult here because evangelicals make up a much smaller proportion of the campus community. When I asked students to describe the religious culture of Top 100 College, this response from a moderate conservative was typical:

> Nonexistent, more or less. When I first came to [Top 100 College], I thought the fact that it was [denomination]-founded actually meant something, but it really doesn't, as far as, like, religious events and, I guess, religious support goes. There are obviously student-led organizations that are faith-based, but they are poorly attended typically

and don't really fulfill [the need] I see on this campus, as in having a real solid Christian community.

While students are required to take one theology course as part of the general education curriculum, in the interviews, a number of students commented that the courses are taught from either a neutral or perhaps even critical perspective. Politically, Top 100 College is quite diverse. On the one hand, the college is located in a politically conservative part of the country, and it is certainly not known for its progressivism in the way that colleges like Oberlin or Reed are. On the other hand, the college itself is more liberal than the state and the community around it, especially on social issues like gay marriage.

Great Books College

Great Books College is a liberal arts college affiliated with a mainline Protestant tradition (not the same tradition as Top 100 College). While the college does not formally subscribe to a "great books" curriculum, the general curriculum places a heavy emphasis on Western literature and philosophy. From the interviews, I got the sense that while many students identify as Christian, most are mainline Protestants who have become disengaged from their faith during their college years. The college embraces its religious heritage perhaps slightly more than Top 100 College, but it remains quite secular compared to the evangelical colleges where I conducted interviews. One student's explanation was revealing on several levels:

> I mean, because this is a smaller liberal arts school with a [mainline Protestant] background, the average student is middle class to upper middle class, just because of the cost of the college, and is either self-identifying as Christian or comfortable enough with Christianity to go to a school that's [mainline Protestant]. Although [Great Books College] isn't very overt about its [mainline Protestant] affiliation, it's still there. You get a prayer before convocation; you get a prayer before graduation. That's what I usually see as the average student. There's not the best representation of minorities because of the cost of it and everything.

Politically, Great Books College is fairly moderate and has tended to discourage overt political displays, including denying political speakers on both sides of the aisle permission to speak on campus.

Directional State University

Directional State University is a large regional public university. As one would expect, the overall campus culture is strongly secular. The college is quite diverse politically, but overall more liberal and less active in comparison to Old Faithful College and New Faithful College. One interviewee, who attends a private evangelical-affiliated college but was taking a course at Directional State University, provided an interesting contrast:

> It's a lot different coming here because I've been [attending] private school my entire life. . . . I'm at a private Christian college, so I've always had that kind of atmosphere. I have friends outside of that atmosphere, so I'm not just a sheltered little person that doesn't know anything, but it's interesting when you have teachers in class that [use profanity], and you can't talk to the guy next to you without [him using profanity]. . . . My teacher, my physics prof, kind of bashes religion every once in a while, and I've never had that before. It's definitely different, for sure.

However, the university has several student organizations that promote the evangelical faith. These groups are probably less visible than the evangelical student organizations at Top 100 College and Great Books College. Nevertheless, if students encounter religion at Directional State University, it is through these groups.

Conclusion

Having established the basic trends in public opinion among young evangelicals, in Part II I turn to testing the theoretical mechanisms proposed in Chapter 1. A mixed-methods approach, combining the use of nationally representative survey data with qualitative interviews, helps provide a rigorous test of my account of public opinion among young evangelicals.

In particular, the interviews discussed in this chapter help flesh out the mechanisms behind the relationships we see in the nationally representative survey data. The interviews also help show the diversity of perspectives among young evangelicals thanks to the variations in subcultural immersion built into the research design. Overall, my hope is that this mixed-methods approach both helps provide a convincing test of my theory as well as offer a rich, flavorful account of public opinion among young evangelicals.

4

How the Evangelical Subculture Influences Public Opinion

In American politics, the assumption that religion (in any of its forms) influences public opinion is ubiquitous. In fact, that assumption rests at the foundation of my theoretical account of public opinion among young evangelicals. In this chapter, I begin the process of testing that theory. In particular, John Zaller's (1992) receive-accept-sample (RAS) model of public opinion discussed in Chapter 1 suggests that any effort to influence public opinion must begin with altering the underlying distribution of considerations held by young evangelicals.

In this chapter, I use both nationally representative survey data and my interviews with young evangelicals about their churches, colleges, and clubs to show that the evangelical subculture alters the distribution of considerations held by young evangelicals in four ways. First, the evangelical subculture builds in-group identity, leading members to think of themselves as evangelicals and therefore making them more likely to adhere to broadly accepted stereotypes regarding evangelicals. Second, the evangelical subculture teaches a number of distinctive beliefs, or "core values," that could alter opinion on political issues. Third, the evangelical subculture discredits the broader culture, making it more likely that adherents will ignore certain secular considerations. Finally, the evangelical subculture delivers explicitly political messages through a variety of institutions. Together, the results provide strong empirical support for my theoretical account of how the evangelical subculture influences the political attitudes of young evangelicals.

Building Group Identity

Any group's attempt to influence public opinion among members begins with building in-group identity. Social identity is at the foundation of several major theoretical approaches to the study of American political behavior. For the Columbia School, or "sociological," perspective, social groups are important because they determine the social networks that individuals are exposed to (Berelson, Lazarsfeld, and McPhee 1954). For the Rochester, or "rational choice," perspective, social groups are important because they can serve as heuristics to help individuals make political choices in the absence of full information (Downs 1957; Popkin 1994; Sniderman, Brody, and Tetlock 1991). Finally, for the Michigan, or "social-psychological," perspective, social groups serve as an important factor in the development of party identification, which in turn exerts a strong impact on public opinion (Campbell et al. 1960; Green, Palmquist, and Schickler 2002; Lewis-Beck et al. 2008). Clearly, then, an important step in the evangelical tradition's ability to affect public opinion is building evangelical identity among its members.

The interviews revealed that the evangelical tradition has a number of mechanisms in place for developing in-group identity. One of the most prominent of these was churches and church-based youth groups. One conservative student at Great Books College explained to me that his church-based youth group was an important social outlet during high school. He remembered, "We pretty much had fun together. We had a weekly group event where we would all get together and play games, worship, talk about God, and eat food, and then outside of that, we always hung out and just played volleyball on the beach, [went] camping, things like that." By creating a community of young people who held common religious beliefs, the youth group made it more likely that individuals would incorporate religion into their identities.

While those who self-identified as evangelical were undoubtedly more likely to attend evangelical colleges, the interviews also made it clear that these colleges had several mechanisms in place for building and reinforcing evangelical identity. Most notably, both Old Faithful and New Faithful colleges require courses that teach the foundations of evangelical religious doctrine. For example, Old Faithful College requires all students to take a course on its affiliated denomination's doctrinal beliefs in their first year. One politically moderate student explained the course as follows:

> Right now I'm in my religion class, and the way they teach it is through the views of [Old Faithful's denomination]. So my professor said at the beginning that he has to teach it that way, but it's up to us to make up our own minds. But he does tell us what the [denomina-

tion] thinks about certain ideas, and what he thinks, and then tells us we need to make up our own minds about what they tell us. . . . Also, through almost every class I've taken so far, I'd say there is some aspect of what [Old Faithful College] stands for.

Students at the two evangelical colleges also reported that professors go out of their way to bring religion into their courses, no matter what the subject matter. One student at Old Faithful College explained how professors brought faith into all of her courses:

Every class that I've had here—say, kinesiology . . .—[is] taught from the Christian perspective; like, "God gave our bodies," and everything's like that. Also, it just came from a historical perspective in a political thought class where we learned about the classics like Aristotle, Plato, and today we learned about John Calvin. So it's like, government from a Christian perspective. God, He's the supreme authority, then He also gave authority to government leaders, . . . things like that. Even in geology class, I had all these devotionals and prayed before class.

In addition, students at New Faithful College explained to me that the college holds professors accountable for adding religious content to their courses, including inquiring about how well professors incorporated faith into the classrooms on the end-of-semester teaching evaluations.

Another way evangelical colleges build identity is through chapel services. At New Faithful College, students are required to attend chapel several days a week, although they get a certain number of "skips" each semester. One student explained to me, "Not every chapel is a sermon, either. Sometimes it will be just people kind of more or less plugging a group or something, so they'll talk about what they've done in the past or what they do on campus, [or they'll host] guest speakers, so it's not like a traditional sermon every time." At Old Faithful College, students are not required to attend chapel. However, chapel still seemed to be an important part of campus life, and many of the students who I spoke with reported they attend frequently. Thus, through incorporating religion across the curriculum and encouraging chapel attendance, we see strong evidence for an institutional commitment to building evangelical group identity among the evangelical colleges where I conducted interviews.

The interviews suggested that these efforts at reinforcing evangelical identity had an impact on students. In the interviews, one of the last questions I asked students was whether they felt their faith had changed as a result of attending their colleges. A frequent refrain among students at evangelical colleges was that their faith had not changed that much in terms of their level of commitment or the orthodoxy of their beliefs. Indeed, I got the sense that there is a strong sorting effect, with the most religiously committed students being more likely to choose to attend an evangelical college. However, students did report that their faith had become deeper, more theologically informed, and more meaningful to them on a personal level. One response from a student at Old Faithful College is typical:

> I think they've gotten stronger because I'm more independent from my parents. I'm learning the . . . small specific things I've grown stronger in and how I made my relationship with Christ my own. . . . [During high school,] it's your relationship with Christ, but it's also your relationship with your parents and Christ. So it's like, because I grew up in a Christian home, they impressed things on me, but then from that point on, I feel like I've grown my faith as my own.

This student's account of having made her faith her own, as well as similar accounts from a number of other students attending evangelical colleges, suggests that the efforts of evangelical colleges at building in-group identity among students are indeed proving successful.

Likewise, the interviews revealed that evangelical groups at secular college campuses had a number of ways of building evangelical identity. Simply holding weekly meetings requires an expression of evangelical identity from members. However, it was clear that the groups' identity-building practices reached far beyond regular meetings. One student leader of InterVarsity at Great Books College revealed the extent of the group's activities:

> At the beginning of the year, we do a new student outreach, so like any other organization, we try to recruit new people. We do, like, a weekly large group event where everybody comes together; there's worship and sometimes a speaker. Otherwise we just hang out and talk about God, and then there's small group Bible studies that go every single week, and then there's different conferences that we go to. We also do [something equivalent to evangelism week]. We do things that are dedicated to trying to reach out to campus, and one of the ways we do that is through proxy station, and it's just like a couple boards that have a theme. . . . I know for the beginning of this year, we talked about "How will you grow?" and then students came up and put a sticker on it . . . mentally, academically, physically, socially, or spiritually. Then they put a sticker on the one they most want, and

then we take them to the next slide and, through that, just get them thinking about God, and then if the opportunity leads/presents itself, then we talk to them about the Gospel. That's not really the whole idea of it; it's just to get people thinking about God and, in that case, "How are you actually growing and developing?" This past one was more of an identity basis: "What do you actually define yourself as?" Things like that.

The interviews also made it clear how the topics of discussion at evangelical clubs often drove home the need for an evangelical identity. Consider another student's description of a talk given at an evangelical club at Old Faithful College:

Student: [The club] I feel really incorporates who you are as a person as well as who you are in faith. So one of the past [meetings was] on relationships, breaking up and getting into relationships, and how we can reflect our faith in God in our relationships, especially when it comes to relationships with non-Christians.
Me: Can you say a little more if you remember the main idea on that talk on relationships, [in terms of] what [the club] asked you to do?
Student: It asked us to be thoughtful in our relationships, and it asked us to be careful in the way that we view relationships. Per se, we could view them as just something for physical attractiveness or something for conformity, but it asked us to view it as something along the lines of what we're comfortable with and also something along the lines of what we know, or what we think, God would want for us and reflect[ing] God in the relationships. And also it really emphasized the fact that in order to really be comfortable in a relationship, especially a strong relationship with a strong faith, you really have to emphasize your faith as an individual first. You have to find what you're comfortable with as an individual before you can find what you're comfortable with in a relationship.

In this section, we have seen how three types of evangelical institutions build a sense of evangelical identity among the younger members of the faith. The task of building in-group identity is an important component in developing the potential for the group-based influence of members' political attitudes, because doing so increases the likelihood that individuals will draw on considerations associated with that identity when forming and expressing political opinions (per the theory developed in Chapter 1). In addition, the various mechanisms of influence discussed in this chapter build upon one another. For example, once individuals self-identify as evangelical, they are more likely to be exposed to and take part in the distinctive beliefs and behaviors profiled in the next section.

Distinctive Beliefs in the Evangelical Subculture

Another key mechanism through which the evangelical subculture can affect public opinion is through the promotion of certain distinctive beliefs (alternatively referred to by some scholars as core values). Distinctive beliefs, as I understand them, are elements of the evangelical faith that (1) represent an important part of what it means to be a member of the faith and (2) help define the boundaries of the group in relation to society. Over time, the distinctive beliefs of a subculture might change as the society around it changes. For example, at one point in time abstinence from alcohol was an important belief for many evangelicals (Warner 2009). While some churches (particularly in the Pentecostal and fundamentalist flavors of evangelicalism) still reject alcohol, overall this belief has become a much smaller part of evangelicalism's identity and distinctiveness than in the past.[1] In addition, while many of these distinctive beliefs have a long historical association with evangelicalism, others are evolving as evangelicalism's place in the American religious landscape changes. Furthermore, some of these distinctive beliefs are unique to evangelicalism, while others are shared with other religious traditions.[2] This is particularly true for the three Protestant religions, which share a number of common theological doctrines.

From the perspective of public opinion theory, these distinctive beliefs help alter the distribution of considerations in the minds of evangelicals compared to their nonevangelical counterparts. However, the degree to which these considerations will matter may vary from issue to issue. Zaller's (1992) accessibility axiom suggests that the more clearly applicable a distinctive belief is to a political issue, the more likely it is to influence public opinion because respondents will be able to recall and more reliably apply the consideration to the issue.

In this section, I highlight some of the most politically relevant religious beliefs of evangelicals using data from the 2007 and 2014 Pew Religious Landscape Studies. Throughout this section, I include comparisons to other large religious traditions to examine whether evangelicals are in fact distinctive in the degree to which they adhere to these beliefs. My theory contends that the evangelical subculture includes several institutions that convey these distinctive beliefs to young evangelicals. To test this aspect of my argument, I supplement the discussion with qualitative evidence from the interviews that demonstrates how churches, evangelical colleges, and evangelical student organizations convey these beliefs to members.

Foundational Beliefs

One important belief that characterizes evangelicals is the faith that the Bible is the Word of God. Indeed, differences in biblical interpretation are one key source of controversy that led to the split between evangelical and mainline Protestantism. As controversy over Darwin's *On the Origin of Species* grew and modernization became more prevalent, evangelical Protestant denominations largely maintained their belief that the account of creation presented in Genesis was literally true and continued to understand the Bible as the Word of God. In contrast, many mainline Protestant denominations grew to understand the Bible as theological authority but not necessarily written by God himself (they might use the term "inspired by") and not necessarily meant to be a literal account of events (e.g., Layman 2001; Smidt 2007, 2013).

The data from the 2014 Pew Religious Landscape Study show that evangelicals are still quite distinctive in their understanding of the Bible. Figure 4.1 shows opinions about the Bible among those younger than thirty by

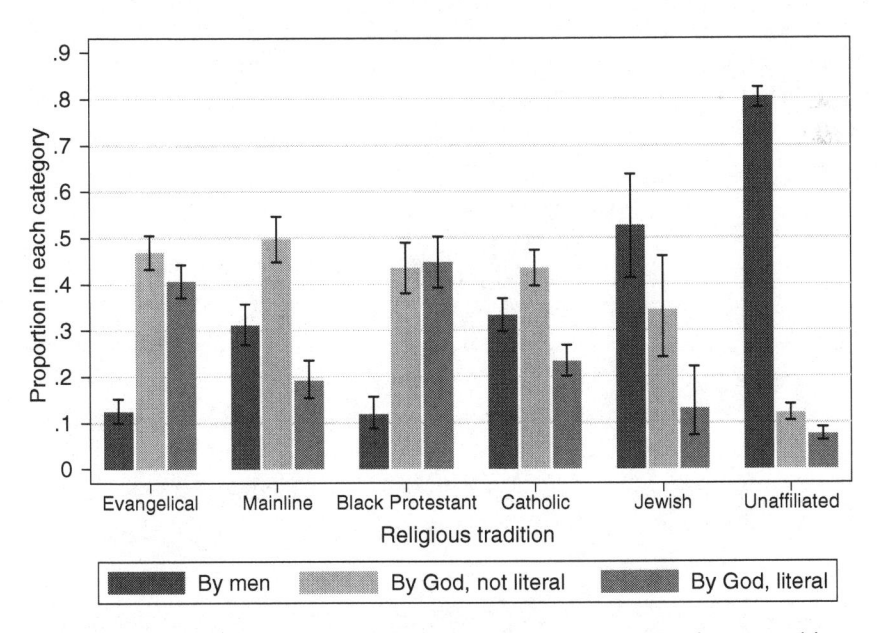

Figure 4.1. Attitudes about the Bible among eighteen- to twenty-nine-year-olds by religious tradition.
Source: Weighted 2014 Pew Religious Landscape Study.
Note: Error bars represent 95 percent confidence intervals.

religious tradition. Respondents were first asked to choose from two options: "[Holy book] is the word of God" or "[Holy book] is a book written by men and is not the word of God." Respondents saw the name of the Holy book associated with their tradition; for example, Jews saw the Torah and Muslims saw the Koran. Those who said that their Holy book was the word of God received a follow-up prompt, asking them to choose whether "[Holy book] should be taken literally, word for word" or "Not everything in [Holy book] should be taken literally, word for word." We see that about 88 percent of young evangelicals said that the Bible was the word of God, and 41 percent of young evangelicals said that the Bible "should be taken literally, word for word." Young evangelicals subscribe to Biblical literalism at a rate comparable to black Protestants, and significantly higher than mainline Protestants, Catholics, Jews, and the unaffiliated ($p < .05$).

Closely connected to evangelicals' faith in the Bible is their tendency to identify as "born-again" Christians. Again, there is considerable variation in what born-again status means. For many evangelicals, it is simply having accepted Christ as their Savior. For others, it may require a more specific event. In the Pentecostal and Charismatic communities, the born-again experience may be accompanied by other behaviors, such as speaking in tongues.

The 2014 Pew Religious Landscape Study reveals that, whatever the precise meaning of "born-again," it is part of the religious identity of young evangelicals. The survey asked, "Would you describe yourself as a 'born-again' or evangelical Christian, or not?" The top panel of Figure 4.2 shows that about 80 percent of evangelicals (as defined by religious tradition) affiliated with the born-again label. The percentage of young evangelicals who identified as born-again was significantly higher among evangelicals than in each of the other Christian groups ($p < .05$).

Another characteristic belief among evangelicals is the importance of sharing their faith with others (Smidt 2007). The bottom panel of Figure 4.2 shows the proportion of each tradition that shares its beliefs with others at least once or twice a month. Given that sharing is also sometimes called "evangelizing," we would expect that young evangelicals often engage in it. Indeed, 56 percent of young evangelicals report sharing their faith at least monthly, significantly more often than do the proportion of mainline Protestants, Catholics, Jews, and the unaffiliated ($p < .05$).

Theological Exclusivism

Another distinctive belief among evangelicals is comparatively higher rates of theological exclusivism (e.g., Smidt 2007). Evangelicals take seriously Christ's declaration that "I am the way and the truth and the life. No one comes to

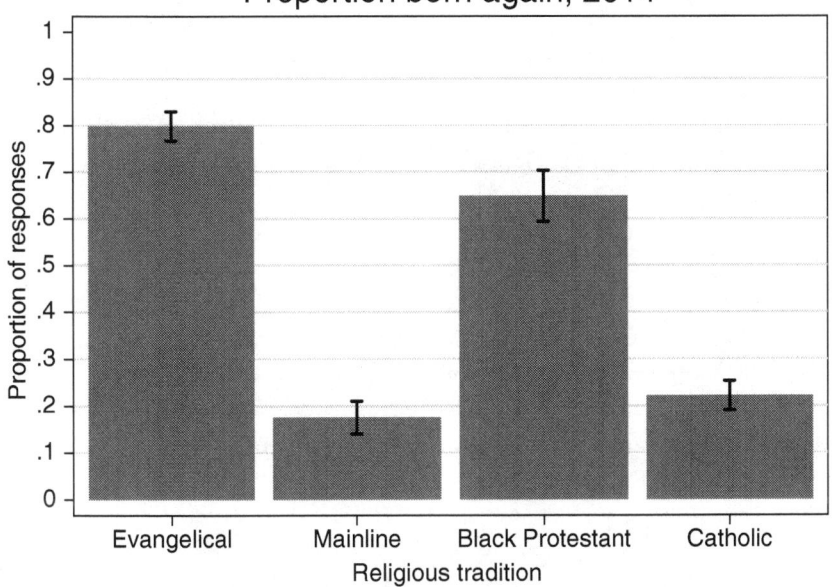

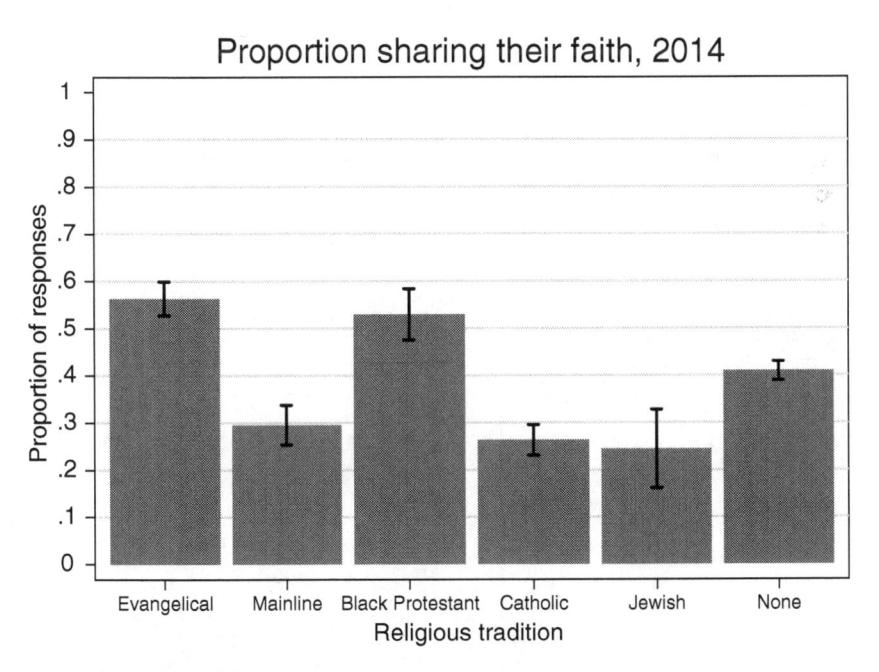

Figure 4.2. Born-again identification and faith sharing among eighteen- to twenty-nine-year-olds by religious tradition.

Source: Weighted 2014 Pew Religious Landscape Study.
Note: Error bars represent 95 percent confidence intervals.

the Father except through me" (John 14:6, NIV). This runs directly counter to the tendency among most Americans to believe that there are multiple denominations, and even religious traditions, that possess core truths (Putnam and Campbell 2010).

This commitment to theological exclusivism is reflected in the survey data. The top panel of Figure 4.3 shows respondents choosing from between two statements that best reflected their views: "My religion is the one true faith leading to eternal life" or "Many religions can lead to eternal life." Fifty-one percent of young evangelicals took the exclusivist position, making them significantly more exclusivist than mainline Protestants (25 percent), Catholics (18 percent), and Jews (16 percent).

A subsequent question provides insight into how particularistic young evangelicals are about interpreting their own faith. The question again asked respondents to choose from between two options: "Only Christian religions can lead to eternal life" or "Some non-Christian religions can lead to eternal life." The results, shown in the bottom panel of Figure 4.3, indicate that young evangelicals (22 percent) are significantly more likely than all the other large traditions to say that only Christian religions lead to an eternal life.

Religion as a Source of Guidance

Consistent with the importance of evangelical identity as discussed earlier in this chapter, evangelicals are also more likely to view religion as a guiding source in their lives. An important teaching of evangelicalism is that an individual's faith in Christ should affect all areas of his or her life. To understand the relative importance of religion to evangelicals, the survey asked how much their religion guides their daily lives. The top panel of Figure 4.4 shows that 73 percent of young evangelicals reported that religion was "very important" to them, which was comparable to the number for black Protestants and significantly higher than all other traditions in the figure ($p < .05$).

In the interviews, I routinely asked students whether they personally identified as an evangelical, and I often followed up by asking them to explain what being an evangelical meant to their daily lives. A number of students gave passionate responses that discussed the importance of religious teachings affecting the totality of their lives, including this articulate conservative student from New Faithful College:

> The personal relationship with Christ, that's the defining thing, and I think definitely over the last four or five years, that's become a lot more important to me. . . . What the [faith] means now for me is

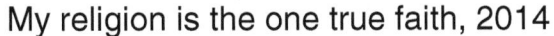

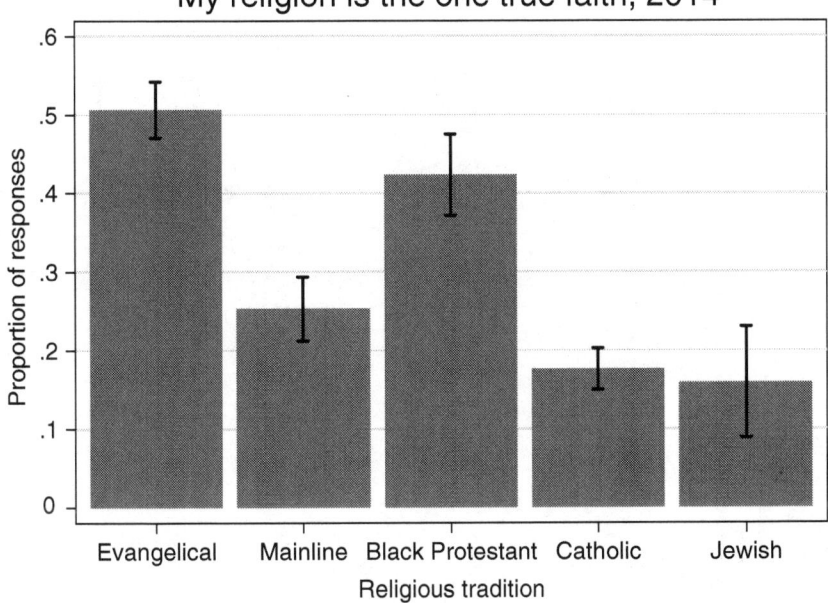

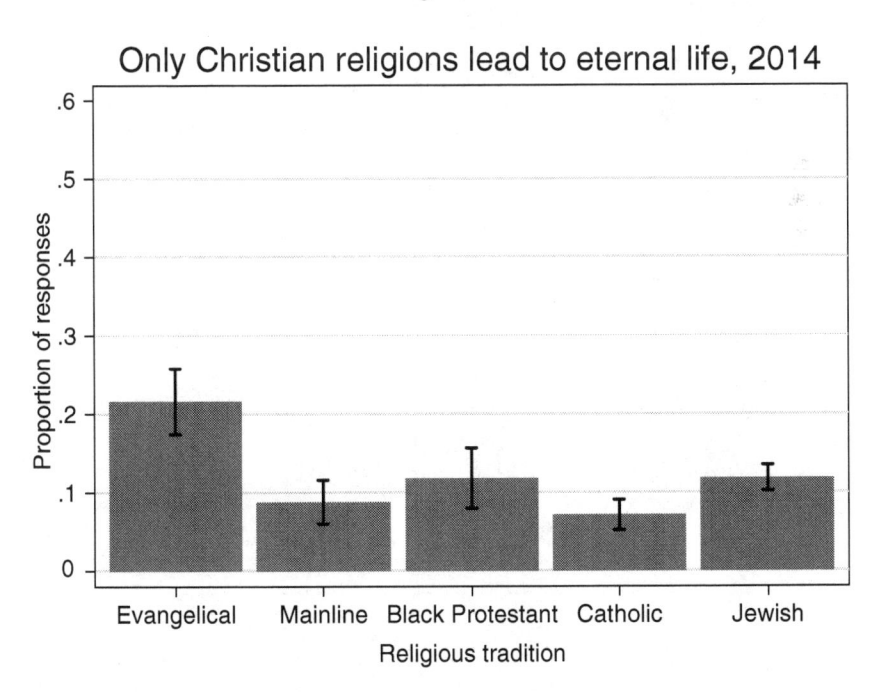

Figure 4.3. Theological exclusivism among eighteen- to twenty-nine-year-olds by religious tradition.

Source: Weighted 2014 Pew Religious Landscape Study.
Note: Error bars represent 95 percent confidence intervals.

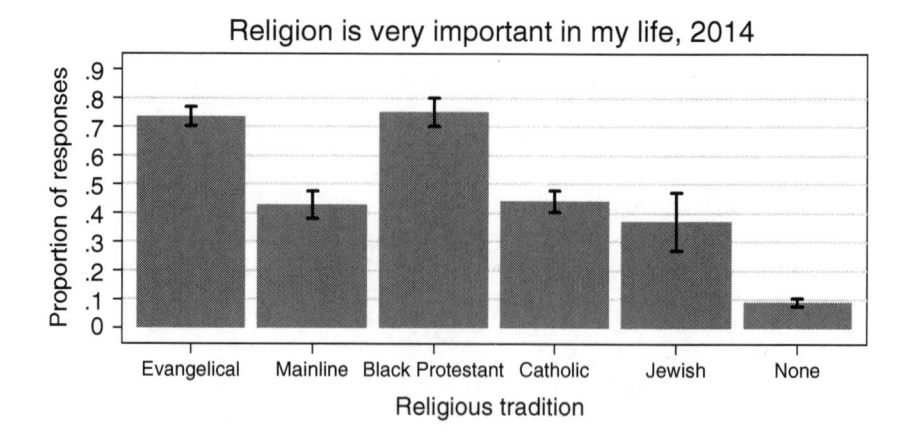

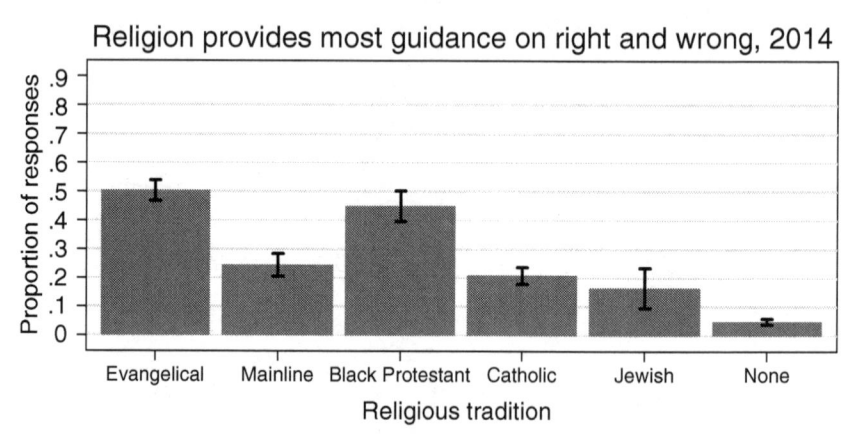

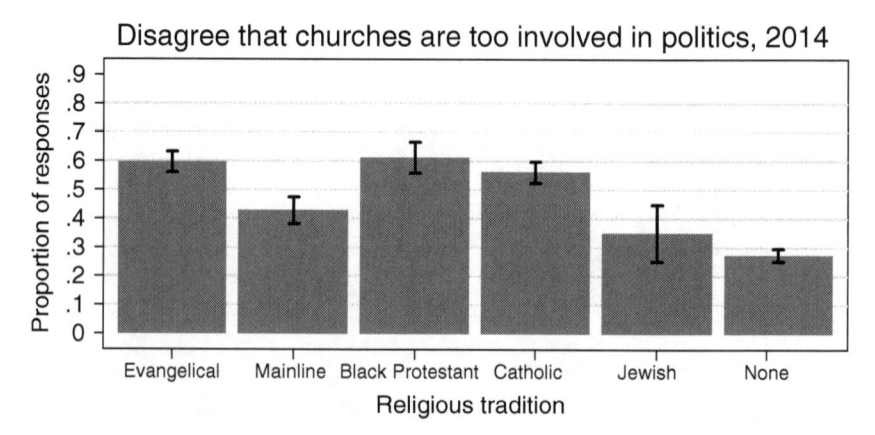

Figure 4.4. Religion as a source of guidance and religious influence on politics among eighteen- to twenty-nine-year-olds by tradition.

Source: Weighted 2014 Pew Religious Landscape Study.
Note: Error bars represent 95 percent confidence intervals.

consistent time in the Word every day, prayer, but really I think it's an understanding for me that Jesus should be the one that satisfies me and that, when I look to other things to satisfy me, they don't fill me completely. I'm a runner, and you know, if I'm looking for my performance on the track to satisfy me, I find, even if I run a great race, a couple days later, I'm empty again. So I think that for me, knowing that Jesus is this running water that fills me up, that's when I become so excited. . . . His love fills me in a way that other things can't, and in return, He's called me to obedience and evangelizing.

One area in particular where many evangelicals let religion influence their daily lives is in their understanding of morality. The Pew Religious Landscape Study asked, "When it comes to questions of right and wrong, which of the following do you look to most for guidance?" Response options included "Religious teachings and beliefs," "Philosophy and reason," "Practical experience and common sense," "Scientific information," or other. The middle panel of Figure 4.4 shows the proportion of respondents who said that religion most influenced their views on right and wrong. About 50 percent of young evangelicals said that religion most influenced their view of morality. Evangelicals were significantly more likely to turn to religion for guidance on morality compared to mainline Protestants, Catholics, Jews, and the unaffiliated ($p < .05$).

Of course, one important way that evangelicals can let their faith influence their daily lives is through their politics. While evangelical Protestantism went through a period of political disengagement following the Scopes Trial, high profile evangelicals in the latter half of the twentieth century, from Billy Graham, Francis Schaeffer, Jerry Falwell, and Pat Robertson on the right to Jim Wallis, Ronald Sider, and Shane Claiborne on the (moderate) left, have one thing in common: they all have encouraged evangelicals to incorporate their religious beliefs into their political behavior (Capps 1994; Claiborne 2006; Claiborne and Haw 2008; Schaeffer 1976; Sider 2008; Wallis 2006). The survey data suggest that their message has largely been absorbed by the evangelical masses. The bottom panel of Figure 4.4 shows the percentage of young people in each large religious tradition who disagreed with the statement, "Churches and other religious organizations are too involved in politics." The graph reveals that about 60 percent of evangelicals disagreed with the statement. Again, evangelicals were comparable to black Protestants but significantly more likely to disagree compared to mainline Protestants, Jews, and the unaffiliated ($p < .05$). This suggests that evangelicals are more likely than other denominations to hold the ideal that religion should guide their attitudes toward politics.

Conservative Attitudes on Morality and Sex

The evangelical commitment to the Bible as authority also manifests itself in conservative attitudes on morality broadly, and sex in particular (Oldfield 1996; Putnam and Campbell 2010; Wilcox 2009). Because evangelicals view the Bible as the preeminent source of guidance on matters of morality, they are inclined to take a moral absolutist position, despite the growing prevalence of moral relativism in society more generally. The basic evangelical belief in moral absolutes can be seen in Figure 4.5. Respondents were asked to choose from between two options: "There are clear and absolute standards of right and wrong" or "Whether something is right or wrong often depends on the situation." Young evangelicals (at 38 percent) were significantly more likely than young people from all other traditions to agree that there are absolute standards of right and wrong ($p < .05$).

The general concerns with morality also translate to specific concerns about sexual behavior. The evangelical position on sexual morality is more complicated than frequently believed. Recent scholarship demonstrates that evangelicals view sex within proper contexts (many would say, heterosexual marriage) as a divine and God-influenced act with profound social implications (DeRogatis 2015). The "culture wars" battles of the latter half of the twentieth century were driven largely by the increasing feeling among committed evangelicals and other religious traditionalists that secular society and the mass media had breached those proper contexts, leading to conflicts over issues such as sex education in public schools, same-sex relationships, and depictions of sex in art and entertainment (Deckman 2004; DeRogatis 2015; Hunter 1991; Putnam and Campbell 2010).

The survey data demonstrate that young evangelicals continue to hold more conservative attitudes than their peers on issues like premarital sex. Because the Pew Religious Landscape Studies did not include any questions directly addressing premarital sex, the data here come from the General Social Survey. Specifically, the question asks respondents to indicate whether premarital sex is "always wrong," "almost always wrong," "sometimes wrong," or "not wrong." In an attempt to strike a balance between a large enough sample of young evangelicals to yield reliable results and a recent enough sample to capture relatively current attitudes among young people, I have pooled the data from 2000 to 2014. The results, shown in the middle panel of Figure 4.5, indicate that during this period, 40 percent of eighteen- to twenty-nine-year-old evangelicals reported that premarital sex was "always wrong," in comparison to 25 percent of black Protestants, 20 percent of mainline Protestants, 5 percent of Catholics, and 3 percent of the unaffiliated (evangelicals were significantly different from each of these traditions, with the exception

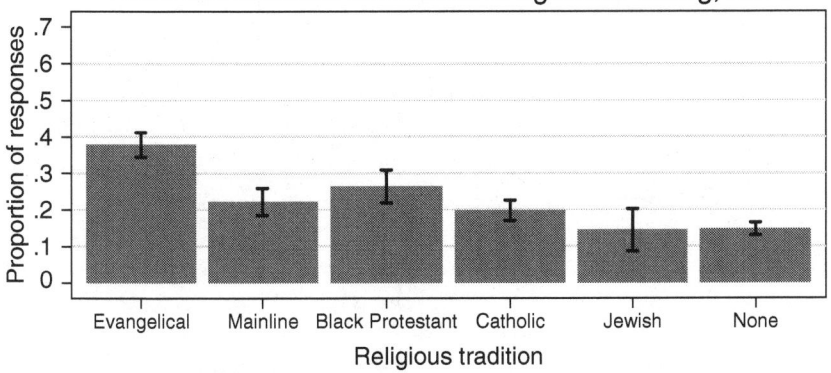

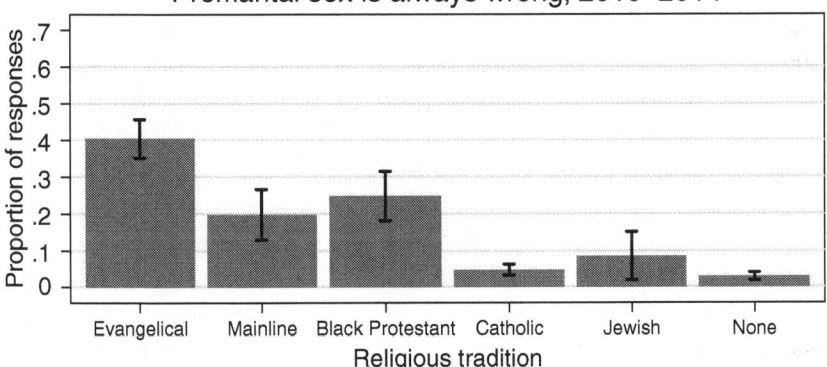

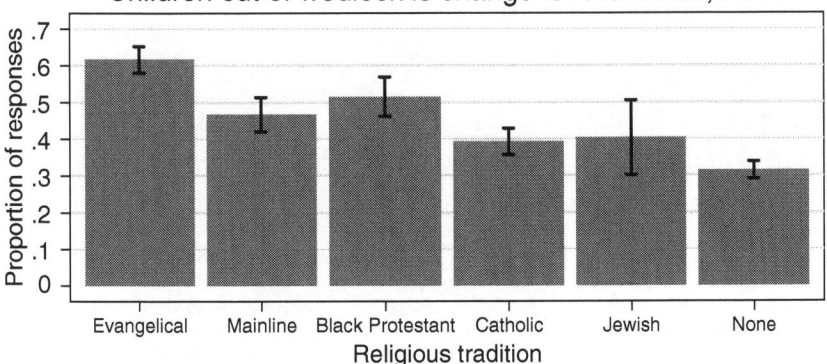

Figure 4.5. Attitudes on morality and sexuality among eighteen- to twenty-nine-year-olds by religious tradition.

Source: Weighted 2014 Pew Religious Landscape Study; weighted 2000–2014 General Social Survey.
Note: Error bars represent 95 percent confidence intervals.

of black Protestants, at $p < .05$). Clearly, then, even young evangelicals hold distinctively conservative attitudes on premarital sex.

Likewise, evangelicals express concern over social trends, such as the increasing number of children born outside of wedlock. In the 2014 Pew data, respondents were asked whether a series of changes had been "a change for the better," "a change for the worse," or "hasn't made much difference." One question asked about "Many people having children without getting married." As shown in the bottom panel of Figure 4.5, about 62 percent of young evangelicals say this has been a change for the worse, which makes evangelicals significantly more conservative on this question than all the other traditions shown ($p < .05$).

Each of the distinctive beliefs discussed has the potential to become politically relevant. Because evangelicals hold these beliefs at higher rates than other traditions, they are more likely to sample them when forming and expressing political attitudes. However, the relevance of each of these distinctive beliefs also depends on the precise issue under consideration. For example, evangelicals' conservative sexual attitudes are far more likely to be relevant toward an issue like abortion as opposed to a noncultural issue like immigration. Thus, while these distinctive beliefs are an important mechanism by which evangelicalism influences public opinion, their effect may be bound by the extent to which individuals can apply these beliefs to specific issues.

Discrediting Secular Culture

Another key task for any subculture is discrediting the dominant culture. Subcultures must distinguish themselves from the dominant culture to attract members and define the subculture's boundaries. As Christian Smith and colleagues (1998) demonstrate, having a clear out-group opponent can help keep the subculture strong in the face of social change.

Discrediting secular culture is particularly important in the case of young evangelicals. The literature on the Millennial generation has named a number of potential causes for their comparatively liberal views, but among the most frequently cited are secularization and the media (e.g., Howe and Strauss 2000; Winograd and Hais 2008, 2011). Naturally, then, any institution with an interest in maintaining conservative political attitudes has an incentive to develop a means for countering the influence of secularization and the media. This is all the more true for evangelicals, as evangelicals have a long history of negative engagement with the media. For example, evangelicals were largely depicted as "backward" during the coverage of the Scopes Trial (Larson 2006), and researchers have found evidence of media bias against Christian fundamentalists in the modern era (Bolce and De Maio 2008).

The evangelical tradition has responded in part by discrediting secular culture and the media through a variety of mechanisms, including local congregations, religious media, and the legal and political system. For example, James Davison Hunter (1991) notes how the media were one locus for the "culture wars" between religious traditionalists and religious progressives. An important side effect of this discrediting process, from the perspective of Zaller's RAS theory of public opinion, discussed in Chapter 1 (Zaller 1992, see also Taber and Lodge 2006), is that young evangelicals will be less likely to receive, and more likely to reject, secular-derived considerations on political issues.

The interviews provided strong evidence that evangelical subcultural institutions are often engaged in teaching about culture. Presentations of the "ideal" relationship between evangelicals and the secular culture varied across universities and clubs, but a critical theme was often apparent. One student at Old Faithful College described how his institution addresses the relationship between evangelicals and secular culture: "We have to engage in culture because culture is created by God and therefore redeemable by God, and so we have to find the redeemable aspects of culture and bring them to light." When I followed up, asking where he had heard that take, he responded:

> I've heard that growing up because my parents are [Old Faithful] grads, all of my relatives are [Old Faithful] grads, most of my teachers were, so that concept, it's an . . . "every square inch belongs to God" kind of thing, and so everything is redeemable. So that I've heard growing up. But it is talked about by [Old Faithful's president and dean, and] my profs say things like that, so it's sort of just an undercurrent.

The interpretation the student presents is consistent with the teachings of Old Faithful's affiliated denomination. It is important to note that in this theology, the secular culture is not irredeemable. Rather, as Old Faithful College teaches, evangelicals have an important role in finding the redeemable aspects of culture (as well as, implicitly, rejecting or fixing the irredeemable aspects).

Likewise, New Faithful College includes a discussion of what it means to be an evangelical in modern society in its core curriculum. Here is how one student described the course:

> Yeah, so there's four Bible gen ed classes, sort of meant to be taken one each year, but not necessarily. You start freshman year with a class called [something equivalent to The Evangelical Church and

Culture] and basically it's an eight-week course: a little bit of church history, mostly evangelical doctrine . . . significant individuals in the evangelical church history, talking a lot about these things. Then it culminates in a paper [about] what does it mean for you to be an evangelical and how does that influence . . . your faith and your life and the actions you've taken so far? So that class is taken by freshmen their first semester . . . just so everyone at college has the same foundation.

Thus, it was readily apparent from the interviews that the evangelical subculture was critical of secular culture, often teaching students to recognize the shortcomings of culture and discussing what place evangelicals hold in modern society.

Subcultural Attitudes among Young Evangelicals

Are these teachings having an effect? Are young evangelicals more critical of secular culture compared to their peers? To answer these questions, we need survey data that can help us understand evangelicals' attitudes toward culture. Drawing on data from the 2007 Pew Religious Landscape Study, Figure 4.6 shows responses of eighteen- to twenty-nine-year-olds to the statement, "I often feel that my values are threatened by Hollywood and the entertainment industry." It is clear from the data that young evangelicals hold significantly more negative attitudes toward the entertainment industry compared to members of other religious traditions. About 42 percent of young evangelicals either mostly or completely agreed that the entertainment industry threatens their values. The group with the next highest rate of threatened values was Catholics, at about 35 percent.

The middle panel of Figure 4.6 shows responses to the question, "Do you think there is a natural conflict between being a devout religious person and living in a modern society, or don't you think so?" (also from the 2007 Pew Religious Landscape Study). About 44 percent of evangelicals said yes, second only to black Protestants (47 percent). Young evangelicals are significantly more likely to see a conflict between being religious and living in a modern society compared to Catholics and Jews (this question was not asked of those without a religious affiliation).

Another way of conceptualizing subcultural values is by examining attitudes about how a religious tradition should respond to the challenges of modernity. The bottom panel of Figure 4.6 shows responses from the 2014 Pew Religious Landscape Study when respondents were asked to choose whether their tradition should "preserve its traditional beliefs and practices,"

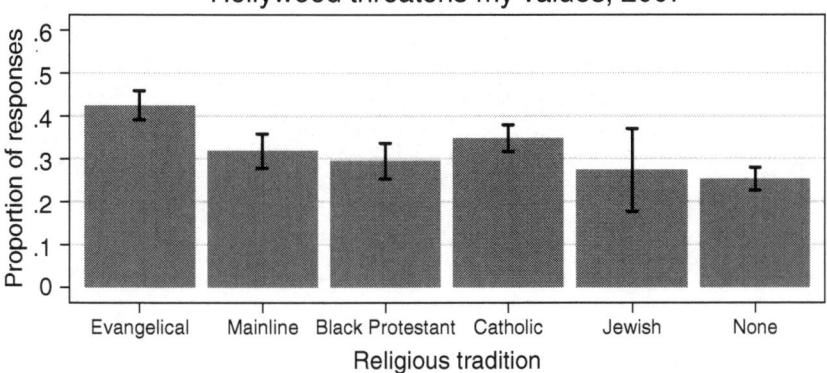

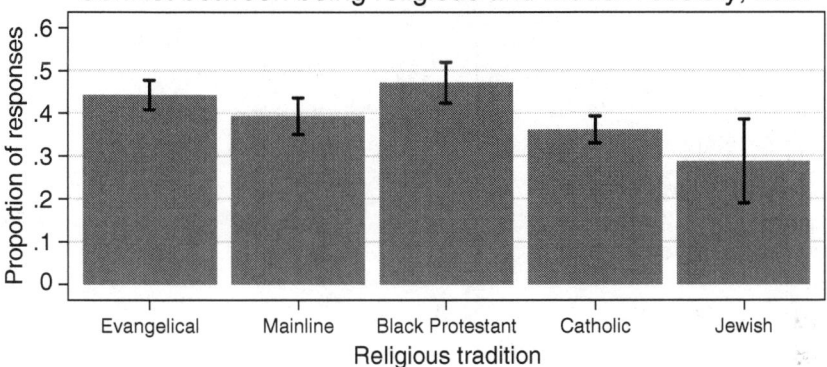

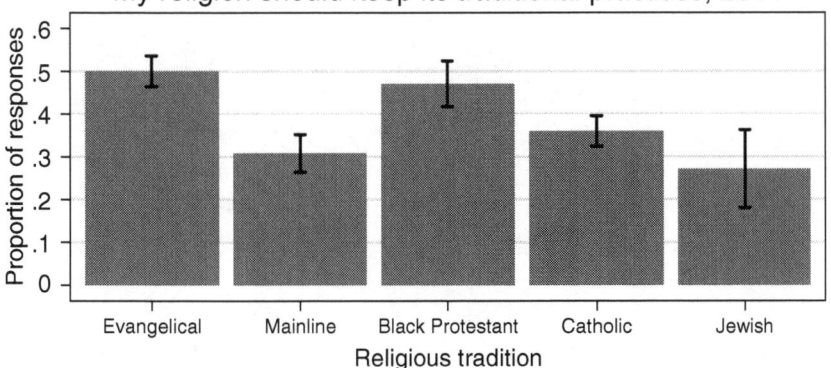

Figure 4.6. Subcultural attitudes among eighteen- to twenty-nine-year-olds by religious tradition.

Source: Weighted 2007 Pew Religious Landscape Study (Hollywood and conflict); weighted 2014 Pew Religious Landscape Study (traditional beliefs).
Note: Error bars represent 95 percent confidence intervals.

"adjust traditional beliefs and practices in light of new circumstances," or "adopt modern beliefs and practices." Young evangelicals were the most likely group to report that their tradition should preserve traditional beliefs and practices (at 50 percent), and they were also the least likely to agree that their tradition should adopt modern beliefs and practices (at 10 percent, not shown in the figure). Again, the results for evangelicals are comparable to the numbers for black Protestants, but well above those who belong to other religious traditions. Together, then, the survey data make it clear that young evangelicals are more likely to hold subcultural attitudes compared to their peers.

The Interviews: Why So Negative?

While the survey data help us establish *that* young evangelicals have a contentious relationship with secular culture, it remains unclear exactly *why* evangelicals have such a comparatively negative view of the society they live in. The data from the interviews can help us better understand the exact nature of evangelical feelings toward mainstream culture. In the interviews, I routinely asked students whether their view of American pop culture was more positive or more negative. Almost all the students responded that they viewed pop culture in a negative light. However, as my subcultural theory would lead us to expect, those with higher levels of religious commitment and subcultural immersion tended to express even more negative views.

A common theme was that the students found American pop culture materialistic, selfish, and corporate. One moderately liberal student at Old Faithful College said:

> A lot of the stuff that's put out there in the big headlines—like the big movies, the big songs, the big magazines, everything like that—seems pretty wrapped up in more shallow issues, shallow in general, very materialistic, very individualistic. . . . There's just stunts by Miley Cyrus and whoever, like "Look at me, look at me"—very foolish things. They get their fifteen seconds of fame, but at the end of the day, it's not really a contribution to society. It just seems cheap.

The negative view that many evangelicals have of secular culture is also related to their feelings about the role of religion in American culture. When I asked students whether the role of religion in the United States was growing or shrinking, almost all the students I spoke to thought it was shrinking. Many students at evangelical colleges indicated that they had even discussed the decline of religion's influence in their coursework. One conservative student at Old Faithful College provided a fairly typical analysis, albeit with a uniquely colorful take on the consequences:

> Honestly, I think [the role of religion in American culture is] shrinking. Even if you just, like, turn on the TV, or go onto YouTube, even, and look at the different music that's out there, I don't think that any of it's really influenced by religion. I mean, very loose morals and stuff. Maybe there's some catchy tunes out there, but if you even go onto news sites . . . there's horrible stuff happening out there. . . . Really, people have gotten away from God and religion, and it's going to bite people in the butt.

Students often said that, in addition to becoming less prevalent, when religion did come up in American culture, it was often presented in a trivial or watered-down fashion. Essentially, the students perceived that Christianity's role in popular culture is increasingly becoming indistinguishable from that of "civil religion" (Bellah 1967; Rousseau 1893), defined by Keith Roberts as "the set of beliefs, rites, and symbols that sacralize the values of the society and place the nation in the context of an ultimate system of meaning" (2004, 356). Many expressed something akin to the thoughts of one liberal evangelical at Top 100 College, who said, "I don't think it does very much anymore, which is sad, because other than when actors at awards ceremonies are standing up on stage and thanking God, you don't really hear about it very much in pop culture. Well, unless you're watching Fox."

A liberal, religiously committed student at New Faithful College expanded on this idea:

> I think that in pop culture, you tend to see caricatures of religion. We tend to take bits and pieces of religion that we like or that speak positively to us, and it becomes engrained in pop culture. We see a lot of eastern religions, for example, kind of get pulled in, with people talking about meditation, and other aspects of Zen Buddhism are kind of prevalent in pop culture. With Christianity, God kind of tends to be portrayed as this distant vague force. . . . I don't see people talking about Jesus as God very much except when they're joking about it, like I see on Comedy Central–type shows a lot.

In short, then, the interviews revealed that young evangelicals have strongly negative attitudes toward popular culture. They see religion's role in society as shrinking, and that only adds to the feeling of embattlement among many evangelicals (e.g., Smith et al. 1998).

Direct Political Cues

Finally, the evangelical subculture has the potential to affect public opinion by directly conveying political messages to adherents, thereby altering their underlying issue considerations. In our complex political landscape, there are hundreds of ways that the evangelical subculture might communicate political messages to adherents. In this section, my goal is simply to (1) demonstrate empirically that the evangelical subculture is engaged in these processes, and (2) to demonstrate that young evangelicals are picking up on these political messages. Therefore, I narrow my focus to two particularly influential ways in which the evangelical tradition communicates political messages to adherents: through broadly held political stereotypes and through the actions of subcultural institutions such as churches, evangelical colleges, and evangelical clubs and organizations.

Social Expectations

The literature in political science has long recognized that social groups play an important role in political behavior (e.g., Berelson, Lazarsfeld, and McPhee 1954; Campbell et al. 1960). In particular, sociodemographic groups can serve as an important heuristic as voters form opinions on candidates and issues (e.g., Popkin 1994; Sniderman, Brody, and Tetlock 1991). For example, research increasingly recognizes the role that social groups play in attitudes toward political candidates. Beyond simply liking or disliking a candidate because of his or her social group memberships, the research suggests that voters use a candidate's gender, race, religion, level of religious commitment, and other traits to make inferences about the candidate's partisanship and ideology (Berinsky and Mendelberg 2005; Campbell, Green, and Layman 2011; Castle et al. 2017; Huddy and Terkildsen 1993). Likewise, knowing whether a particular social group supports a matter of public policy can dramatically affect voter attitudes toward policies (e.g., Adkins et al. 2013; Kinder and Kam 2009; Sniderman, Brody, and Tetlock 1991). In short, the social expectations for groups can be a powerful source of political attitudes.

Perhaps the most important way groups matter is serving as a reference in the development of party identification (Green, Palmquist, and Schickler 2002). Since the 1950s, a steady stream of evangelical elites have worked hard to connect evangelical identity to conservative politics. Jerry Falwell, Pat Robertson, James Dobson, Phyllis Schlafly, and others established a pattern of nationally visible evangelicals taking far-right wing positions (Capps 1994; Martin 2005; Wilcox 1992; Williams 2010). Likewise, Republican politicians, including Ronald Reagan, George W. Bush, Mike Huckabee,

Sarah Palin, Rick Perry and others, touted their evangelical Christian beliefs in office and on the campaign trail (e.g., Holmes 2012; Medhurst 2008).[3] Indeed, the literature on religion and politics confirms that both evangelicals and "highly religious people" have become an important part of the Republican Party's public image (Campbell, Green, and Layman 2011; Castle et al. 2017).

The interviews suggest that young evangelicals are well aware of the stereotype that evangelicals are politically conservative. In the interviews, I routinely asked students about political stereotypes of evangelicals. Nearly all students identified evangelicals with conservative politics and the Republican Party, even those who were fairly liberal in their own views. One conservative student from New Faithful College explained:

> As evangelicals, we've taken the lead from a lot of well-known authors and pastors who take these more conservative choices, so, you know, people read these books and they hear these sermons online, and they tend to subscribe to the theology that these people are teaching, whether it be right or wrong. I think the conservative evangelical standpoint is the one that we hear most often, so [it's] the one we're most comfortable with and the most acceptable for Christians.

While most students were not quite this articulate, this student's response is particularly interesting because it highlights the role of the subculture (specifically, evangelical books and websites) as one potential source of the political stereotyping of evangelicals.

I also asked the students whether there seemed to be any issues that evangelicals stereotypically cared a lot about. Overwhelmingly, students cited abortion, gay marriage, and "social issues" as the issue areas most closely associated with evangelicals. In fact, several students highlighted these "culture war" issues as the primary reason why evangelicals were allied with the Republican Party. One student at Old Faithful College provides a typical example of this line of thought:

> Well, the Republican Party tends to be not as big for gay marriage, more pro-life—not all of them—but they tend to be more pro-life, from what I've noticed. I might just know a lot of conservative people, but more evangelicals tend to fall on the conservative side. So while not all of them might have [a conservative affiliation], I feel like they tend to line up, which might just be because, as far as social issues, they tend to agree more. So then they decide to agree more on other issues as well.

This sentiment is consistent with findings from nationally representative survey data that suggest that both elite- and mass-level party sorting on the basis of views on cultural issues was one factor driving evangelicals toward involvement in conservative politics (Killian and Wilcox 2008; Layman 2001).

When I followed up and asked respondents why they thought evangelicals cared about abortion and gay marriage so much, the impact of evangelicalism's distinctive beliefs was apparent: many students drew on biblical stories or passages to explain why evangelicals cared so much about these issues. One student at Great Books College provided a response that was typical:

> There's definitely biblical evidence that they cite and that they adhere to as showing that God is in the image of man and God has created us in his image, and that there's biblical evidence that . . . you are that image when you are still inside your mother's womb. So that's a very touchy thing to mess with when you're talking about destroying the image of God. It's equated to murder.

Likewise, when I asked why evangelicals cared so much about gay marriage, one liberal evangelical at Old Faithful College answered, "Again, it's in the Bible. 'A man should not lie down with another man as he would with a woman' is in Deuteronomy, I believe.[4] So that's one of their big hang-ups in America right now, is gays shouldn't be allowed to marry." The fact that this student was able to quote biblical passages on the subject despite his skepticism of the "stereotypical" point of view is remarkable and testifies to the importance of the subculture in forming attitudes on these issues.

While scholars dating back to Max Weber have noted a theoretical link between religion and economic attitudes, in practice the young evangelicals in the interviews were much less likely to identify economic issues as a core concern. When one libertarian student at Great Books College indicated that evangelicals were typically Republican, I asked him why. His response was interesting in that he explicitly rejected a connection between evangelicalism and economic policy:

> Well, Christian values tend to be more socially conservative, and the church doesn't concern itself as much with economics or money. The church, at least that I belong to, is very, very pro-life. It tends to be against gay rights, but that's more of a "hate the sin, love the sinner" type mentality. There's an opposition to homosexuality without being opposed to the people.

Another student at Great Books College, who was deeply conservative on economic issues, took a similar stance on the relationship between the church and economic policy:

> For me, and a lot of other evangelicals my age, we are very fiscally conservative and such, but, like, I wouldn't say that it's because I am a Christian. So there are issues a lot of us are passionate about. But otherwise it goes back to the same things, like pro-life. There's things like prayer in school . . . and, obviously, gay marriage.

The fact that these students explicitly downplayed a connection between evangelicalism and economic attitudes provides anecdotal evidence in favor of my issue hypothesis. In other words, the evidence suggests that the necessary issue constraint needed for individuals to connect the tradition's distinctive beliefs to political issues is harder to come by with regard to economic issues (e.g., Layman and Green 2005).

Political Messages from Subcultural Institutions

Beyond the public image of evangelicalism as politically conservative (particularly on social issues), the data from the interviews suggest that evangelical institutions have a variety of ways of communicating political messages to adherents. During my conversations with young evangelicals, I routinely asked students whether they had experienced various institutions taking positions on political issues. I summarize my findings by the type of institution: churches, colleges, and evangelical clubs.

Churches

Consistent with the literature's finding, most students indicated that their churches rarely discuss politics directly from the pulpit. However, it was also clear that churches had developed a number of mechanisms for conveying political messages to members. One of the most frequently referenced categories of activities in the interviews was church-sponsored events with political implications. One of the most common types of events within this category were those supporting expectant mothers and/or opposing abortion. For example, a moderately liberal student at Old Faithful College described this event hosted by her home church:

> They did an event . . . called Bikers for Babies. . . . There are a lot of bikers in the church—I mean motorcyclists—and they rode

downtown to [a local] pregnancy resource center . . . and did some sort of fund-raiser there. I think a big part of that was . . . it was all a big pro-life thing.

The social networks within churches can also be a source of political messages. A politically conservative student at Old Faithful College explained that one member of her church had went out of her way to communicate her views on abortion by encouraging members to sign a petition before and after services:

She had her sheet with her, and she'd go up to each individual person and tell them what it was about and how it was hoping to get rid of abortion in [their state]. Then she gave them the option of thinking about it and if [they] wanted to sign it next week—she gave them time to think about it. She wanted people to sign it because she was very strong toward the idea, but she didn't force anyone to.

This description fits well with the literature's more general emphasis on how the social networks within churches can be just as important as sermons and sponsored events for conveying political messages (e.g., Djupe and Gilbert 2009; Putnam and Campbell 2010; Wald, Owen, and Hill 1988, 1990).

Even liberal students had experienced their churches hosting events on abortion. A religiously committed student at New Faithful College recounted an activity that her church had hosted:

I think the most political we ever got was regarding . . . there was an organization we supported that . . . was basically supposed to be a resource for women with unwanted pregnancies to help them get connected to adoption agencies and things like that. . . . We would do this fund-raiser where . . . congregation members are given a baby bottle, and they collect spare change in it from either themselves or their coworkers, and then there's a day when everyone brings it in and the money is donated.

This anecdote serves as an excellent example of how changes in framing might relate to the formation of public opinion on abortion. Collecting change in a baby bottle may make respondents more likely to think that mothers would choose abortion out of financial need and not because of rape, incest, or reasons of health. Such a distinction could be relevant to public opinion on abortion, as most individuals are more predisposed to support legal abortions in the latter cases than the former (e.g., Jelen and Wilcox 2003). This is just one example of how seemingly "apolitical" activities within church walls can have an important impact on the way that evangelicals think about political issues.

During the interviews, most students reported that if their churches advocated on any issue, it was abortion. But several respondents reported that their churches delivered direct political messages about other issues as well. While I do not believe these examples to be typical of evangelical churches today, the fact that they came up in the interviews is nonetheless noteworthy, in that they help provide a fuller picture of the types of advocacy churches are engaged in.

One student at Great Books College reported that an assistant pastor at his church occasionally offered programs on creationism and evolution. The student described both the pastor and the program in detail:

> He personally, definitely, takes a position [in favor of] creationism, so it does affect how his debates are structured, but he does try to have programs that are friendly to those who want to question his position. He's also focused on youth outreach, so he also has a lot of youth programs like "Let's have a debate about all this." . . . I remember one was a debate, and he had this one guy who was a creationism expert come in, and they had another person who played devil's advocate, but I don't remember where he was from or all that. And sometimes he'll have an opportunity where kids who come to the program can ask him questions about what they've heard in class, and he'll just kind of field those.

While evangelicals have de-emphasized the issues of creationism and intelligent design in the wake of courtroom defeats in cases such as *Epperson v. Arkansas* (1968) and *Edwards v. Aguillard* (1987), the fact that local pastors are still teaching these suggests how important they once were in the evangelical subculture.

One politically liberal gay evangelical at the secular Top 100 College, who is becoming more distant from his faith, recounted that his pastor occasionally delivers antigay messages from the pulpit. Like the pastor speaking on creationism, the literature and my interviews suggest that this sort of open discussion of homosexuality from the pulpit is uncommon. Nevertheless, I include this example for the sake of demonstrating that the mechanisms for the evangelical subculture to deliver political messages exists. The student recounted the following:

> There's me and one other person at the church who people know that [we're] gay, but [the pastor will still say things like,] "If you're gay, you're gonna go to hell." Or "They're trying to legalize gay marriage, and they're gonna mess up the marriage that God has created for a man and a woman. . . . You could do civil unions but don't mess up marriage." . . . I feel like they are very hard and very open about being against those things. And he would preach like, "In the Word of God—I'll read it to you; this is what it says. . . . Some pastors might want to preach and just say something random, but I'm taking it to the book, and we're going to analyze the book for what it is." So I think they take a more conservative perspective of the Bible, and when they preach it, they definitely show that conservative side of it as well.

At least one student reported that his pastor also took liberal positions on some issues at the pulpit. The student, who attends Old Faithful College, explained that his pastor

> would do it very subtly because he was far more left than the majority of the members were, so he was very cautious of what kind of politics he would preach in his sermons, but knowing him and knowing the way he talked about things, I personally could see subtle hints of what he was talking about. . . . He talked a lot about equality, how Jesus taught equality, so whenever he was preaching on the Beatitudes in Matthew 5, he would bring up equality through that, and he would subtly [explain that] "we should treat everybody in this country equally" in his sermon.

On the one hand, this statement provides an important alternative perspective, demonstrating that evangelical churches are not uniformly conservative. On the other hand, though, the fact that this Midwestern pastor felt the need to be so subtle about advocating liberal ideas in his sermons suggests that the norms of political conservatism among evangelicals have become so strong that pastors who wish to advocate for more liberal causes may find it difficult to do so without generating push back from congregants.

Colleges

In Chapter 1, I also argue that the evangelical tradition had developed and encouraged specific institutions, such as evangelical colleges and evangelical clubs on secular campuses, designed to communicate subcultural values to young evangelicals in particular. Therefore, we would expect to see evidence in the interviews that students at evangelical colleges perceived their colleges to have a political agenda.

As in the case of churches, many students reported that they were unaware of their college's political leanings. However, others were able to marshal evidence that their college did support one party or another. The nature of this evidence varied wildly. Often, it was disconnected from specific programs at the college. For example, one student at Old Faithful College pointed to a key set of donors, who are well-known around campus, as strong Republicans who donate to conservative candidates.

In other cases, students pointed out how colleges used special programs to advocate a political position. Several students observed that homosexuality was a subject of on-campus conversation and debate. At one time, evangelical colleges may not have felt the need to address homosexuality. However, as the LGBT rights movement has gained salience and support among public opinion, evangelical colleges seem increasingly compelled to address the issue. One moderate student at Old Faithful College explained:

> Student: They do a lot of talks on it. I think there's a few coming up soon. Also, let's say a family comes and visits and a family asks about it, we do tell them what [Old Faithful] believes and stands for on those issues. . . .
> Me: How would you sum up [Old Faithful]'s stance on homosexuality?
> Student: We accept the person but not the lifestyle. It's more of, like, loving the sinner, not the sin.

In the interest of clarifying, the college's official position on homosexuality as explained on its website is that same-sex attraction (without accompanying sexual activity) is not sinful in and of itself. However, the college condemns sexual activity between gay couples (and all sexual activity outside of heterosexual marriage).[5]

Another student at Old Faithful College, who was fairly conservative, explained one way in which these views were communicated to students: "At the beginning of the year, there were these different seminars that freshmen could go to, and one of them was on homosexuality, and I feel that they really emphasized not only the [affiliated denomination's] view but the popular Republican view on homosexuality in that lecture." In short, then, Old Faithful College used special seminars to communicate its subcultural position on homosexuality to students.

Of course, as I note in Chapter 4, Old Faithful College is theologically moderate for an evangelical college. So, we would expect some liberal influences pushing students the other way. Several students viewed the faculty as espousing more liberal views than the administration or the student body. One conservative student at Old Faithful explained that his philosophy professor identified himself as a Democrat during class. This student noted, "He would explain his views as a Democrat and then challenge why we would be a Republican, given the way he thought."[6] If nothing else, this anecdote serves as another reminder that even if the evangelical subculture as a whole tends to lean toward the political right, the diversity within the evangelical subculture means that the political messages evangelicals receive are by no means monolithic.

While some students at New Faithful College mentioned that they did not think the college was politically active, for others the connection between New Faithful and conservative politics was all too clear. Several students mentioned that the college was actively taking sides on a narrow issue in the "culture wars."[7] The college had recently hosted a series of forums on the issue, and it was clear that students were informed about the specifics of the college's position. In addition, one of the interviewees mentioned that the college had sponsored a number of alumni speakers who had worked in politics and that most were conservative.

The ways that evangelical colleges communicate messages may seen more distinctive when juxtaposed against the activities of the nonevangelical colleges. At Top 100 College, most of the students perceived the administration and faculty as quite liberal, on average. Several interviewees mentioned that the college's president had recently written an editorial in the local newspaper taking the liberal position on a state-level "culture wars" debate. The student culture at Top 100 is also quite liberal, at least compared to the other evangelical colleges where I conducted my interviews (as I explain in the introduction to Part II, it is probably quite moderate when compared to other colleges nationwide). In the interviews, several students referenced Top 100's very active gay-straight alliance student organization. One of the club's annual events, which at least two students described to me during the course of our interviews, is a mock wedding of three couples (one gay, one lesbian, and one heterosexual) hosted in a prominent on-campus location on National Freedom to Marry Day.

The students at Directional State University generally did not perceive the administration as particularly politically active. However, as I note in the Introduction to Part II, the students generally perceived the college's culture as being secular and moderate to liberal politically. As a campus with a much greater number of commuters and a higher percentage of part-time students, the levels of group activity at Directional State were lower than at the private colleges where I interviewed. In addition, Directional State had neither the faith-based motivation for political action that the evangelical colleges had nor the latitude to engage in state politics that Top 100 College had. In short, it is unsurprising that students sensed fewer political messages coming from Directional State, despite what was likely a liberalizing environment.

Student Clubs

In general, there was less evidence of student clubs delivering explicitly political messages. One member of InterVarsity at Great Books College noted that the group rarely takes sides on particular political issues. He explained that although specific group members were interested in issues like abortion and the Israel-Palestine conflict, "they try to keep things pretty neutral because everybody's from different backgrounds." One factor in the relative lack of issue advocacy in these organizations may be the fact that they are mostly student-run and therefore have a less well-defined agenda coming from adult leadership than other aspects of the subculture. Whatever the reason, the interviews suggested that the effect of student clubs is probably primarily from generating an evangelical identity and teaching evangelicalism's distinctive beliefs, as opposed to direct issue advocacy.

Conclusion

In this chapter, I provide empirical evidence for my theoretical account of how the evangelical subculture engages in four key processes that together allow it to exert considerable impact on the political attitudes of evangelicals by altering the distribution of considerations they draw from as they express opinions on political issues. First, the evangelical tradition builds evangelical social group identity among its members. Second, the evangelical tradition teaches its members distinctive beliefs, many of which could have implications for politics. Third, the evangelical tradition discredits secular culture, thereby reducing the likelihood that evangelicals would rely on secular considerations. Finally, the evangelical subculture delivers explicitly political messages. Together, then, there is strong evidence that immersion in the evangelical subculture could alter the distribution of opinion considerations, thereby influencing their political beliefs.

The results of this chapter should be of interest to a variety of audiences. For social identity theorists, the findings provide insight into how social groups may use institutions to help develop in-group identity in the absence of clearly identifiable external traits, such as race, ethnicity, and gender (Castle et al. 2012). Future research may examine how other subcultures, ranging from the Tea Party to the LGBT community, use similar institutions to build in-group identity that can then shape political behavior.

The findings in this chapter also set the stage for future analyses. In this chapter, we see how the evangelical subculture uses subcultural institutions to make it more likely that respondents will draw on religious considerations, and less likely that respondents will draw on secular considerations, as they form opinions on political issues. In Chapter 5, I test the core of my argument that engagement in the evangelical subculture leads to greater conservatism among young evangelicals, especially on measures of political identity and cultural issues.

5

Testing Subcultural Immersion's Impact on Public Opinion

To those who associate Millennials with political liberalism, Paul Franklin[1] is something of a mystery. He is politically knowledgeable, active in politics, and uniformly conservative on social, economic, and foreign policy issues. What explains Paul's views? My subcultural theory of public opinion among young evangelicals developed in Chapter 2 would lead us to expect that Paul is deeply involved in the evangelical subculture. Indeed, throughout my hour-long semistructured interview with Paul in the spring of 2014, it became clear that his religious beliefs and upbringing were the most important source of his political conservatism. Paul's parents were committed evangelicals, he attended evangelical Christian schools, and he was about to graduate from New Faithful College at the time I interviewed him. My theory suggests that immersion in the evangelical subculture, and exposure to the new issue considerations discussed in Chapter 4, caused Paul's conservatism. So far, however, I have not provided evidence that it is immersion in the evangelical subculture, specifically, that is causing young evangelicals to remain more conservative than their peers on most issues.

In this chapter, I provide a more rigorous test of the core of my theory of public opinion among young evangelicals introduced in Chapter 1. I expect to find that evangelicalism exerts an impact on individuals' political attitudes. However, we should not expect evangelicalism to influence attitudes among all adherents or on all issues equally. In Chapter 1, I introduce two hypotheses that would help us predict and explain where the evangelical subculture's impact would be the strongest. First, the issue hypothesis predicts that evangelicalism has a larger impact on those political identities and issues that have been a more important part of evangelicalism's identity and distinctiveness. Second, the commitment hypothesis predicts that those, like Paul, who have been more engaged in the evangelical subculture tend to be more conservative than their less engaged counterparts, particularly in terms of political identity and cultural issues. In the pages that follow, I provide a stronger test of these hypotheses by looking at the impact of religious commitment on issue attitudes and issue salience, controlling for other possible explanations.

In addition, my argument contains a causal claim that immersion in the evangelical subculture *causes* greater conservatism. To test the causal aspects of my argument, I rely on panel data, which allow us to observe individual-level change over time. Specifically, I employ data from the 2010–2014 Cooperative Congressional Election Study Panel Survey. I find strong evidence that immersion in the evangelical subculture leads to more conservative attitudes on cultural issues.

Quantifying the Impact of Evangelical Subcultural Engagement

In Chapter 2, I show that young evangelicals remain quite similar to both older evangelicals and previous generations of young evangelicals on attitudes that have been at the heart of evangelicalism's political identity, including Republican identification, conservative ideology, and conservative views on abortion. In Chapter 3, I show that to the extent young evangelicals are becoming more liberal on issues like gay marriage, this liberalization seems to be concentrated among infrequent attendees, thereby suggesting that forces outside the subculture are driving the change.

Implicit in these analyses, and explicit in my commitment hypothesis, is the assumption that immersion in the evangelical subculture is causing the conservatism. While this assumption probably resonates with most readers, we should not assume it to be correct without evidence. A variety of other things besides immersion in the subculture could be causing evangelicals to hold conservative attitudes. For example, one possibility is that evangelicalism leads to Republican Party identification, and then Republicanism leads to conservative left-right ideology and conservative attitudes on most issues. If this was true, once we account for party identification, religious commitment would not have much of an impact on issue attitudes or issue salience. Another possible explanation for the relative conservatism of evangelicals is that evangelicals disproportionately live in the South, which has a comparatively conservative political culture. Again, if this account was correct, once we control for the fact that evangelicals disproportionately live in the South, religious commitment would not have much of an impact on evangelicals' attitudes.

Therefore, a more rigorous test of my commitment hypothesis is clearly necessary. If subcultural immersion (in the form of religious commitment) really is at the heart of evangelicalism's impact, then we should find that religious commitment exerts a statistically significant impact on issue attitudes and issue salience, even after controlling for party, region, and a variety of other alternative explanations. However, we must also keep in mind the issue hypothesis. Specifically, religious commitment is most likely to show an effect on the political identities and issues that have been an important part of evangelicalism's identity and distinctiveness: Republicanism, conservatism, and, specifically, conservative attitudes on abortion and gay marriage.

To provide a convincing test of these hypotheses, I again rely on data from the 2014 and 2007 Pew Religious Landscape Study. I use a series of regression models with the sample limited to evangelicals between the ages of eighteen and twenty-nine. The dependent variables are those that I on focus on throughout the book: partisanship, ideology, and attitudes on abortion, gay marriage, homosexuality, the environment, welfare, military strength, and isolationism. Each dependent variable is recoded to range from zero (the most liberal response available) to one (the most conservative response available) to provide a consistent basis for interpreting and comparing results.

Besides their large sample size, another advantage of these surveys is that they include a number of other variables that serve as useful controls. Specifically, I control for gender (a dummy variable for females), income, education, region (a dummy variable for the South, with all other regions as the comparison group), and race (dummy variables for Hispanic, Asian, and Mixed/Other, with whites as the comparison group). To provide an even stricter test of my hypotheses, I control for party identification in the models for ideology and the issues, and I control for ideology in the models for party and the issues.[2] All independent variables are also recoded to range from zero to one.

I measure subcultural engagement with a standard scale of religious commitment, made up of frequency of attending religious services, the degree of guidance religion provides in one's life, and frequency of prayer.[3] Together, these items create a reliable measure of engagement within the evangelical subculture.[4] Furthermore, although we do not have access to questions about more specialized behaviors, like how often an individual uses media designed for evangelical audiences, we would expect these to share a strong positive correlation with the religious commitment scale I use.

The commitment hypothesis and the issue hypothesis lead us to expect to find that the coefficients for religious commitment are positive and statistically significant for party affiliation, ideology, abortion attitudes, gay marriage, and views on homosexuality. In contrast, we would expect to find that religious commitment exerts a much smaller influence on attitudes on noncultural issues such as the environment, welfare, immigration, the military, and isolationism.

In several cases, the coding of the dependent variables means that it is theoretically appropriate to use either logistic regression (gay marriage) or ordered logistic regression (abortion). Unlike ordinary least squares regression, the coefficients for these types of regression are difficult to interpret in substantive terms. Therefore, I discuss the results in terms of predicted probabilities. The actual regression results are shown in the Chapter 5 Appendix.

Overall, the results provide strong support for my hypothesis. Beginning with party identification, Figure 5.1 shows that, when holding all other variables in the model constant, the average young evangelical with the minimum level of religious commitment has a predicted partisanship of .38 (in substantive terms, an independent-leaning Democrat). In contrast, the average young evangelical with the maximum level of religious commitment has a predicted partisanship of .69 (in substantive terms, very nearly "Republican" identification). Overall, then, moving from the minimum level

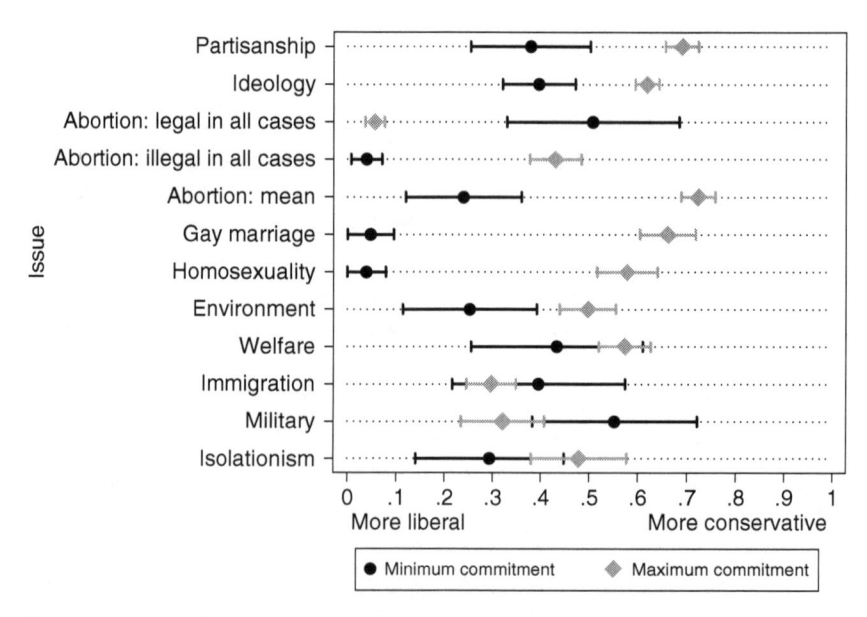

Figure 5.1. The effect of religious commitment on issue attitudes among eighteen- to twenty-nine-year-old evangelicals (with controls), 2014.
Source: 2014 Pew Religious Landscape Study.
Note: Error bars represent 95 percent confidence intervals.

of religious commitment to the maximum increases partisanship by about .31 points (this effect is statistically significant at $p < .001$).

Figure 5.1 shows that religious commitment also exerts a strong impact on ideology among young evangelicals. After controlling for the other variables in the model, the average young evangelical with minimum religious commitment has a predicted ideology of .40, while the average young evangelical with maximum religious commitment has a predicted ideology of .62. This means that the effect of religious commitment on ideology among young evangelicals is .22 (statistically significant at $p < .001$).

As we would expect, religious commitment also appears to have a strong impact on attitudes toward abortion among young evangelicals. Here, the dependent variable is a four-point scale, ranging from "legal in all cases" to "illegal in all cases." Therefore, I use ordered logistic regression to estimate the probability that an evangelical would fall into each category. Figure 5.1 shows that as religious commitment moves from its minimum to its maximum value, the probability that a young evangelical believes abortion should be legal in all cases declines from .51 to .06. Likewise, the probability that a young evangelical believes abortion should be illegal in all cases rises from .04 among the least committed to .43 among the most committed. I then use ordinary least squares regression to obtain a clear one-number summary of the impact of religious commitment on abortion attitudes (shown in Figure 5.1 with the label "Abortion: mean"). As the figure shows, the effect of moving from the minimum to the maximum religious commitment is an increase of about .48 ($p < .001$) in predicted abortion attitudes.

Religious commitment also has a strong impact on attitudes toward homosexuality. Figure 5.1 shows that, after controlling for the other variables in the model, a young evangelical with minimum religious commitment has a .04 probability of believing that society should discourage homosexuality. An otherwise identical young evangelical with the maximum level of religious commitment has a .58 probability of believing that society should discourage homosexuality. Overall, then, the total effect of religious commitment is about a .54 increase in the probability of saying that homosexuality should be discouraged ($p < .001$).

The results were similar on the question of same-sex marriage. Figure 5.1 shows the probability of opposing gay marriage. Holding the other variables in the model constant, the regression equation predicts that a young evangelical with the minimum level of religious commitment has a .05 probability of opposing gay marriage, while an otherwise identical young evangelical with the maximum level of religious commitment has a .66 probability of opposing gay marriage. This means that moving from the minimum to the maximum level of religious commitment among young evangelicals leads to a .61 increase in the probability of opposing same-sex marriage ($p < .001$).

The impact of religious commitment was quite different on noncultural issues. Beginning with the environment, Figure 5.1 shows the probability of a respondent taking an antienvironment position in the jobs-environment trade-off. After controlling for other factors, a young evangelical with minimum religious commitment has a .25 probability of responding that "stricter environmental laws and regulations cost too many jobs." An otherwise identical young evangelical with the maximum possible religious commitment has a .50 probability of taking the antienvironment position. Overall, moving from minimum to maximum commitment increases the probability of a young evangelical taking an anti-environment position by about .24 ($p < .05$).

Next, on the topic of welfare, Figure 5.1 shows the probability of a young evangelical agreeing with the statement, "Government aid does more harm than good by making people too dependent on government assistance." The results indicate that, controlling for other factors, religious commitment has only a comparatively small and not statistically significant impact on welfare attitudes. The figure shows that a young evangelical with minimum religious commitment has a .43 probability of taking the antiwelfare position, compared to a .57 probability for a young evangelical with maximum religious commitment. However, the large standard errors here mean that we cannot be certain that religious commitment affects welfare attitudes once we control for partisanship, ideology, income, and other relevant variables.

Similarly, when it comes to immigration, Figure 5.1 shows the likelihood of young evangelicals taking the position that increasing immigration has been "a change for the worse." After controlling for partisanship, ideology, race/ethnicity, and other relevant factors, a young evangelical with a minimum level of religious commitment has a .40 probability of saying increasing immigration has been a change for the worse. An otherwise comparable young evangelical with the maximum level of religious commitment has a .30 probability of saying that increasing immigration has been a change for the worse. After accounting for the control variables, religious commitment appears to decrease anti-immigrant attitudes by about .10, although the effect is not statistically significant.

Continuing the now-familiar theme, religious commitment also appears to have a weak impact on attitudes toward the military-diplomacy trade-off. Figure 5.1 shows the probability of agreeing with the statement, "The best way to ensure peace is through military strength" (Pew Religious Landscape Study 2007). After controlling for other factors, the model predicts that a young evangelical with minimum religious commitment has a .55 probability of agreeing with this statement, compared to a probability of .32 for young evangelicals with maximum religious commitment. Overall, the wide standard errors mean that the impact of religious commitment on attitudes toward the military among young evangelicals is weak and not statistically significant.

Finally, Figure 5.1 shows the effect of religious commitment on the likelihood of agreeing with the statement, "We should pay less attention to problems overseas and concentrate on problems here at home" (Pew Religious Landscape Study 2007). After controlling for other factors, the probability of a young evangelical with minimum religious commitment taking the isolationist stance is .29, compared to .48 for a young evangelical with maximum commitment. Overall, the effect is moderate in size (.18) and is not statistically significant.

The results in this section provide strong support for the commitment hypothesis. Even after controlling for a variety of rival explanations, religious commitment seems to affect issue attitudes among young evangelicals across a variety of issues. While cross-sectional data cannot provide definitive evidence of causality, the analysis here lends support to my contention that subcultural immersion (measured by religious commitment) influences political identities and issue attitudes, even when controlling for partisanship, ideology, and other sociodemographic explanations.

The results also provide strong support for my issue hypothesis. The effects of immersion are consistently strong and statistically significant for both partisanship and ideology. Immersion has an even stronger relationship to conservative attitudes on cultural issues like abortion, social acceptance of homosexuality, and same-sex marriage. In contrast, immersion has a weak and inconsistent pattern of influence on noncultural issues. On environmental policy, religious commitment clearly increases conservatism. On most other noncultural issues, including welfare, immigration, the military, and isolationism, religious commitment does not have a statistically significant impact once we account for rival explanations.

Subcultural Immersion and Issue Salience

We also might wonder how subcultural immersion affects issue salience. To test this, I use data from the Public Religion Research Institute's Millennial Values Survey, 2012. To control for the effects of partisanship and other potential covariates, I use a series of logistic regression models, where the dependent variable is whether the respondent said an issue was a "critical issue" (coded 1) or "one among many"/"not that important" (coded 0). The independent variables in the model are nearly identical to those in the previous section; they include party, ideology, a dummy variable for women, income, education, a dummy variable for Southern residence, and dummy variables for Hispanic and mixed/other race. The main independent variable of interest is religious commitment. The data are limited to evangelicals ages eighteen to twenty-four.[5] Because logistic regression coefficients are difficult to interpret substantively, I discuss the results in terms of predicted probabilities (the full model results are shown in the Chapter 5 Appendix).

The results suggest that immersion is an important factor in the salience of abortion attitudes among young evangelicals. As we would expect, the more religiously committed a young evangelical is, the more likely he or she will consider abortion a "critical issue." Specifically, Figure 5.2 shows that moving from the minimum religious commitment to the maximum increases the probability of labeling abortion a critical issue from .16 to .53 ($p < .05$).

Perhaps somewhat surprisingly, after controlling for other factors, religious commitment leads to a statistically significant decrease in the likelihood of labeling the federal deficit a critical issue ($p < .05$). As Figure 5.2 shows, the probability of a young evangelical with the minimum religious commitment declaring the deficit a critical issue is .91, compared to just .56 among the most highly committed young evangelicals. While surprising at first, this finding may be reflective of the relative unimportance of economic policy to the identity of the evangelical subculture discussed in previous chapters.

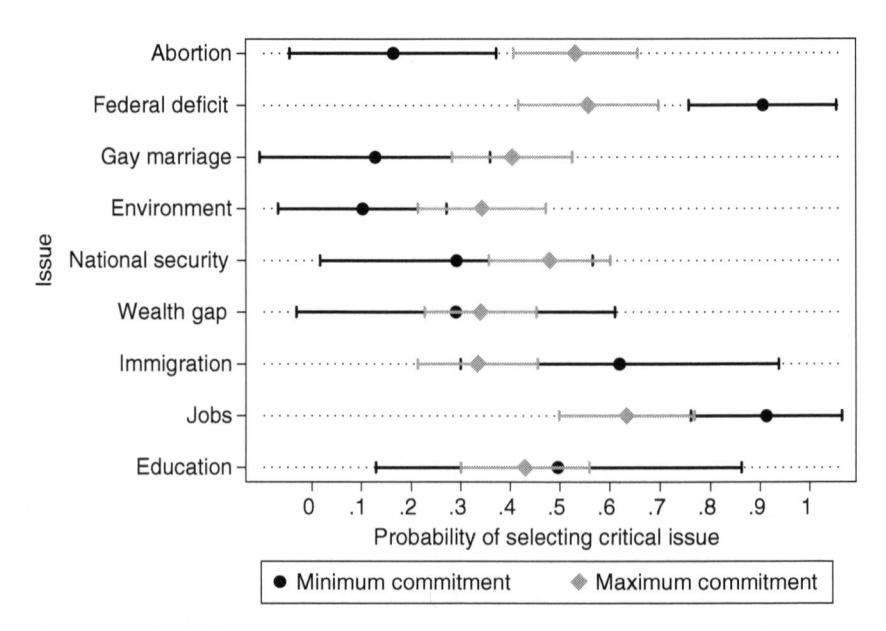

Figure 5.2. The effect of religious commitment on issue salience among eighteen- to twenty-nine-year-old evangelicals (with controls).

Source: Public Religion Research Institute Millennial Values Survey, 2012.
Note: Error bars represent 95 percent confidence intervals.

On most other issues, the impact of religious commitment on issue salience is not statistically significant. Perhaps the most surprising among these issues is the attitudes toward same-sex marriage. The probabilities shown in Figure 5.2 indicate that religious commitment has a sizable impact on the probability of declaring gay marriage a critical issue, with the probability rising from .13 among those with the minimum commitment to .40 among those with the maximum commitment. However, the confidence intervals around the estimates are quite wide, and therefore the effect is not statistically significant.

There were also several noncultural issues for which religious commitment appears to increase salience, although the results are not statistically significant. One such issue is the environment. The model predicts that the probability of a minimum-commitment young evangelical declaring the environment a critical issue is .10, compared to .34 for an otherwise equally high-commitment young evangelical. Another such issue is national security, where the probability of a minimum-commitment young evangelical considering it a critical issue is .29, compared to .48 for a maximum-commitment evangelical. Finally, religious commitment appears to lead to a slight increase in the salience of the wealth gap, from .29 among low-commitment evangelicals to .34 among high-commitment evangelicals.

There are also a few issues where religious commitment appears to decrease salience, although again the effects are not statistically significant. These include immigration, where the probability of labeling it a critical issue falls from .62 at the lowest level of commitment to .33 among the most highly committed. Another such issue is jobs, where the predicted probability of considering it a critical issue falls from .91 among the least committed to .63 among the most committed. Finally, on education, the probability of considering it a salient issue falls from .50 among those with the minimum level of commitment to .43 among those with the maximum level of commitment.

While the results in this section are perhaps weaker than anticipated, the findings nevertheless add support to both the commitment hypothesis and the issue hypothesis. Young evangelicals who are more immersed in the subculture are more likely to consider abortion a critical issue, and they are less likely to consider the federal deficit a critical issue. On most other issues, immersion appears to have little effect on salience once we account for other potential explanations.

The Question of Causality

Up to this point in this chapter, I use nationally representative survey data to demonstrate that evangelicals who are more engaged in the evangelical subculture are more conservative, particularly on political identities and cultural issues. However, my argument regarding the impact of subcultural immersion contains a causal claim: subcultural immersion *causes* young evangelicals to become more conservative. So far, the data have not been able to address this causal aspect of my argument because they have measured attitudes at only one point in time.

Defending the causal aspect of my argument is particularly consequential in light of recent developments in the literature on religion in American politics. For several decades, survey researchers assumed that the causal relationship between religion and politics was *unidirectional*, with religion affecting political attitudes but political attitudes exerting no influence on religion. For example, Bernard Berelson, Paul Lazarsfeld, and William McPhee (1954) argued that the social context of religion helped "remind" individuals of their group's partisan and candidate preferences in the months before an election. The assumption of a unidirectional relationship makes sense in light of the early sociological and social-psychological models' understandings of the impact of social identities like race, gender, and religion on the development of partisanship (e.g., Campbell et al. 1960; Green, Palmquist, and Schickler 2002; Lewis-Beck et al. 2008).

While the importance of social groups to the formation of political identities and issue attitudes remains unquestioned, over time scholars came to more fully understand that partisanship and ideology were important social identities in and of themselves (Campbell et al. 1960; Conover and Feldman 1981; Green, Palmquist, and Schickler 2002; Greene 1999, 2004). Typical of the group warfare predicted by social identity theory (e.g., Tajfel 1981, 1982), research on polarization suggests that Republicans and Democrats increasingly view each other as negative reference groups (Iyengar, Sood, and Lelkes 2012). Given the strength of partisanship and ideology as social identities in and of themselves, we might predict that the relationship between religion and political identity would become *bidirectional* rather than unidirectional. That is, we might expect—in addition to evangelicals and religious traditionalists sorting into the Republican Party and religious modernists and seculars sorting into the Democratic Party—Republicans to increase their religiosity and Democrats to decrease their religiosity so that they more closely conform to their preferred party's image.

Indeed, research has found strong support for this bidirectional theory of the relationship between religion and politics (which I will refer to as the "political religion hypothesis"). For example, in a landmark paper, Michael Hout and Claude Fischer (2002) argue that the increasing association between religion and conservative politics is leading liberals to drop their religious affiliations, particularly in mainline Protestant and Catholic denominations. Following up on this research, Stratos Patrikios (2008) analyzes evangelicals in the American National Election Studies and finds strong evidence in favor of the political religion hypothesis: while increasing church attendance appears to lead to a more conservative ideological identification, conservatives also appear to have increased their attendance. However, the existing studies are not flawless. In particular, Patrikios (2008) suffers from very small sample sizes (fewer than three hundred respondents) and does not test whether church attendance or religious commitment appears to affect partisanship or attitudes on cultural issues.

The political religion hypothesis itself actually fits well with my subcultural theory. Throughout this book, I frequently suggest that the evangelical tradition responded to the cultural liberalism of the 1960s by making Republican Party affiliation, ideological conservatism, and conservative attitudes on cultural issues part of its distinctive identity. Thus, it would be no surprise to find that political liberals or those who are pro-choice would sort out of the evangelical tradition because the tradition's newly clarified political identity did not fit with their preexisting attitudes. Indeed, this sorting effect may be one of the mechanisms that helps the evangelical subculture maintain the relative consistency over time that we see in the time-series data in Chapter 2. However, whether the kind of political sorting described by the political religion hypothesis is occurring or not, *the key for my theory is that we should find the opposite is true as well: those who become more immersed in the subculture should become more Republican, more likely to self-identify as ideologically conservative, and more likely to express conservative attitudes on cultural issues.*

Thus, to fully defend my subcultural theory, I need to show that the subculture's influence holds even after accounting for the political religion hypothesis. One strategy for providing a more convincing test of causal claims involves the use of panel data, in which the same set of individuals is interviewed at multiple points in time. Having multiple measures of attitudes over time allows us to examine the causes of variation within individuals as independent variables change. In this case, I rely on data from the 2010–2014 Cooperative Congressional Election Study Panel Survey (CCES), an internet survey of nine thousand five hundred Americans conducted by the firm YouGov (Schaffner and Ansolabehere 2015). The benefits of this data set include a large sample and three waves of responses (2010, 2012, and 2014). The political religion hypothesis would lead us to expect to find some evidence that political identities and issue attitudes cause a change in religious attendance. However, my subcultural theory would lead us to expect to also find evidence that increased church attendance leads to increased conservatism and conservative issue attitudes, even after accounting for the political religion hypothesis.

To test my theory with the CCES data, I use a series of three-wave cross-lagged structural equation models. Unlike most of the analyses in this book,

I do not restrict the data to young evangelicals for several reasons. In terms of theory, my goal is simply to test whether immersion in the evangelical subculture in general leads to greater political conservatism. As a practical matter, sample size was also a relevant consideration, particularly because structural equation models tend to require larger samples than ordinary least squares regression.[6] Limiting the data to those who belong to evangelical denominations during all three waves reduces the sample size to 1,517. The principle independent variable is religious commitment, which is again a scale made up of church attendance, frequency of prayer, and religious importance.[7]

Figure 5.3 shows the results for the relationship between religious commitment and partisanship.[8] As we would expect, both partisanship and religious commitment appear quite consistent over time ($p < .001$). The political religion hypothesis also receives support: evangelicals who became more Republican increase their church attendance in both waves ($p < .05$). Turning to the main effect of interest, the effect of church attendance on partisanship is not statistically significant during the 2010–2012 wave, but it is significant between 2012 and 2014 ($p < .05$). Given that we are looking at the effect of church attendance on partisanship among all age categories, it is not surprising that we find understated effects. Researchers who study political socialization recognize that partisanship is most malleable when individuals are in their teens and twenties (Jennings and Niemi 1981; Neundorf and Smets 2017); after that partisanship is consistent over time (Green, Palmquist, and Schickler 2002).

The results for ideology, shown in the bottom panel of Figure 5.3, are similar. Again, we see that both ideology and religious commitment are stable over time. The political religion hypothesis is clearly supported: evangelicals who become more conservative tend to increase their church attendance, and the effect is statistically significant in both time periods ($p < .05$). Church attendance does not have a statistically significant impact on ideology during the period from 2010 to 2012, but the effect is significant ($p < .05$) from 2012 to 2014. Given the similarity of the patterns for partisanship and ideology, we might speculate that church attendance has a greater impact on political identities during nonpresidential election cycles, when political messages from other sources are more limited.

Religious commitment appears to have had an even stronger impact on cultural issue attitudes. Figure 5.4 shows the relationship between religious commitment and attitudes on abortion. Again, it is evident that both religious commitment and attitudes on abortion are consistent over time. The political religion hypothesis is again supported: abortion attitudes strongly affect religious commitment in both 2010–2012 ($p < .001$) and 2012–2014 ($p < .05$). However, the commitment hypothesis also receives strong support,

Party identification

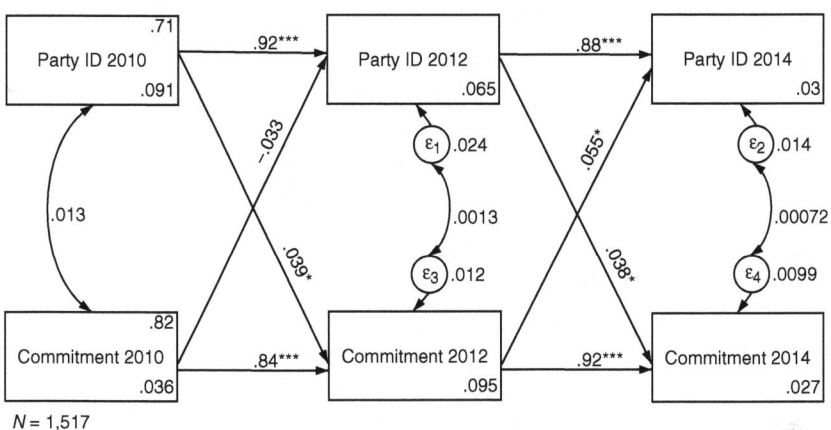

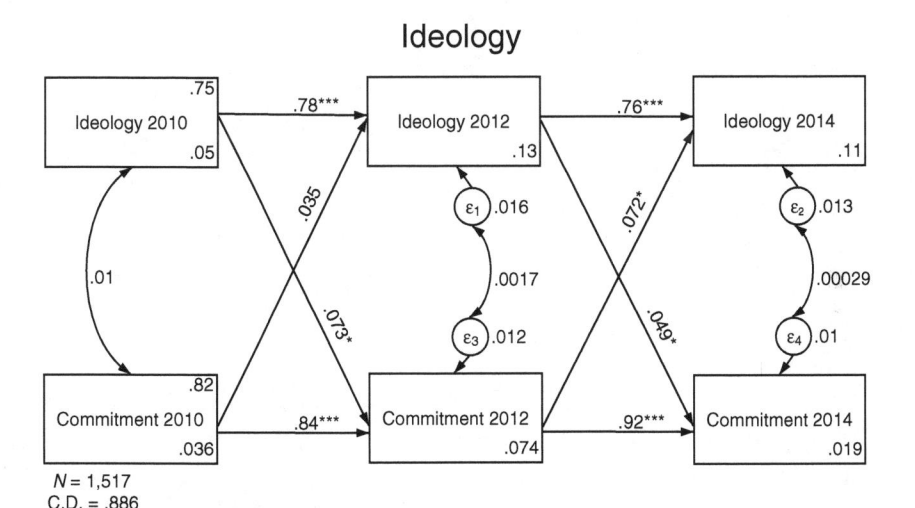

[Path diagram showing Party ID 2010 (.71, .091), Party ID 2012 (.065), Party ID 2014 (.03) across top; Commitment 2010 (.82, .036), Commitment 2012 (.095), Commitment 2014 (.027) across bottom. Path coefficients: Party ID 2010 → Party ID 2012 = .92***; Party ID 2012 → Party ID 2014 = .88***; Commitment 2010 → Commitment 2012 = .84***; Commitment 2012 → Commitment 2014 = .92***; Party ID 2010 ↔ Commitment 2010 = .013; cross-lagged: −.033, .039*, .055*, .038*. Error terms: ε₁ .024, ε₂ .014, ε₃ .012, ε₄ .0099, with covariances .0013 and .00072.]

N = 1,517
C.D. = .921

Ideology

[Path diagram showing Ideology 2010 (.75, .05), Ideology 2012 (.13), Ideology 2014 (.11) across top; Commitment 2010 (.82, .036), Commitment 2012 (.074), Commitment 2014 (.019) across bottom. Path coefficients: Ideology 2010 → Ideology 2012 = .78***; Ideology 2012 → Ideology 2014 = .76***; Commitment 2010 → Commitment 2012 = .84***; Commitment 2012 → Commitment 2014 = .92***; Ideology 2010 ↔ Commitment 2010 = .01; cross-lagged: −.035, .073*, .072*, .049*. Error terms: ε₁ .016, ε₂ .013, ε₃ .012, ε₄ .01, with covariances .0017 and .00029.]

N = 1,517
C.D. = .886

Figure 5.3. The causal relationship between religious commitment and partisanship/political ideology among evangelicals (all ages).
Source: Weighted 2010–2014 Cooperative Congressional Election Study Panel Survey.
Note: *$p < .05$; **$p < .01$; ***$p < .001$.

as religious commitment exerts a significant impact on abortion attitudes in both 2010–2012 ($p < .05$) and 2012–2014 ($p < .01$).

The relationship is similarly strong for same-sex marriage. One interesting observation is that attitudes on gay marriage seem somewhat less consistent over time compared to the other identities and attitudes we have looked at. This finding is probably reflective of the general liberalization of

Abortion attitudes

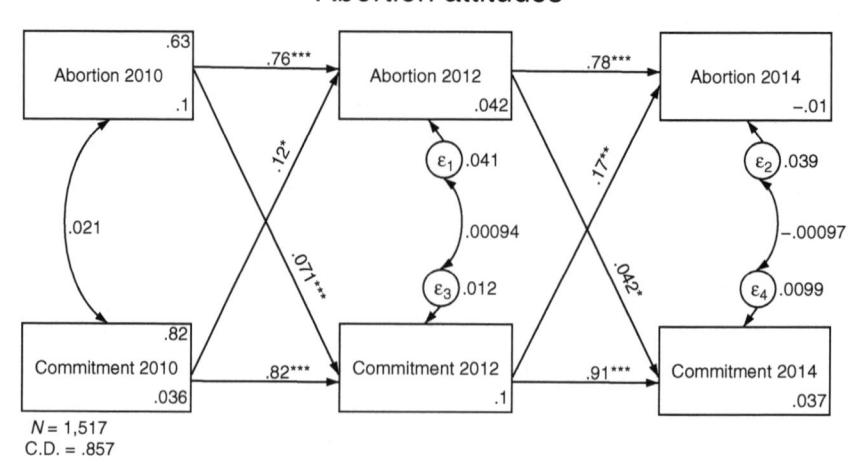

[Path diagram showing: Abortion 2010 (.63, .1) → Abortion 2012 (.042) via .76***; Abortion 2012 → Abortion 2014 (−.01) via .78***; Commitment 2010 (.82, .036) → Commitment 2012 (.1) via .82***; Commitment 2012 → Commitment 2014 (.037) via .91***; Abortion 2010 ↔ Commitment 2010: .021; cross-lag Abortion 2010 → Commitment 2012: .071***; Commitment 2010 → Abortion 2012: .12*; Abortion 2012 → Commitment 2014: .042*; Commitment 2012 → Abortion 2014: .17*; error covariances: ε₁ .041, ε₃ .012, .00094; ε₂ .039, ε₄ .0099, −.00097]

N = 1,517
C.D. = .857

Gay marriage attitudes

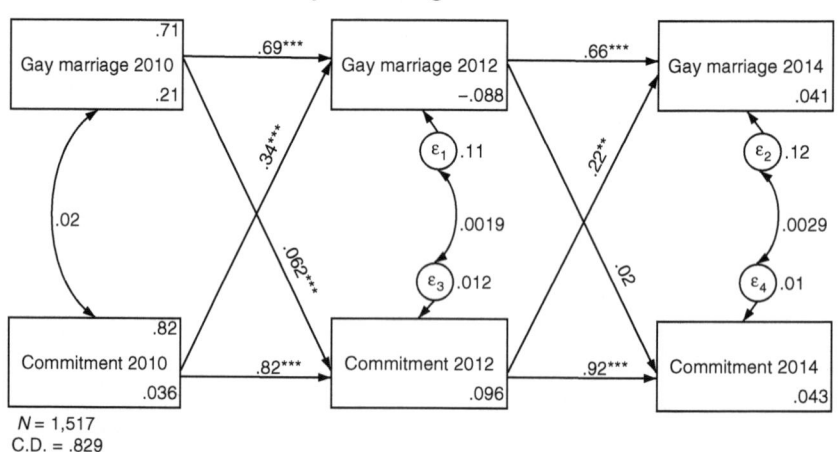

[Path diagram showing: Gay marriage 2010 (.71, .21) → Gay marriage 2012 (−.088) via .69***; Gay marriage 2012 → Gay marriage 2014 (.041) via .66***; Commitment 2010 (.82, .036) → Commitment 2012 (.096) via .82***; Commitment 2012 → Commitment 2014 (.043) via .92***; Gay marriage 2010 ↔ Commitment 2010: .02; cross-lag Gay marriage 2010 → Commitment 2012: .062***; Commitment 2010 → Gay marriage 2012: .34***; Gay marriage 2012 → Commitment 2014: .02; Commitment 2012 → Gay marriage 2014: .22**; error covariances: ε₁ .11, ε₃ .012, .0019; ε₂ .12, ε₄ .01, .0029]

N = 1,517
C.D. = .829

Figure 5.4. The causal relationship between religious commitment and abortion/gay marriage attitudes among evangelicals (all ages).
Source: Weighted 2010–2014 Cooperative Congressional Election Study Panel Survey.
Note: *$p < .05$; **$p < .01$; ***$p < .001$.

attitudes on gay marriage over the period examined. The political religion hypothesis is clearly supported in the bottom panel of Figure 5.4, as gay marriage attitudes affect religious commitment in both 2010–2012 ($p < .001$) and 2012–2014 ($p < .10$). However, we also see support for the commitment hypothesis: religious commitment affects attitudes on same-sex marriage in both 2010–2012 ($p < .001$) and 2012–2014 ($p < .01$).

In this section, we see the strongest evidence yet that immersion in the evangelical subculture, as measured by religious commitment, leads respondents to become more conservative. While the relationship between religious commitment and partisanship/ideology is moderate and seems to depend on political cycles, the relationship between religious commitment and attitudes on cultural issues is strong and consistent. Given the evidence amassed through Chapters 4 and 5, we should be reasonably confident that it is immersion in the evangelical subculture that is causing the distinctively conservative attitudes on cultural issues that we see among young evangelicals.

Conclusion

This chapter tests the core of my subcultural theory of public opinion among young evangelicals. Survey data show that, even controlling for a variety of alternative explanations, religious commitment has a significant impact on partisanship, ideology, and cultural issue attitudes among young evangelicals. On noncultural issues, religious commitment's impact is weaker and less consistent. I also demonstrate that, even after controlling for rival explanations, religious commitment leads to greater issue salience for cultural issues like abortion. Finally, using panel data, I show that engagement in the evangelical subculture leads to Republican identification, ideology, and conservative attitudes on cultural issues. Together, the results of this chapter provide strong support for my subcultural theory of public opinion among young evangelicals.

These results speak to the growing literature on the relationship between religion and political attitudes. While recent trends in the literature have recognized religious sorting among political partisans as an important phenomenon in American politics, the findings presented here suggest that the classical model of religious influence in American politics still holds true as well (particularly when it comes to cultural issues). In the years ahead, studying the bidirectional relationship between religion and politics, including understanding when each tends to take the lead role, will likely be a high priority among scholars of religion and politics.

The results also showcase how my subcultural theory, and the issue hypothesis in particular, can help us understand patterns in the impact of subcultural immersion across a variety of issues. One of the most consistent findings so far has been the uniquely strong influence of immersion on conservative attitudes on cultural issues. As long as cultural issues remain an important part of the in-group identity and distinctiveness of evangelicals, we should expect young evangelicals (especially those who are deeply immersed in the subculture) to continue to exhibit distinctively conservative attitudes.

6

Public Opinion among Liberal Young Evangelicals

Rachel Carter[1] is the Democratic Party's dream: a politically active liberal Millennial who is passionate about issues like the environment and food access. In high school, she became interested in political causes like the Save Darfur campaign. In college, Rachel moved from bystander to activist, working for an interest group concerned with immigration reform. Rachel looks like a stereotypical young Democrat, except for one detail: she self-identifies as an evangelical Christian, and she is passionately involved in both her church and New Faithful College. Rachel, then, is representative of the liberal young evangelicals that have captivated political observers in recent years. How does my subcultural theory of public opinion among young evangelicals explain Rachel and others like her? Are these exceptions to the rule a reason to question my theory? Or can my subcultural theory help us understand highly committed liberal young evangelicals as well?

In this chapter, I suggest that my subcultural theory can also help us understand patterns of public opinion among liberal young evangelicals. Specifically, I develop the idea that, nested within the broad evangelical subculture, is a narrower liberal evangelical subculture (where possible, I refer to the "evangelical tradition" instead of the "evangelical subculture" to reduce confusion). However, I argue that this liberal evangelical subculture remains bound by many of the norms of the larger evangelical tradition. Specifically, I show that even committed liberal evangelicals tend to be more moderate than their nonevangelical counterparts, especially on cultural issues. I attribute this fact to the continuing influence of the evangelical tradition's commitment to cultural conservatism. Given the salience of cultural issues to evangelical identity over the past fifty years, I argue that maintaining conservatism on cultural issues reduces the tension between individuals' social identities as liberal and evangelical.

Furthermore, I argue that committed liberal evangelicals tend to emphasize noncultural issues on which the evangelical tradition's public image is not as clearly defined. At the individual level, emphasizing noncultural issues provides another means of reducing cognitive dissonance among seemingly conflicting social identities. Using data from the Public Religion Research Institute's 2012 Millennial Values Survey, I show that committed liberal young evangelicals tend to downplay the salience of cultural issues like abortion and instead focus on issues that do not conflict with the public image of evangelicalism, such as the environment and the wealth gap. Thus, this chapter suggests that even committed liberal evangelicals are bound by the norms of the evangelical subculture discussed throughout this book.

Theorizing Liberal Evangelicals

At one time, the idea of a committed liberal evangelical might not have seemed so outlandish. During the 1970s, for example, Jimmy Carter provided a highly salient example of a highly committed, politically liberal evangelical. Since the rise of the New Christian Right, however, evangelicals have become inextricably linked with conservatism and the Republican Party (Adkins et al. 2013; Campbell, Green, and Layman 2011; McDermott 2009). Indeed, in a world where social groups are increasingly sorted along partisan lines (Green, Palmquist, and Schickler 2002), we generally think of evangelicals as having other social group identities that "fit" together: Republican, conservative, white, Southern, religiously committed, anti-abortion, and so on. In contrast, Democrats and liberals are often part of a second set of mostly contradictory identities, which include African Americans, northeasterners, union members, and the nonreligious (e.g., Campbell, Green, and Layman 2011, 45). *Thus, we would generally expect to find that liberal evangelicals are quite rare and tend to have lower levels of religious commitment compared to their more conservative counterparts.*

Nevertheless, in recent years American politics has seen a "revival" of sorts among politically liberal evangelicals. Perhaps the most visible face of this movement has been Jim Wallis, the founder of the evangelical group Sojourners. Wallis, Tony Campolo, Ronald Sider, and others have written numerous books that present a considerably more liberal viewpoint than that of the New Christian Right. The next generation of these liberal evangelicals, including best-selling author Shane Claiborne, have likewise garnered mainstream attention for breaking political stereotypes of evangelicals.

I argue that this liberal movement is itself a subculture, nested within the broader evangelical tradition. Understanding liberal evangelicals as a subculture is useful for a variety of reasons. On one hand, it highlights that these liberal evangelicals are distinctive compared to their conservative counterparts. Liberal evangelicals have a somewhat different set of theological influences (including many of the authors mentioned). Their religious, political, and social beliefs also may be different from those of their more conservative counterparts in a variety of ways. At the same time, though, the "subculture" label highlights the fact that liberal evangelicals are bound by many of the same core theological, social, and political commitments as the larger evangelical tradition. The differences, while important, are largely variations in emphasis. For example, evangelicals of all stripes generally agree on the authority of the Bible, but liberal evangelicals are probably more likely to emphasize Jesus Christ's teachings on social justice and stewardship compared to their more conservative cousins. In short, the notion of a liberal evangelical subculture captures both the shared commitment to certain core values as well as the distinctive aspects of how their faith affects their political beliefs.

Liberal evangelicals may be more likely to experience some level of tension or cognitive dissonance as a result of belonging to two (or more) seemingly contradictory social groups. Cognitive dissonance is the psychological tension or conflict individuals feel as a result of holding a series of seemingly conflicting beliefs or attitudes at the same time (Festinger 1957). According to cognitive dissonance theory, when individuals feel inconsistency between multiple identities they are motivated to resolve that tension for the sake of their psychological comfort. The father of cognitive dissonance theory, Leon Festinger, describes this drive in vivid imagery: "Cognitive dissonance can be seen an as antecedent condition which leads to activity toward dissonance reduction just as hunger leads to activity oriented toward hunger reduction" (1957, 3). We would expect the desire to resolve dissonance to be particularly strong in the context of modern American politics, where various social groups play a powerful role in forming attitudes toward the parties, candidates, and policies (e.g., Campbell et al. 1960; Green, Palmquist, and Schickler 2002; Kinder and Kam 2009; Popkin 1994; Sniderman, Brody, and Tetlock 1991). Thus, *cognitive dissonance theory predicts that we should see evidence of liberal evangelicals taking a variety of steps to relieve the dissonance or tension between their identity as liberals and their identity as evangelicals.*

There are several strategies that individuals might use to reduce their levels of cognitive dissonance (Festinger 1957; McLeod 2014). One such strategy is acquiring new information. For example, committed liberal evangelicals might seek out biblical passages that appear to justify liberal policy positions, or they might read works by authors like Jim Wallis, Tony Campolo, Ronald Sider, or Shane Claiborne in an effort to support the idea of consistency between liberalism and evangelicalism. Another strategy is changing one or more attitudes to eliminate the dissonance. For example, committed liberal evangelicals might either (1) become more conservative or (2) leave the faith altogether. In fact, scholars have cited the link between religion and political conservatism as one reason why many young liberals are leaving religion behind (Hout and Fischer 2002; Putnam and Campbell 2010).[2] Finally, individuals may de-emphasize certain issues in an attempt to reduce the salience of any dissonance they feel. In short, we would expect to see evidence of liberal evangelicals employing each of these strategies.

Committed Liberal Evangelicals in Demographic Perspective

Just how widespread are liberal evangelicals? And just how big a role does religious commitment play in the ideology of young evangelicals? Answering these questions is key to understanding just how widespread the liberal evangelical subculture is. Therefore, I turn to data from the 2014 Pew Religious Landscape Study. To facilitate an easy comparison, I divide evangelicals into three tertiles, based on their level of religious commitment.[3] Figure 6.1 shows trends in ideology among evangelicals between the ages of eighteen and twenty-nine. The data reveal that those who identify as liberal or very liberal make up just 15 percent of all evangelicals in this age group. The data also reveal that liberal evangelicals are heavily concentrated among the lowest tertile of religious commitment, where 21 percent of respondents identify as liberal. In contrast, among the middle and highest tertiles of commitment, just 12 percent and 10 percent of young evangelicals identify as liberal (these differences are significant at $p < .05$). In this section, like the more extensive discussion in Chapter 2, I find that Republican Party affiliation and political conservatism are still the norm among young evangelicals (and, as we see in Chapter 3, this is even more true among those with the highest levels of religious commitment). So, while it is important to study the committed liberal young evangelicals, it is also important to recognize that such individuals constitute a small percentage of young evangelicals.

Issue Attitudes among Committed Liberal Evangelicals

My subcultural theory can help us understand patterns in public opinion among liberal evangelicals. Earlier in this chapter, I note that by understanding liberal evangelicals as a subculture, we recognize that even liberal young evangelicals are bound by many of the same stereotypes as the broader evangelical culture. As I have highlighted elsewhere in this book, cultural issues

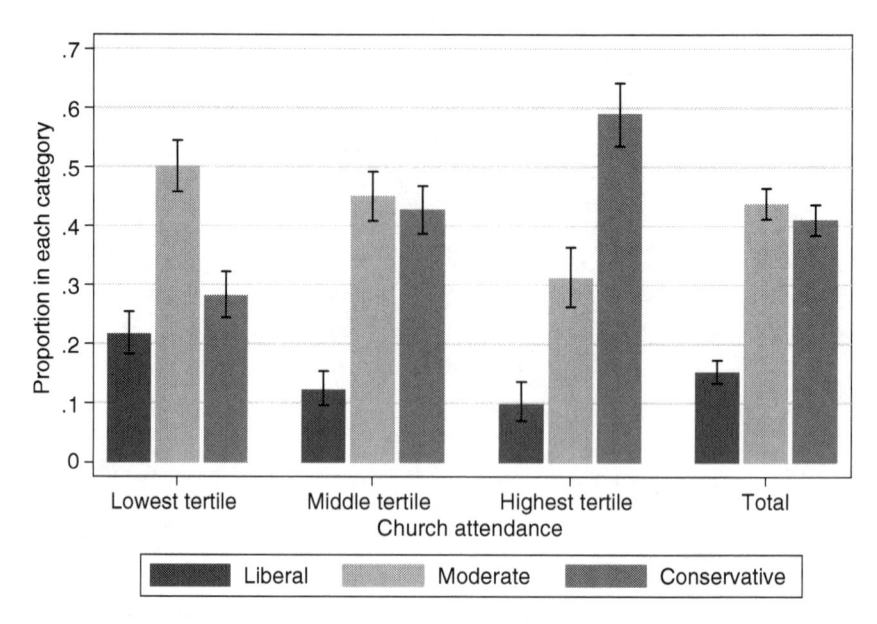

Figure 6.1. Church attendance and ideology among eighteen- to twenty-nine-year-old evangelicals.
Source: Weighted 2014 Pew Religious Landscape Study.
Note: Error bars represent an 85 percent confidence interval, meaning that overlapping intervals create a 95 percent test.

like abortion and gay marriage were among the most important factors driving evangelicals and other religious traditionalists toward the Republican Party in the last quarter of the twentieth century (Adams 1997; Hunter 1991; Killian and Wilcox 2008; Layman 2001). In fact, several commentators have observed that conservatism on abortion is approaching the level of an "unofficial litmus test" among evangelicals (e.g., Martin 2005; Scanzoni, n.d.; Williams 2010). Given the salience of these issues to evangelicals, *we would expect to find evidence that even committed liberal evangelicals retain relatively conservative attitudes on cultural issues.* In doing so, they help reduce the cognitive dissonance between their evangelical identity and their liberal identity by remaining more consistent with the public image of evangelicalism on the issues that are most important to evangelicalism's political identity.

Anecdotal evidence suggests that even high-profile liberal evangelicals, like Jimmy Carter, have more moderate views on cultural issues. Speaking to Fox News correspondent Jonathan Serrie in 2005, Carter discussed his views on abortion:

> When I took my oath of office as president, I swore to uphold the laws and Constitution of the United States as interpreted by the Su-

preme Court. So I enforced Roe versus Wade, and I did it without embarrassment or anguish. At the same time, I never have believed that Jesus Christ would approve abortions, with a few possible exceptions. I didn't ever approve the use of federal funding, for instance, for abortions, and I tried everything I possibly could to discourage the need for abortions. (Fox News 2005)

Carter made even more of a distinction between church and state when discussing his views on gay marriage:

My own belief is that there should be a distinction between so-called gay marriages, which I look upon as a possibility of a church-ordained blessing of God on a union, which I think should be between a man and a woman. But at the same time, that people who do have gay union in a court or in secular terms not relating to religion, should be treated with complete equality. (Fox News 2005)

Clearly, Carter does not represent the staunch cultural conservatism of evangelical icons like Falwell, Robertson, and Schlafly. However, Carter also does not endorse cultural liberalism as fully as many subsequent Democratic Party elites.

Likewise, many of the intellectual leaders of the evangelical church who are cited as "liberals" remain comparatively conservative on cultural issues. Jim Wallis maintains a conservative perspective on abortion, although he also encourages evangelicals to support a "seamless garment" approach to life (2006, 301). Shane Claiborne and Tony Campolo also oppose abortion and speak of the need for a consistent ethic of life, which Claiborne colorfully describes as a "from the womb to the tomb" approach (Claiborne 2013). While they offer critiques of the dominant evangelical tradition's seemingly narrow focus on the issue, they nevertheless maintain the broader subculture's basic opposition to abortion.

Attitudes among moderate to liberal evangelical elites on gay rights are more complicated (see "7 Burning Issues" 2008). Shane Claiborne has condemned the harsh language of the Westboro Baptist Church when it comes to homosexuality, and he speaks clearly about the need to care for the LGBT members of the community (Evans 2013). However, he has stopped short of a full endorsement of gay marriage. In 2010, when asked his position on gay marriage, Claiborne responded:

I'm not a pastor so it doesn't come out that people would ask me to marry them in a same-gender relationship. Personally, I would not be able to do that if I were a pastor, but I also don't have any shame in saying, "I've got a pastor friend who would love to marry you." (Roberts 2010)

Jim Wallis is more liberal on gay marriage compared to most of the other high-profile moderate-to-liberal evangelicals. Although Wallis opposed gay marriage for many years, in 2013 he reversed his position on the issue:

> We are losing marriage in this society. I'm worried about that—among low income people, but all people. How do we commit liberals and conservatives to re-covenanting marriage, reestablishing, renewing marriage? I think we should include same-sex couples in that renewal of marriage, [but] I want to talk marriage first. Marriage needs some strengthening. Let's start with marriage, and then I think we have to talk about, now, how to include same-sex couples in that deeper understanding of marriage. I want a deeper commitment to marriage that is more and more inclusive, and that's where I think the country is going. (Kaleem 2013)

Wallis's statement is particularly interesting because although he supports gay marriage, his justification primarily involves saving "marriage" as a concept, rather than any affirmative advocacy on behalf of LGBT rights. With this in mind, even Wallis could be labeled less progressive than many of the secular voices advocating for gay marriage.

To provide a more systematic test of the hypothesis that committed liberal evangelicals remain comparatively more conservative on cultural issues, I turn to data from the 2014 Pew Religious Landscape Study. One way of grasping the cross-pressured nature of committed liberal evangelicals on abortion is by comparing them to less-committed liberal evangelicals. Therefore, I have divided young evangelicals into two categories of religious commitment: low commitment and high commitment.[4] Figure 6.2 shows abortion attitudes, coded as whether abortion should be "legal in some cases" or "illegal in all cases," among liberal young evangelicals by level of religious commitment. It is clear from the figure that church attendance has a strong impact on abortion attitudes among liberals: 16 percent of low-commitment liberal young evangelicals said that abortion should be illegal in all cases, compared to 27 percent of liberal young evangelicals who attend a few times a year or more.

An alternate way of testing whether committed liberal evangelicals maintain relatively conservative attitudes on abortion may be to compare them to liberal young people from other religious traditions. The bottom panel of Figure 6.2 shows abortion attitudes among liberal eighteen- to twenty-nine-

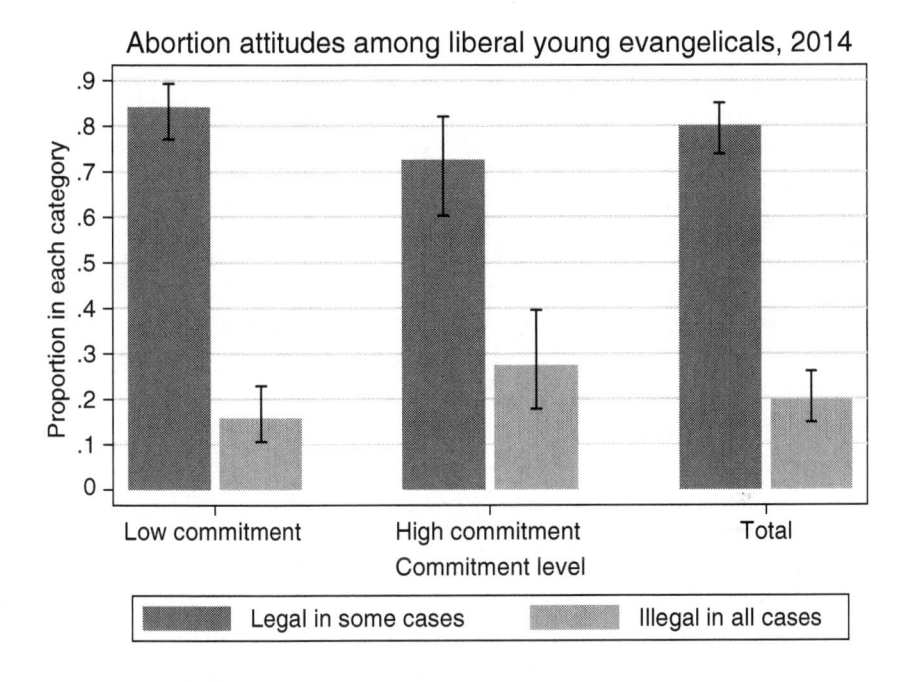

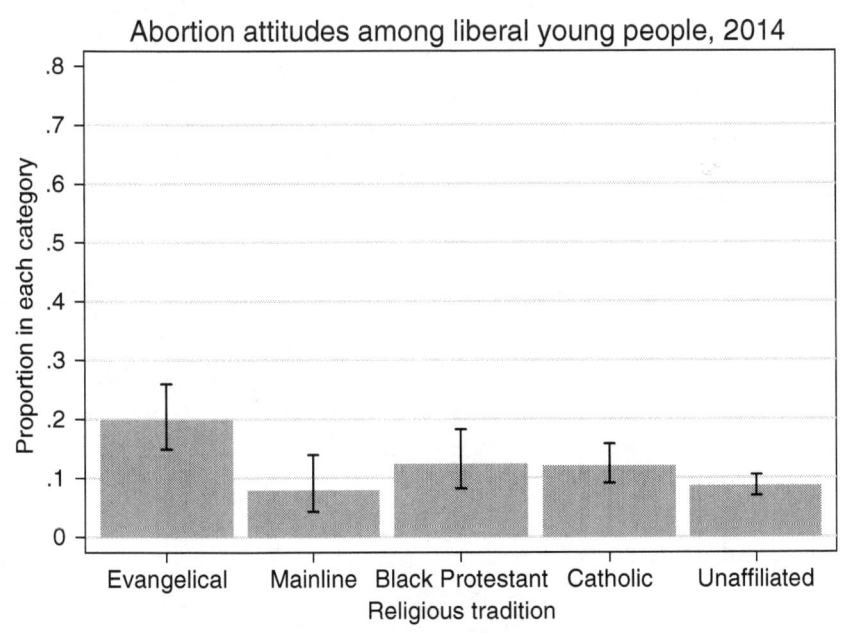

Figure 6.2. Abortion attitudes among liberal young evangelicals and liberal young people.

Source: Weighted 2014 Pew Religious Landscape Study.
Note: Error bars represent an 85 percent confidence interval, meaning that overlapping intervals create a 95 percent test.

year-olds from various religious traditions. Liberal evangelicals are again distinctive: 20 percent oppose abortion in all cases, compared to 12 percent of committed Catholics, 12 percent of black Protestants, 8 percent of mainline Protestants ($p < .05$), and 7 percent of the unaffiliated ($p < .05$). The fact that liberal evangelicals are that much more conservative than liberal Catholics is all the more surprising because opposition to abortion is also an important commitment within the Catholic religious tradition (see Smith 2008).

Respondents were also asked about their attitudes on same-sex marriage. The results suggest that liberal evangelicals are more conservative on gay marriage compared to their less-committed counterparts. Figure 6.3 shows that 22 percent of low-commitment liberal young evangelicals oppose same-sex marriage, compared to 43 percent of high-commitment liberal young evangelicals. The bottom panel of Figure 6.3 shows the percentage of liberal young people from each large religious tradition who oppose same-sex marriage. The results indicate that liberal evangelicals are significantly more likely to oppose same-sex marriage than liberals from the mainline Protestant, Catholic, and unaffiliated traditions ($p < .05$). The gulf between evangelicals and Catholics is particularly striking, as the Catholic Church (as an institution) has also traditionally opposed gay marriage (e.g., Smith 2008). In conjunction with the results for abortion, the findings presented here suggest that evangelicalism's subcultural impulse might help explain this gap between evangelicalism and Catholicism, despite their generally similar doctrinal opposition to sexual liberalism.

Figure 6.4 shows attitudes on the environment among young evangelicals. Specifically, respondents were asked about the trade-offs between jobs and the environment. Religious commitment seems to affect opinion among liberals much less here: 37 percent of low-commitment liberal evangelicals took the antienvironmental position, compared to 32 percent of high-commitment liberal evangelicals. The bottom panel of Figure 6.4 shows views on the environment among liberals from the large religious traditions. Here, evangelicals are not as distinctive: the percentage of evangelicals who take the antienvironment position is similar to the figures for black Protestants (34 percent) and Catholics (32 percent), and is only significantly different compared to the unaffiliated (17 percent, $p < .05$).

Liberal young evangelicals are also comparable to young liberals in their attitudes on social welfare. The top panel of Figure 6.5 shows that commitment has little impact on opinion: 31 percent of low-commitment liberal young evangelicals said that welfare does more harm than good, compared to just 33 percent of high-commitment liberal young evangelicals. The bottom panel shows the percentage of young liberals from each large tradition who said that welfare does more harm than good. Here, liberal young evangelicals

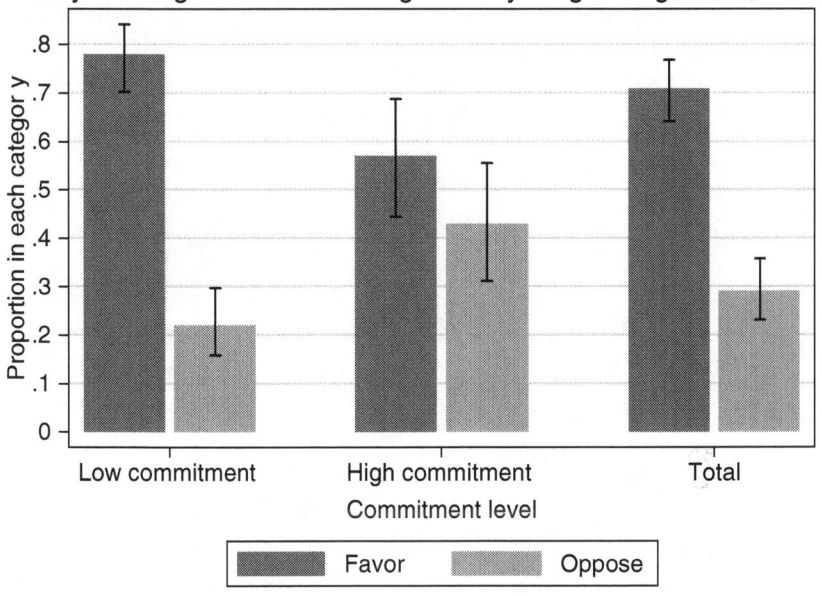

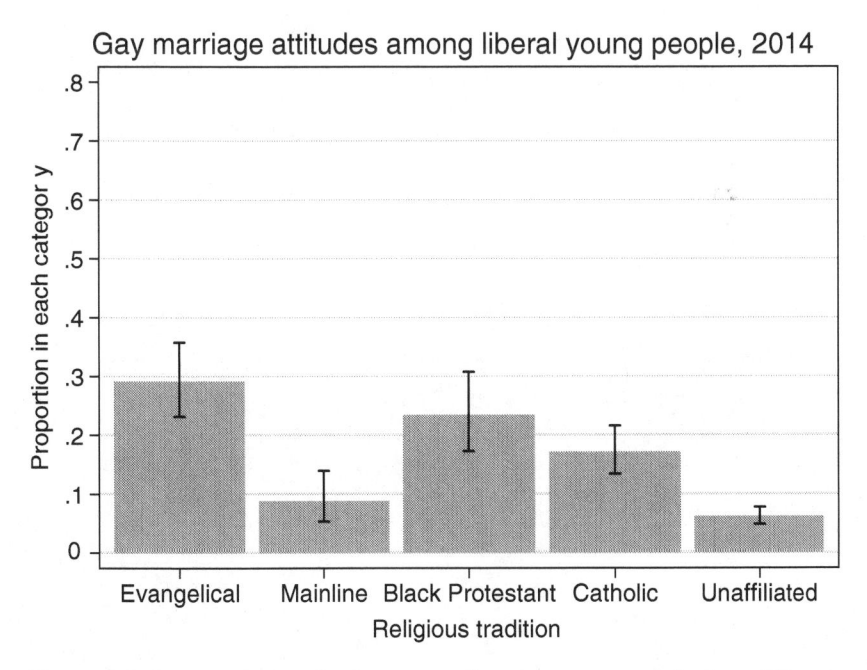

Figure 6.3. Gay marriage attitudes among liberal young evangelicals and liberal young people.

Source: Weighted 2014 Pew Religious Landscape Study.

Note: Error bars represent an 85 percent confidence interval, meaning that overlapping intervals create a 95 percent test.

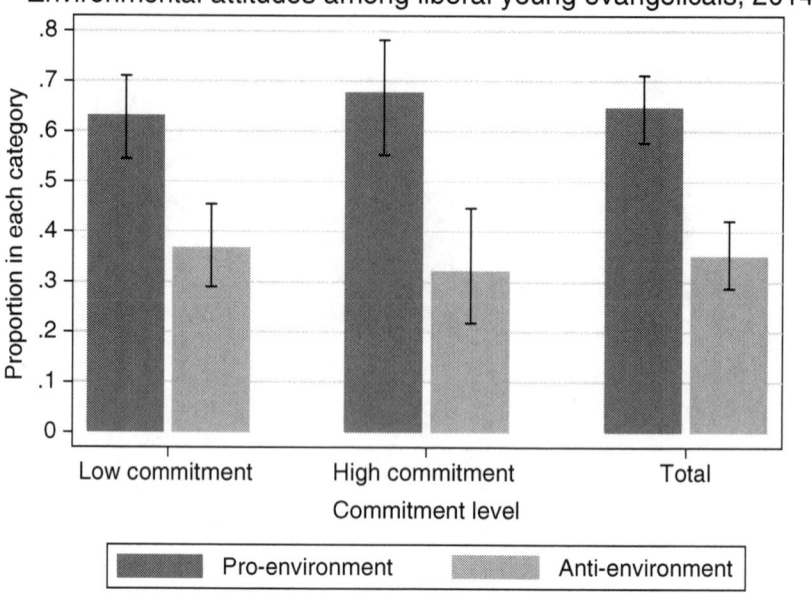

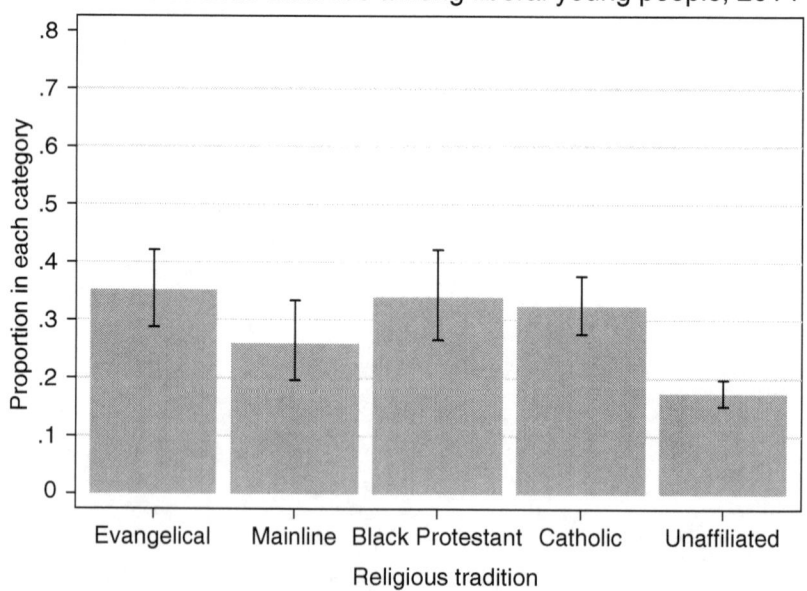

Figure 6.4. Environmental attitudes among liberal young evangelicals and liberal young people.

Source: Weighted 2014 Pew Religious Landscape Study.

Note: Error bars represent an 85 percent confidence interval, meaning that overlapping intervals create a 95 percent test.

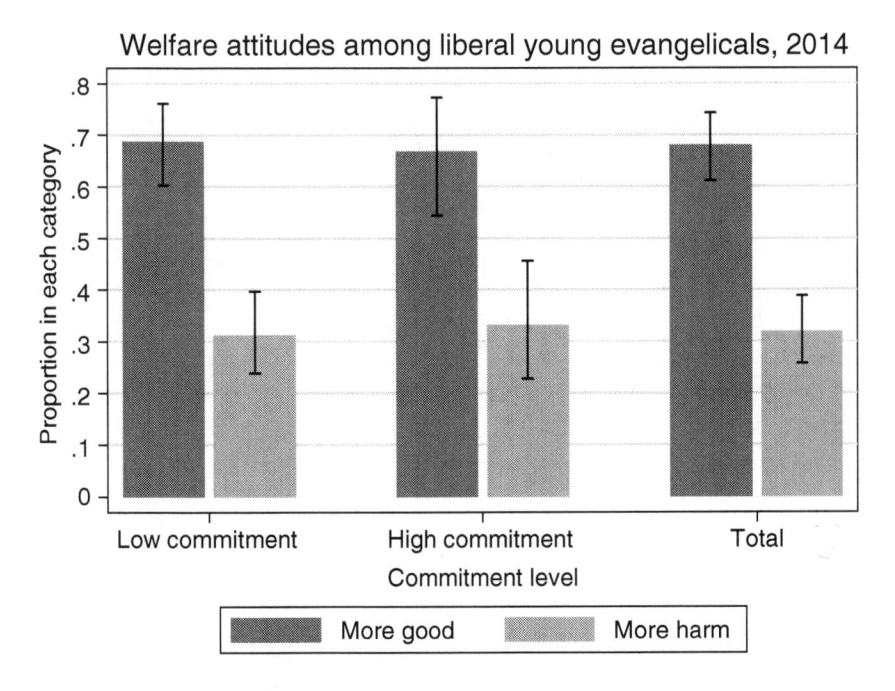

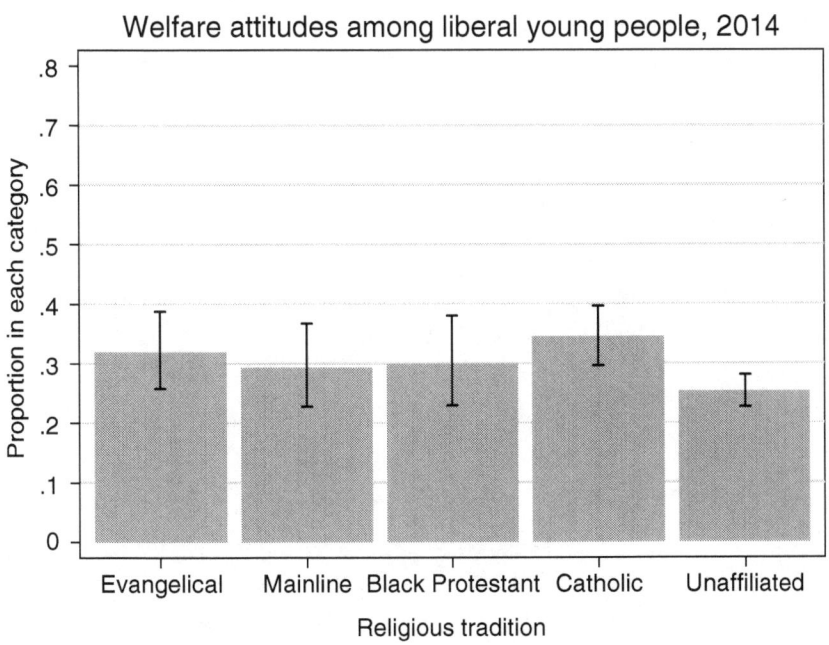

Figure 6.5. Welfare attitudes among liberal evangelicals and liberal young people.

Source: Weighted 2014 Pew Religious Landscape Study.
Note: Error bars represent an 85 percent confidence interval, meaning that overlapping intervals create a 95 percent test.

are statistically indistinguishable from liberal young people from the other large religious traditions.

Figure 6.6 shows immigration attitudes among liberal young evangelicals. Again, religious commitment appears to have little impact. Among low-commitment liberal young evangelicals, 28 percent said that immigration has been a change for the better. Among their high-commitment counterparts, the number that holds conservative attitudes on immigration rises to 31 percent. The bottom panel of Figure 6.6 shows that liberal young evangelicals do remain distinctive compared to other traditions for their comparatively high opposition to immigration. Twenty-nine percent of liberal evangelicals said that immigration has been a change for the worse, which is significantly greater ($p < .05$) than all other large religious traditions.

Figure 6.7 indicates attitudes on the trade-off between diplomacy and military strength. The top panel shows a small attendance divide among liberal young evangelicals: 28 percent of low-commitment liberal young evangelicals said that a strong military is the best source of peace, compared to 18 percent of high-commitment liberal young evangelicals. The bottom panel compares liberal young evangelicals to liberal young people from other large traditions. Here, evangelicals (25 percent) are significantly more likely to favor a strong military as a means of peacekeeping compared to mainline Protestants (11 percent) and the unaffiliated (10 percent).

Finally, Figure 6.8 indicates attitudes on the internationalist-isolationist continuum. The top panel of Figure 6.8 shows only a very small divide based on religious commitment: 29 percent of low-commitment liberal young evangelicals take the isolationist perspective, compared to 33 percent of high-commitment liberal young evangelicals. The bottom panel again compares liberal young evangelicals to liberal young people from other traditions. The data show that liberal young evangelicals hold isolationist attitudes at a similar rate to liberal young people from other traditions, suggesting that evangelicals are hardly distinctive on this question.

Are Liberal Evangelicals Distinctive? A Multivariate Analysis

Of course, the aforementioned analysis consists of bivariate results. Can we be confident that it is actually evangelicalism, and not other covariates, that is making evangelicals stand out from other liberals on certain issues? To answer this question, I set up a series of models using the 2014 Pew Religious Landscape Study data (again, supplemented by the 2007 Pew Religious Landscape Study data when necessary). The sample consists of liberals ages eighteen to twenty-nine from select faith traditions. The dependent variables are attitudes on abortion, gay marriage, homosexuality, the environment, welfare,

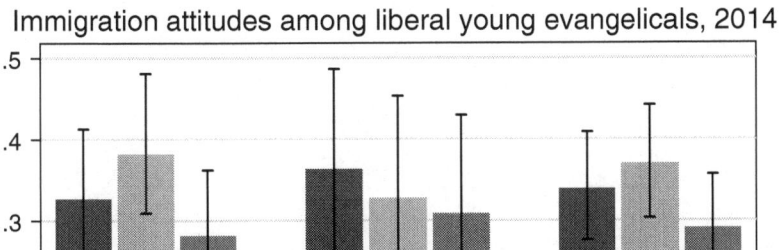

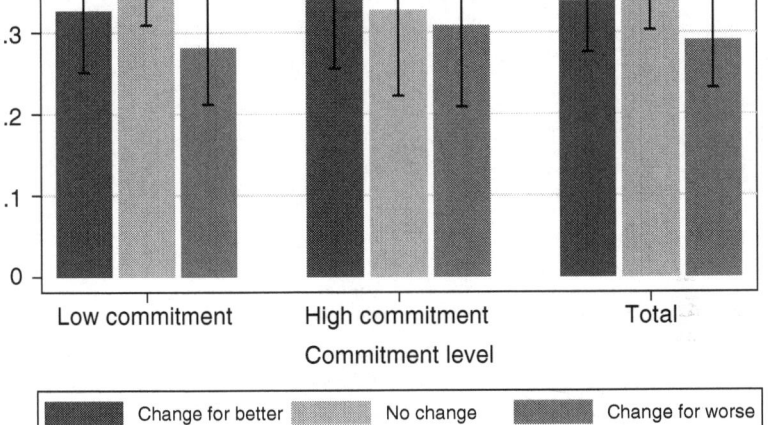

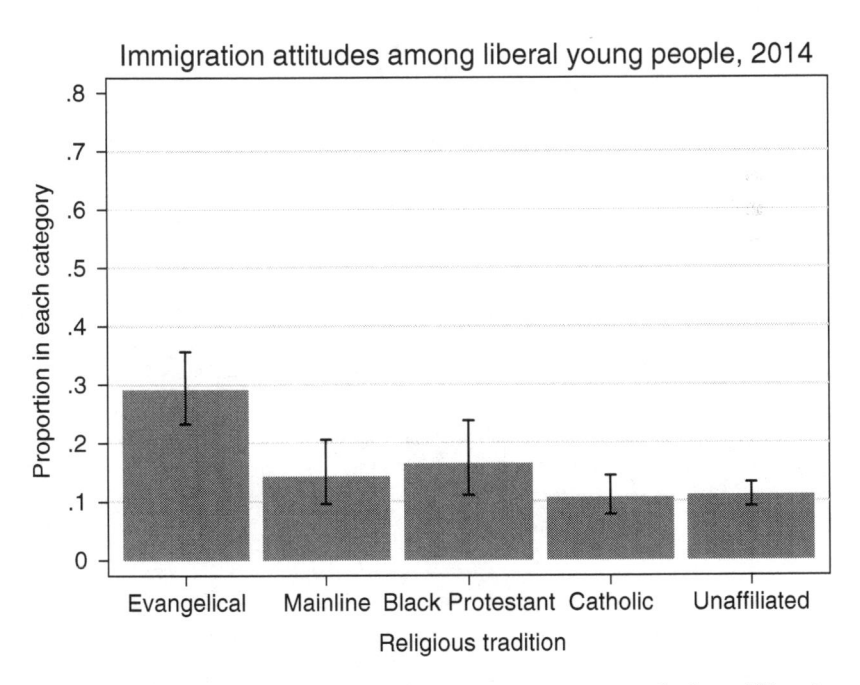

Figure 6.6. Immigration attitudes among liberal young evangelicals and liberal young people.

Source: Weighted 2014 Pew Religious Landscape Study.
Note: Error bars represent an 85 percent confidence interval, meaning that overlapping intervals create a 95 percent test.

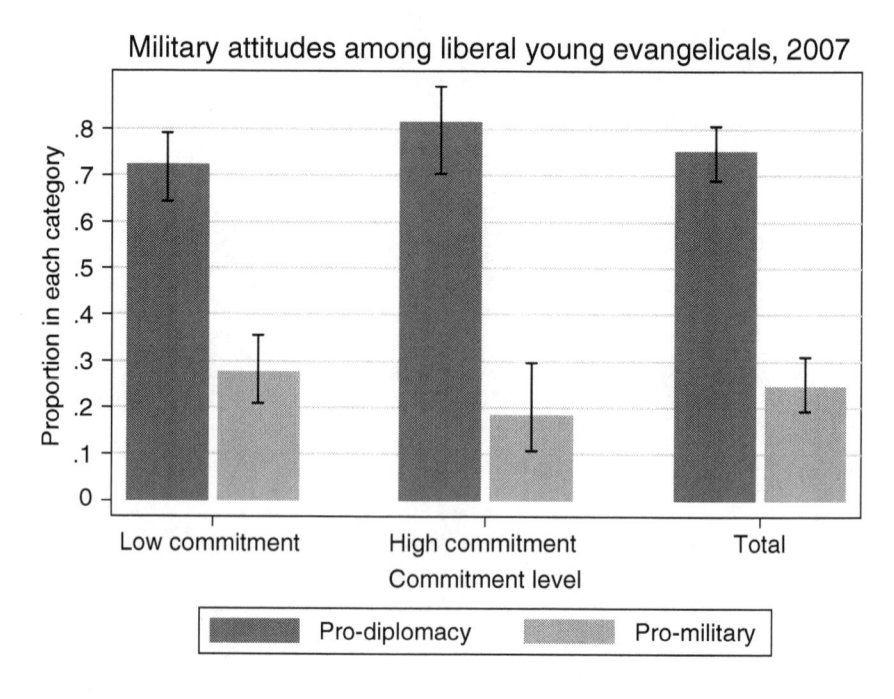

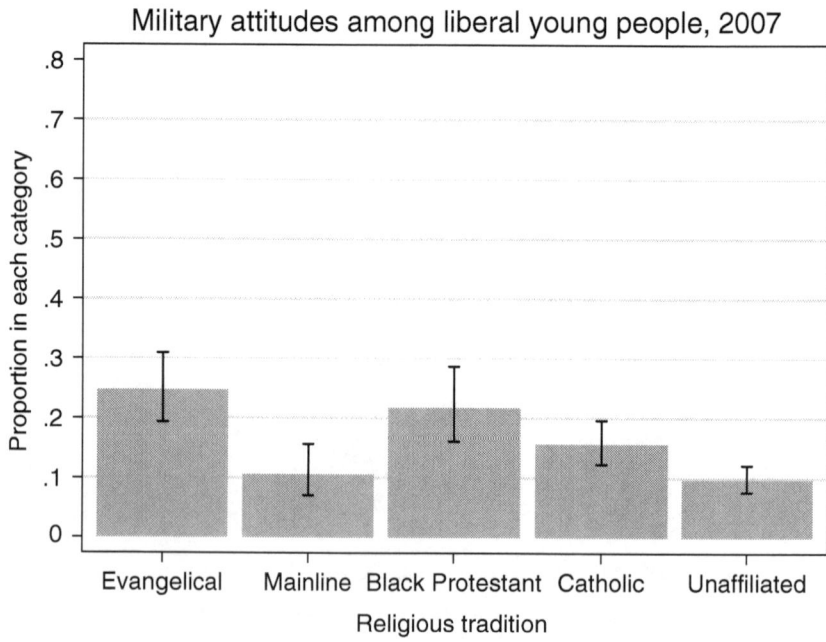

Figure 6.7. Military attitudes among liberal young evangelicals and liberal young people.

Source: Weighted 2007 Pew Religious Landscape Study.
Note: Error bars represent an 85 percent confidence interval, meaning that overlapping intervals create a 95 percent test.

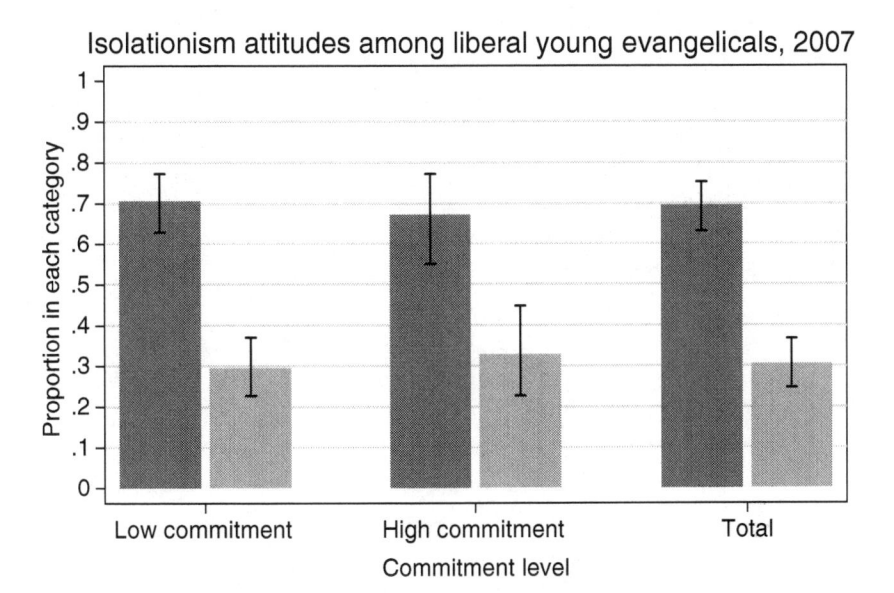

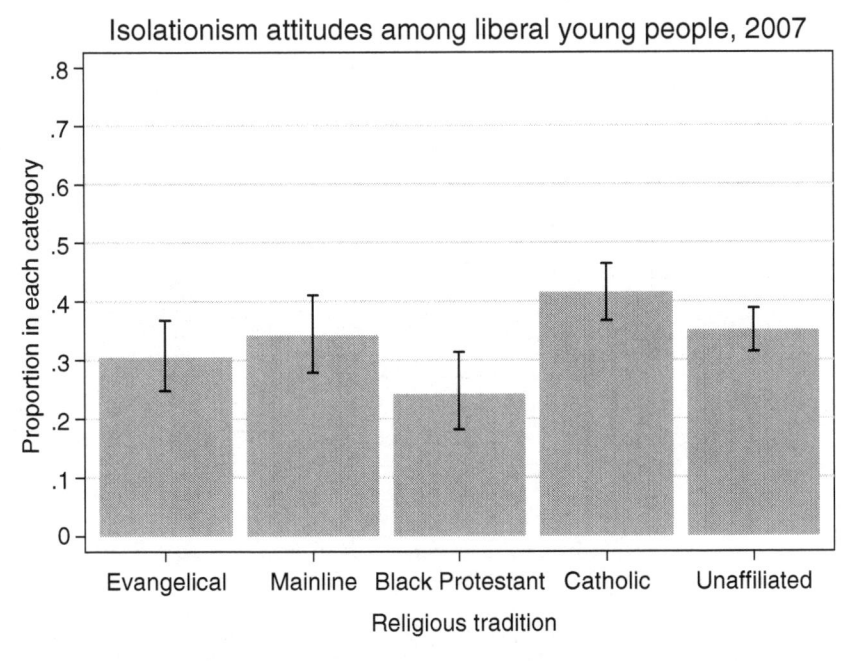

Figure 6.8. Isolationism among liberal young evangelicals and liberal young people.

Source: Weighted 2007 Pew Religious Landscape Study.
Note: Error bars represent an 85 percent confidence interval, meaning that overlapping intervals create a 95 percent test.

162 / CHAPTER 6

immigration, diplomacy, and isolationism. Independent variables that I control for include party identification, gender (a dummy variable for females), income, education, region (a dummy variable for the South, with other regions as the comparison category), and race/ethnicity (dummy variables for black, Hispanic, Asian, and mixed/other, with whites as the comparison category). Finally, I include a dummy variable for membership in the evangelical tradition.

Figure 6.9 summarizes the central findings in terms of predicted probabilities (full results are available in Tables A6.1 and A6.2 in the Chapter 6 Appendix). Beginning with cultural issues, it is clear that liberal young evangelicals are distinctive compared to other young liberals even after controlling for other factors. Figure 6.9 shows that the predicted probability of a liberal young evangelical saying that abortion should be illegal in most or all cases is .41, compared to .32 among nonevangelicals ($p < .05$). The gap in attitudes toward gay marriage is even larger: the probability of a liberal young evangelical opposing abortion is .25, compared to .10 among comparable nonevangelicals ($p < .05$). Finally, the probability of a liberal young evangelical saying that society should discourage homosexuality is .27, compared to .07 among an otherwise comparable nonevangelical ($p < .05$).

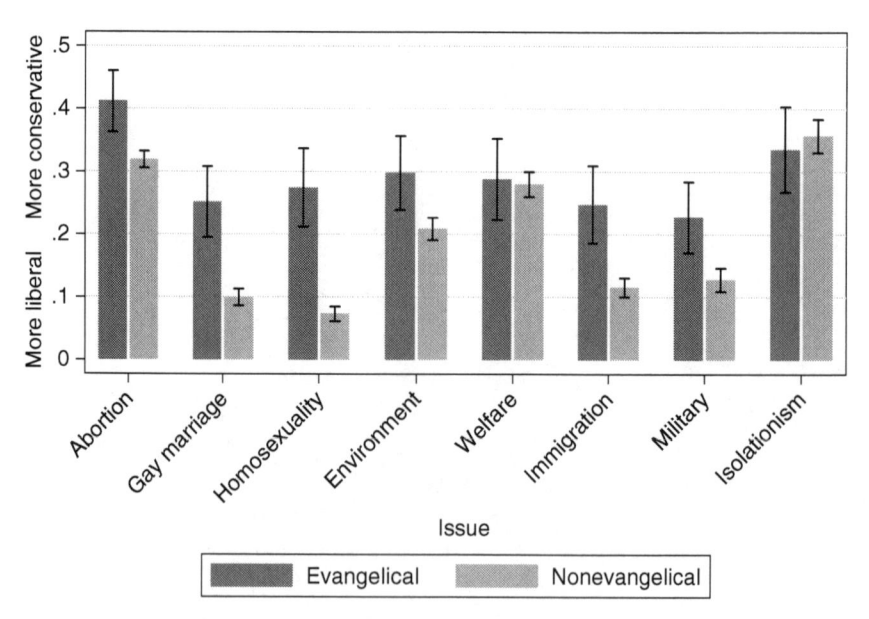

Figure 6.9. Effect of evangelicalism on issue attitudes among eighteen- to twenty-nine-year-old liberals (with controls).
Source: Weighted 2007 and 2014 Pew Religious Landscape Study.
Note: Error bars represent an 85 percent confidence interval, meaning that overlapping intervals create a 95 percent test.

Figure 6.9 indicates that the differences between evangelical and nonevangelical liberals are less consistent on noncultural issues. On the environment, the probability of a liberal young evangelical taking the antienvironment stance is .30, compared to .21 for an otherwise identical nonevangelical ($p < .05$). On welfare, the difference in the probability of saying welfare does more harm than good between evangelicals (.29) and nonevangelicals (.28) is substantively small and not statistically significant. On immigration, the probability of a liberal young evangelical saying that the increasing number of immigrants has been a "change for the worse" is .24, compared to .11 among nonevangelicals ($p < .05$). Turning to the foreign policy items from the 2007 Pew Religious Landscape Study, the model indicates that the probability of a liberal young evangelical saying that a strong military was the best way to ensure peace is .23, compared to .13 among nonevangelicals ($p <. 05$). Finally, liberal young evangelicals had a similar probability of favoring isolationism compared to otherwise equal nonevangelicals (.34 to .36, respectively).

In short, the data in this section provide evidence that the evangelical subculture's strong norm of conservatism on cultural issues influences public opinion even among liberal evangelicals. At the individual level, the data also support the idea that one way in which committed liberal evangelicals work through their cognitive dissonance is by maintaining relatively more conservative attitudes on abortion compared to other liberals.

Evidence from the Interviews

The tension that committed liberal young evangelicals feel on cultural issues was also apparent in the interviews. The interviews reveal the myriad mechanisms that committed liberal young evangelicals have developed for resolving the cognitive dissonance between their identities. For example, in a derivative version of Festinger's classic "acquire new information" technique (1957), some of the students attempted to redefine the meaning of certain political labels so that their beliefs appear more consistent. Rachel, the highly committed young evangelical we met at the start of this chapter, explained her position on abortion to me as follows:

> I'm very definitely pro-life. . . . I've always been pro-life. . . . It's a matter of what I think the best way of preventing abortion is. I think that we would do better to provide more sex education, more resources for mothers who are facing financial hardship or emotional hardship, rather than just straight-up trying to restrict or ban abortion.

This response is interesting from a psychological standpoint because Rachel continues to identify herself as pro-life to conform to the public image or the "unofficial litmus test" for evangelicals, but her endorsement of sex education and resource provision, and her implied willingness to support the continued legality of abortions, speaks to her embrace of the liberal viewpoint on the issue.

Another strategy used by committed liberal evangelicals to resolve the tension between their liberal worldview and their faith is justifying their positions in terms of evangelicalism's distinctive beliefs, just as their more conservative counterparts would. During our conversation, one liberal evangelical at Old Faithful College discussed his support for gay marriage. When I asked where he thought his views on the subject came from, he responded, "I guess [from] my reading of scripture, especially when Jesus talks about treating people the way you want to be treated—not discriminating against them because they're different than you, which is the way he acted toward [people]." A politically liberal gay evangelical at Top 100 College put forward a similar explanation when I asked him whether his faith played a role in his liberal political ideology:

> Student: Maybe not my faith but my perception of God. . . . I have always been taught that God loves everyone and a specific emphasis on the teachings of Christ. I guess my mother's church also had more of an emphasis on the New Testament and Christ's teachings than they did on the Old Testament, so I grew up with this preconceived notion of how Jesus treated people and that I should try to be like him. That probably made me a bit more liberal. . . . I feel like he would have voted for Obama.
> Me: What sort of traits about Jesus and the way he treated people do you think translate into politics?
> Student: The one that I always come back to is "let he who is without sin cast the first stone" and that entire debacle with Mary. It's something that people forget all too often. That was one of the biggest things that he did.

Together, these examples show how some liberal young evangelicals draw on distinctive beliefs like biblical authority to reduce the tension between their religious and political identities.

A related strategy for integrating religious and political identities involves adding more information by making a more pronounced distinction between personal views and beliefs about public policy. One highly committed, fiscally liberal student at Top 100 College explained his attitudes on gay marriage as follows:

> I explained earlier that I was liberal in a fiscal way, [but] I would say that I'm more conservative in a social way because . . . when you do take the gospel literally, there are certain things that you believe that you can't necessarily advocate for. . . . For example, you could go with gay marriage. The gospel does say that that's not the way to be. That's something that you just, you know—if you take the gospel literally, you read that . . . you're given that, and you go from there. I personally think that . . . we try to establish this separation of church and state, and so, for me to say, legally, two homosexuals can't get married, that's not right for me to say because that's a legal institution.

Rachel took a very similar position:

> Theologically, I'm not sure how I feel about homosexuality. . . . As far as marriage, though, I'm in favor of allowing gay marriage because I think our country is and should be governed by the Constitution, and I think the Constitution guarantees equal rights, equal right to life, liberty, and the pursuit of happiness. I don't think it's fair or equal to deny gay couples the right to marry based upon my own faith convictions.

Both of these students showcase the typical evangelical beliefs in the authority of the Bible and the relevance of religious beliefs to political perspectives. At the same time, they each stop short of the notion that one's personal faith should inform government policy. While the response from the student at Top 100 College is anecdotal, it suggests that one difference between conservative and liberal evangelicals is that liberals may be more disposed to give up on the evangelical commitment to regulating morality as a way to maintain their personally conservative attitudes on issues while at the same time maintaining liberal attitudes on those same issues in the larger social context.

Issue Salience in the Liberal Evangelical Subculture

Another implication flowing from my understanding of liberal evangelicalism as a subculture is that liberal evangelicals may tend to emphasize noncultural issues. In Chapter 1, I briefly note that the evangelical subculture as a whole allows, and to some extent may even reward, liberalization on noncultural issues. If evangelicalism was distinctive on every political issue, the costs of membership might become too high and/or the evangelical ability to mobilize in the presence of embattlement might suffer. Furthermore, if it were to emphasize distinctiveness on every issue, the subculture might risk becoming too "countercultural" and thereby lose some of its ability to stay engaged in society. Thus, a more successful strategy for evangelicalism may be allowing liberalization on noncultural issues.

In addition, de-emphasizing cultural issues and instead emphasizing new issue groups may provide benefits for liberal evangelicals at the individual level. Reducing the importance of cognitions is one strategy individuals might use to decrease cognitive dissonance (Festinger 1957; McLeon 2014). In our case, de-emphasizing cultural issues and instead focusing on issues like the environment or poverty may help reduce the tension between the competing identities of liberal and evangelical.

Anecdotal evidence seems to support the notion that liberal evangelical elites have tended to focus on noncultural issues. Although liberal evangelicals like Shane Claiborne, Jim Wallis, Tony Campolo, and Ronald Sider clearly do discuss cultural issues, their primary emphasis seems to be communicating the relevance of biblical teachings to problems like poverty and war that were downplayed by the New Christian Right. For example, Claiborne has taken the stance that cultural issues are not as essential to evangelicalism as the New Christian Right would believe. He said, "We're careful not to get hijacked by those but to recognize that these are real issues. They're not ideologies to us" (Roberts 2010). Elsewhere, he said cultural issues were not something that his community was willing to "die on the hill for" (Manson 2011). In distinguishing his style of evangelicalism from right-wing evangelicals, Tony Campolo wrote, "Most Red Letter Christians are unwilling to become single-issue voters whose politics are determined solely by abortion" (2008, 121).[5] In short, their position is a far cry from the Christian Right's emphasis on the issue.

Furthermore, when they do discuss cultural issues, they tend to talk about them in a way that reinforces their thesis of economic liberalism as an important evangelical value. For example, Campolo frequently emphasizes the economic roots of many abortions (Claiborne 2013), and he favors increased social welfare policies, including free contraceptives and paid maternity leave, as a means of reducing the economic pressures that lead expectant parents to choose abortions (Campolo 2008, 121–122). Thus, rather than primarily speaking of abortion as a sign of cultural decline or a moral evil (in the rhetorical style of the New Christian Right), many publicly visible liberal evangelical elites discuss the issue as a public policy problem with economic roots and economic solutions.

Evidence from the interviews also supports my hypothesis that committed liberal evangelicals are more likely to emphasize issues besides abortion and gay marriage. During the interviews, I routinely asked the students whether there were any political issues they were particularly passionate about. A clear pattern emerged of committed liberal evangelicals emphasizing noncultural issues.

One liberal student at Old Faithful College explained the reason for his passion for environmental issues, saying, "From what I've seen and what I've read, we are just not taking good care of [the earth]. Especially as a Christian, believing that we are here to take care of this good earth that God has created and has kind of put us in charge of—it kind of kills me to see what we are doing to our atmosphere, our forest, what we're doing to our oceans, everything like that."

This quote serves as a nice starting point because the impact of evangelicalism's distinctive beliefs on his views is clear. First, the student is connecting views on the environment to the biblical narrative that God charged humans with caring for the earth (in doing so, he is modeling the subculture's emphasis on biblical authority). Second, perhaps even more interestingly, this student actually seems to feel some aspect of embattlement with society on the issue of creation care.

Another theme apparent from the interviews is that liberal evangelicals are more likely to bring up economic or social welfare issues. In Chapter 4, I discuss how for most of the young evangelicals I met, economic issues were not that salient. Some even explicitly argued that evangelicalism was not that concerned with economic issues. The committed liberal evangelicals who I spoke with provided an exception to this pattern. A liberal student at Top 100 College described why he felt economic policy issues were particularly important:

> I think it's interesting because a lot of conservative religious people tend to identify with the conservative, or Republican, party. I don't fully understand that because . . . when it comes to my faith, you know, Jesus teaches so much about distributing your wealth . . . to the poor, and just within the Bible it talks about not giving in to this love of money, not hoarding money, and so, I have a difficult time understanding why there's that apparent connection there. That so many conservatives are so wealthy and so well-off, and yet they are conservatively religious and fail to identify with that particular teaching.

Again, in this quote we see a pattern of liberal evangelicals drawing on the larger tradition's distinctive beliefs, like biblical authority, but applying them to different types of issues.

By far the most politically active liberal evangelical I met was Rachel. Rachel became an intern at an evangelical immigration-reform organization, and through that experience she became passionate about the issue. In my interview with her, it was clear that she was connecting some of the distinctive beliefs of the evangelical tradition to the issue of immigration. When I asked her why she was passionate about immigration, she explained:

It wasn't an issue I thought about a lot before my internship, to be honest. I always had the sense that our current immigration system was not terribly effective: obviously a lot of issues regarding undocumented immigration, and just the system is very convoluted and difficult and expensive. But once I started working for [the organization], I started to see the more human and spiritual dimension of it. I really started to see in the Bible the way that God talked about immigrants, the way immigrants are a very vulnerable population, and God also tells us that we are to love, and care for, and speak on behalf of the least of these, those who are oppressed, those who are vulnerable. So the more I learned about it, the more I saw the ways in which our system tore apart families through deportations, denied bright, brilliant, wonderful students the opportunity to get an education or to make something of themselves. And the way that in our society, often the rhetoric we use regarding immigrants is so hateful—even within the church, it's very hateful; it's deeply disturbing. And now I count among some of my dear friends some undocumented immigrants that I've met through working there. So it's also personal for me. But the more I learn about it, the more I see that it's a matter of justice, and biblical justice.

Rachel's response is particularly interesting because it highlights many of the themes of this section, including an emphasis on the Bible as authority and an ongoing sense of embattlement with the larger society (exemplified in the critique of society's rhetoric toward immigrants). Rachel's position on immigration also highlights the important role that organizations within the liberal evangelical subculture play in making their issue concerns more appealing to young evangelicals interested in advocacy. Whereas the connection between evangelicalism's distinctive beliefs and cultural issues has been repeatedly emphasized by the New Christian Right, the connection between evangelicalism's core values and immigration remains far less clear to most evangelicals at the mass level. Thus, Rachel's story highlights how organizations within the liberal evangelical subculture may play a more important role in connecting the tradition's distinctive beliefs to noncultural issues.

Survey Data Analysis

To provide a more systematic test of the hypothesis that committed liberal evangelicals tend to de-emphasize cultural issues, I turn to the Public Religion Research Institute's 2012 Millennial Values Survey data, which include a series of measures of issue salience. For each issue, respondents were asked whether they would consider it a "critical issue," "one among many," or "not that important." Table 6.1 shows the percentage of respondents selecting "critical issue" by ideology for evangelicals and nonevangelicals ages eighteen to twenty-four.[6] While the sample size for liberal evangelicals is much smaller than ideal (a further testament to their rarity), the data nonetheless reveal a variety of interesting patterns. First, it is clear that young people (no matter their ideology) are concerned about jobs and unemployment. This finding should not be surprising given the employment crisis among Millennials (Sanburn 2014; Weissman 2014).

Second, when comparing issue priorities between liberal and conservative evangelicals, a number of differences are apparent. Focusing on cultural issues, the responses show that liberal evangelicals are much less likely to declare abortion a critical issue (26 percent) compared to their conservative counterparts (56 percent). Likewise, liberal young evangelicals are less concerned about gay marriage compared to conservative young evangelicals (7 percent to 47 percent, respectively). This finding supports my argument that liberal evangelicals may de-emphasize cultural issues to reduce their cognitive dissonance.

We also see differences between liberal evangelicals and liberal nonevangelicals on cultural issues. In particular, liberal evangelicals remain more likely to consider abortion a critical issue (26 percent) compared to liberal nonevangelicals (15 percent). Surprisingly, the relationship runs in the opposite direction for gay marriage: just 7 percent of liberal evangelicals consider it

TABLE 6.1. ISSUE SALIENCE AMONG EIGHTEEN- TO TWENTY-NINE-YEAR-OLDS

	Evangelicals			Nonevangelicals		
	Liberal	Moderate	Conservative	Liberal	Moderate	Conservative
Abortion	25.6	28.4	56.3	14.5	15.8	28.1
Gay marriage	7.4	19.1	46.9	20.7	17.8	23.8
Education	39.1	47.1	43.6	60.5	52.4	58.2
Immigration	31.5	35.4	44.1	26.4	31.6	43.9
Federal deficit	66.8	61.6	69.8	47.6	55.7	55.9
Jobs and unemployment	50.9	83.2	68.2	78.3	76.7	76.7
National security	23.8	40.0	48.4	23.7	31.6	45.9
Growing gap between the rich and the poor	41.8	41.2	25.5	54.7	37.6	32.1
Environment	27.5	39.7	17.7	45.4	33.4	31.4
N	34	144	173	523	769	370

Source: Weighted Public Religion Research Institute Millennial Values Survey, 2012.
Note: Percentage reflects the percentage of respondents labeling the issue a "critical issue." Response options for each item included "Critical issue," "One among many," and "Not that important."

a crucial issue, compared to 21 percent of liberal nonevangelicals. On most other items, liberal evangelicals rate the issues similarly important compared to liberal nonevangelicals.

To examine whether these trends persist once demographic differences are accounted for, I ran a series of logistic regression models for evangelicals in which the dependent variable was whether the respondent labeled each issue a "critical issue." The independent variable of interest is a five-point measure of ideology. I control for gender (with a dummy variable for females), family income, education, race/ethnicity (dummy variables for Hispanic, mixed, and other), and religious commitment. Because it is difficult to gauge effect size from logistic regression coefficients, I display the results in terms of the predicted probability that otherwise-identical "very liberal" and "very conservative" evangelicals would declare each issue a "critical issue" (full results are shown in Tables A6.3 and A6.4 in the Chapter 6 Appendix). The results have been organized in terms of the probability that a liberal evangelical would declare each a "critical issue."

Figure 6.10 confirms that liberal evangelicals are significantly more likely to declare the environment a critical issue compared to conservatives. In contrast, conservative evangelicals are more likely to declare abortion,

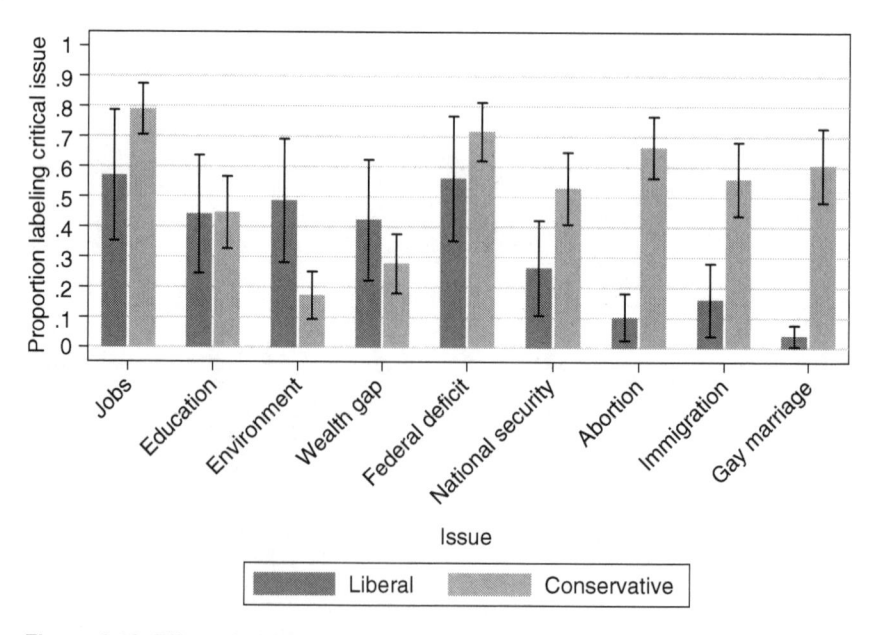

Figure 6.10. Effect of ideology on issue salience among eighteen- to twenty-nine-year-old evangelicals (with controls).
Source: Weighted 2007 and 2014 Pew Religious Landscape Study.
Note: Error bars represent an 85 percent confidence interval, meaning that overlapping intervals create a 95 percent test.

immigration, and gay marriage critical issues. For the other issues covered in the Public Religion Research Institute's 2012 Millennial Values Survey, it appears that evangelicalism does not seem to be the driving factor in differences in issue salience among young liberals. Together, these results provide strong support for my argument that, even after controlling for a variety of alternative factors, liberal evangelicals tend to de-emphasize the importance of cultural issues compared to their conservative counterparts.

Conclusion

Much of this book has focused on the increasing connection between membership in the evangelical subculture and political conservatism. This chapter helps us understand the implications of that connection for the 15 percent of young evangelicals who continue to identify as politically liberal. The data reveal that, even when it comes to the most liberal young evangelicals, existing accounts only partially explain their views.

As we might expect, liberal young evangelicals appear to be more interested in noncultural issues such as the environment and the wealth gap. As we see in the interviews, many liberal young evangelicals have developed passionate views on noncultural issues based on the distinctive beliefs of evangelicalism, including a reliance on the Bible as the authority in all matters of life. In addition, while the data in earlier chapters indicate that young evangelicals in general do not seem to be giving up on cultural issues, abortion and gay marriage appear to have lower salience among liberal young evangelicals. My subcultural theory helps understand the reasons behind these trends: both are a means by which liberal evangelicals can resolve the tension between their (seemingly) conflicting social identities.

In contrast, a less expected discovery is the fact that even liberal evangelicals remain more conservative on social issues compared to their nonevangelical peers. The findings in this chapter suggest that one of the most enduring legacies of the New Christian Right may be the building of cultural conservatism into the political image of young evangelicals. By raising the salience of cultural issues among evangelicals to biblical proportions (pun intended), the New Christian Right may have created a legacy that long outlasts its direct political influence. The evidence I present here suggests that even if the number of committed liberal evangelicals begins to grow, such individuals will likely remain comparatively more conservative on cultural issues and such individuals will primarily limit their activism to noncultural issues. Even among the committed liberal young evangelicals, the values of the evangelical subculture appear to exert a substantial effect.

Conclusion

As we see in the Introduction and Chapter 1, in recent years there has been much debate about the political attitudes of young evangelicals. Some observers asserted that young evangelicals were much more liberal than older generations, while others argued that young evangelicals were as conservative as ever. Still others suggested that young evangelicals were leaving the culture wars behind and focusing on a new set of issues. To date, few academic studies have attempted to solve the various aspects of this debate.

In this book, I develop a subcultural theory of public opinion among evangelicals. Fusing John Zaller's (1992) receive-accept-sample theory and Christian Smith's (1998) subcultural theory of evangelicalism, I explain how the evangelical subculture builds evangelical identity, teaches its own distinctive values, discredits secular culture, and delivers explicitly political messages. Together, these processes give the evangelical tradition the potential to influence public opinion among its members. However, the strength of evangelicalism's effects varies based on several contextual factors.

I propose two overarching hypotheses. First, my issue hypothesis predicts that evangelicalism's influence is strongest on measures of public opinion that have been central to evangelicalism's identity and distinctiveness, including partisanship, ideology, and cultural issue attitudes. Second, my commitment hypothesis suggests that the evangelical subculture's impact is strongest among those who are the most deeply immersed in the subculture. I then test various aspects of these theories.

This Conclusion provides a brief review of key findings and then discusses the implications of my research along two lines: first, the future of evangelicalism's role in American politics, and, second, how my theory might be extended to help us understand other groups within American politics. This discussion highlights the potential long-term implications of this book for our understanding of evangelicals, as well as American politics more generally.

A Brief Review of Key Findings

In Chapter 2, I examine time series data for signs of change in the political attitudes and public opinion of young evangelicals. Consistent with the expectations from my issue hypothesis, I find that young evangelicals' mean partisanship, ideology, and abortion opinions have not really changed since the 1970s. On other issues, I find that young evangelicals are more liberal compared to older evangelicals today. However, for most issues, this appears to be an age-based effect. Only on gay marriage, welfare, and immigration do we find evidence that young evangelicals are becoming more liberal over time. In addition, I find little evidence that young evangelicals are altering their issue priorities: pocketbook issues and cultural issues like abortion are important concerns, while immigration, the wealth gap, and the environment are fairly low on their list of priorities.

In Chapter 3, I examine whether any change among the evangelical tradition is driven by internal or external forces. Using regression analysis to model change among high-commitment and low-commitment evangelicals, I find that for most issues, age-based differences seem to be concentrated among low-commitment evangelicals. We see change concentrated only among high-commitment evangelicals on two issues: immigration and the diplomacy-military trade-off. In short, the patterns in the data suggest that for most issues, any change we see is likely driven by factors external to evangelicalism.

Given the strong initial support for my theory's predictions, in Part II, I turn to a more detailed test of various aspects of my theory. In Chapter 4, I show that evangelicalism has at least four mechanisms to change the underlying distribution of considerations held by members. First, the evangelical subculture builds in-group identity, leading members to "think like evangelicals" when it comes time to express political attitudes. Second, the evangelical subculture teaches a number of distinctive beliefs, including the authority of the Bible, the evangelical tradition's influence throughout a person's life, and conservative attitudes on sexuality, that could serve as relevant considerations when forming opinions about political issues. Third, the evangelical subculture discredits the secular culture, possibly leading adherents to discount secular considerations when forming opinions. Finally, the evangelical subculture delivers explicitly political messages to the young members of the tradition through its public image, churches, and evangelical colleges. This chapter was crucial for demonstrating the subculture's potential to affect public opinion among young evangelicals by both introducing new considerations and discrediting existing considerations from secular sources.

In Chapter 5, I test whether immersion in the subculture explains why evangelicals are distinctive. Using survey data, I show that, even after controlling for a number of alternative explanations, immersion in the subculture exerts a major impact on evangelicals' partisanship, ideology, and attitudes toward cultural issues. On issues that have not been as important to the political identity of evangelicalism, including welfare, immigration, and militarism, the effect of immersion in the subculture is much smaller. I also find that immersion in the evangelical subculture plays an important role in increasing the salience of cultural issues like abortion in the minds of young evangelicals. Finally, using panel data, I test my theory against the "political religion hypothesis" of Michael Hout and Claude Fischer (2002). While I find strong support for the political religion hypothesis, I also find strong support for my commitment hypothesis: it appears that immersion within the evangelical subculture leads to more conservative political identities and more conservative attitudes on cultural issues.

In Chapter 6, I investigate how my theory helps explain public opinion among liberal young evangelicals. I argue that there is a liberal evangelical subculture that is in some ways distinct from the dominant (conservative) evangelical tradition but in other ways is still bound by many of the same norms. I show that liberal evangelicals remain more conservative than other liberals on cultural issues like abortion and homosexuality, and that liberal evangelicals tend to de-emphasize cultural issues and instead advocate on issues that do not conflict with the public image of evangelicalism, including the environment and social welfare programs. Finally, at the individual level, I show how the political behavior of liberal evangelicals also tends to reduce cognitive dissonance by easing the tension among their (seemingly) conflicting social group identities.

The Future of Evangelicals in American Politics

The analysis in this book casts severe doubt on the narrative of a new generation of liberal young evangelicals. As we see in Chapter 2, young evangelicals have been tremendously consistent over time in terms of their partisanship, ideology, and attitudes on abortion. Young evangelicals also do not seem to be altering their issue priorities: they continue to rank the environment, the wealth gap, and immigration relatively low on their list of priorities. In short, owing in part to the impact of the evangelical subculture, young evangelicals are more like their parents on most issues than conventional wisdom might lead us to believe.

With a new wave of politically liberal evangelicals not likely in the cards, what then is the future of evangelicalism's role in American politics? As with anything in the social science, we must proceed with tremendous caution in predicting the future. Nevertheless, in this section, I briefly highlight several potential scenarios and provide my (subjective) evaluation of the likelihood of each scenario occurring.

First, it is possible that evangelicals may once again adopt a strategy of political withdrawal—or what Campbell, Green, and Monson (2014) call "separation." Some scholars, including Ted Jelen (1991), have suggested that evangelicals follow a cyclical pattern of engagement, defeat, and withdrawal. The most recent period of withdrawal was punctuated by the public embarrassment of fundamentalism in the wake of the Scopes Trial (Jelen 1991; Larson 2006).

Indeed, the defeat of the New Christian Right's agenda should give evangelicals plenty of reason to contemplate withdrawal. While evangelicals were tremendously successful at mobilizing into politics during the 1980s and 1990s, much of the New Christian Right's agenda has gone unfulfilled. Although the Christian Right has been successful at placing restrictions on abortion in various state legislatures, they have yet to overturn the fundamental legality of abortion as established in *Roe v. Wade* (1973). After *Obergefell v. Hodges* (2015), gay marriage is legal in all fifty states. Teacher-led prayer in public schools and a variety of other accommodationist policies have been declared unconstitutional by the United States Supreme Court. While the New Christian Right certainly won its share of battles in state legislatures around the country, overall it looks as if liberals have won the "culture war."

In addition, evangelicals have suffered multiple political defeats over the past several election cycles. First, the core interest groups that anchored the New Christian Right have weakened considerably from their heyday. Second, George W. Bush's reelection in 2004 was the last time the Republican Party nominated a candidate who truly fit the mold of evangelical politics. Third, the Democratic Party won major victories in the 2006 congressional elections and twice elected Barack Obama president. The Democrats also obtained major policy victories, including the passage of the Affordable Care Act. Even Donald Trump's victory in the 2016 Presidential election may be read as a defeat of traditional evangelical politics. While Trump aligned himself with Jerry Falwell Jr., son of Jerry Falwell, and other evangelical conservatives, his personal behavior and his previously stated policy positions often fell short of the ideals of the Christian Right.

Despite these apparent political defeats, evangelicals remain as engaged in politics as ever, thus giving reason to question whether the cyclical theory of evangelical political engagement still holds. Evangelicals played an important part in the 2008 and 2012 Republican primaries and were one of the core blocks of Mitt Romney's constituency. Evangelicals also played an important role in the Tea Party's emergence in 2010 (Campbell and Putnam 2011). Finally, evangelicals were an important driving force behind Donald Trump's victory in 2016. In short, evangelicals show no sign of returning to the separatist strategy of the 1920s.

There are several possible reasons why evangelicals have not readopted a strategy of withdrawal. One potential reason is that evangelical elites like Billy Graham, Francis Schaeffer, and Jerry Falwell so profoundly changed evangelical thought through their invitation to engagement that the separatist philosophy has become discredited within the mainstream of evangelicalism. Another potential explanation comes from sociology: perhaps the close association between the Democratic Party and cultural modernism makes it more likely that evangelicals will remain engaged in party politics because of the threat that the opposing coalition represents. Finally, from a political science perspective, perhaps the continuing involvement of evangelical activists in the Republican Party (e.g., Layman 2001) has made it difficult for evangelicals to sever the tradition's conservative image. Whatever the reason for the continued engagement of evangelicals, I personally find it highly unlikely that we will see another evangelical withdrawal equivalent to that of the post-Scopes era.

Another scenario, which I view as more likely, is that we will see subtle shifts in the political behavior of evangelicals in the coming decades. The data from Chapters 2 and 3 suggest that evangelicals will remain reliably Republican and ideologically conservative in the coming years. However, there is reason to believe that evangelicals might change their patterns of advocacy on other issues, including gay marriage. As we see in Chapter 2, young evangelicals are more liberal on gay marriage compared to previous generations. Even though most of the change is concentrated among infrequent attendees, evangelicals who oppose same-sex marriage may find that they no longer have a coalition large enough to justify continued opposition. In fact, given the growing support for LGBT rights in the country as a whole, the distinctively conservative attitudes on homosexuality and gay marriage that once helped the evangelical subculture's distinctiveness may now prove a liability in the effort to recruit new members. Therefore, while I expect evangelicals to maintain their general cultural conservatism, I would not be surprised to see evangelicals begin to de-emphasize gay marriage in their political agenda. In fact, the relative lack of push-back to the Supreme Court's decision in *Obergefell v. Hodges* (2015) suggests that this trend may already be under way.

Finally, it is possible that we may see a shift in the dynamics of the "culture wars." Up until now, most of the "battles" in the culture wars have revolved around evangelicals and other religious traditionalists fighting for the ability to use the institutions of government to enact their preferred policies on others. Outlawing abortion (via a Constitutional amendment or other means) and same-sex marriage (while discouraging homosexuality), teaching creationism and intelligent design alongside evolution in public schools, and legalizing teacher-led prayer in the schools were all priorities of the first wave of the New Christian Right (e.g., Deckman 2004; Hunter 1991; Leege et al. 2002).

As the percentage of religiously unaffiliated Americans grows and evangelicals become more of a political minority, the culture wars may enter a new phase. Rather than fighting for religious accommodation, evangelicals and other religious traditionalists may increasingly find themselves fighting for religious liberties (Castle 2018b). A few recent cases suggest this trend may already be beginning. First, in the wake of the Department of Health and Human Services (HHS) mandate requiring employers (but not churches) to cover contraceptives in their insurance plans, a number of Christian colleges and Christian-owned businesses sued, arguing that being forced to cover contraceptives violated their religious free exercise. In *Burwell v. Hobby Lobby* (2014), the United States Supreme Court decided that corporations with religious objections could be exempted from the HHS mandate on the basis of religious liberty.[1]

The second recent controversy began around whether private businesses should have a right to deny services for religious reasons. For example, should evangelical Christians in the wedding industry, including bakers and photographers, have a right to deny services to lesbian and gay couples? In spring 2015, Indiana passed a version of a state-level Religious Freedom Restoration Act that opponents suggested could have given businesses legal cover to discriminate against the LGBT community (Guerra and Evans 2015; Montanaro 2015). The controversial bill was signed into law by Indiana's Republican Governor, Mike Pence. However, objections from businesses including Apple, Angie's List, and the National Collegiate Athletic Association led Indiana to revise its bill. Even more recently, the United States Supreme Court heard the case *Masterpiece Cakeshop v. Colorado Civil Rights Commission* (2018), in which Masterpiece Cakeshop owner Jack Phillips argued that the First Amendment's guarantee of religious liberty allows his business to refuse service to LGBT couples despite Colorado's antidiscrimination laws.

The court ruled narrowly in favor of Phillips, finding that the Colorado Civil Rights Commission did not sufficiently respect his right to free exercise. However, the ruling left open the possibility that state laws might respect religious free exercise but nevertheless require businesses to serve LGBT couples. Although these battles are just beginning, the examples discussed here suggest that important shifts may be taking place in the way evangelicals fight the "culture wars."

Extending the Theory

This book also makes a contribution to the study of public opinion through the subcultural theory of public opinion among young evangelicals, as well as the accompanying commitment hypothesis and issue hypothesis. Clearly, the theory is helpful to explain patterns in where we do, and do not, see change among young evangelicals. Future work may wish to extend this basic theoretical framework to the study of other religious subcultures. For example, my theory may prove helpful for understanding public opinion among Mormons, who David Campbell, John Green, and Quin Monson (2014) have described as a subculture. Like evangelicals in the 1930s and 1940s, Mormons went through a period of quiescence but have recently become much more visible in American politics through Mitt Romney's candidacy for president in 2012.

Applying the subcultural theory of public opinion to Mormons bears the potential to generate new insights. For example, one of the distinctive beliefs of Mormons is the continuing revelation of religious doctrine through a living prophet (Campbell, Green, and Monson 2014). The belief in a living prophet creates a built-in ability to adapt when certain elements of the subculture begin to conflict strongly with the larger culture in a way that threatens the subculture's viability. For example, early in the history of the Church of Jesus Christ of Latter-Day Saints (LDS), polygamy was a part of the faith. As the practice became more widely known, these "plural marriages" became the source of increasing tensions with the federal government. In particular, it became clear that the federal government was unwilling to grant statehood until the practice was abolished.[2] In 1890, then–Church President Wilford Woodruff issued a manifesto ruling the practice of polygamy void, and the LDS Church has subsequently instituted a policy of excommunicating members found to be practicing plural marriage. From the perspective of my subcultural theory, the potential for the living prophet to modify church doctrine is a useful institution that allows the church to retain subcultural beliefs that give it an advantage within the marketplace (for example, the

Mormon tradition's emphasis on family) and jettison subcultural beliefs that prove a liability to the denomination.

Catholicism may be another fruitful area for study. Modern American Catholicism is certainly not a subculture in and of itself. The increase in socioeconomic status among Catholics, Catholics' movement from ethnic enclaves to assimilation, and John F. Kennedy's presidency are among the twentieth century developments that helped move Catholics into the mainstream of American culture (Prendergast 1999; Steinfels 2007; Wilson 2007). However, theologically conservative subcultures exist within Catholicism. In many ways, these conservative subcultures behave much like evangelicals, including relying on Catholic-centered media and seeking out only the most theologically conservative Catholic colleges for their children.[3] These theologically and culturally conservative Catholics played an important role working alongside evangelicals in the "culture wars" (e.g., Hunter 1991). Alternatively, there are liberal Catholic subcultures that vigorously campaign on a myriad of social justice issues, including social welfare and capital punishment. While not explicitly addressing them from a subcultural theoretical perspective, Gregory Smith's (2008) distinction between social justice priests and personal morality priests essentially uses the variation in these subcultures to study the political influence of priests. Thus, my subcultural theory might help us identify and account for trends in mass-level political behavior among Catholics.

My subcultural theory may also be of interest to those who study religious countercultures, such as the Amish. Because of their insular nature and high level of political withdrawal, countercultural groups like the Amish have been understudied in American politics. My subcultural theory presents an excellent opportunity to engage in research with the Amish and other countercultures. Many of the principles of my subcultural theory would also apply, but even more so: Amish teachings strongly discredit the secular culture and institute powerful countercultural norms (e.g., Hostetler 1993; Kraybill 2001). As with evangelicals, we would expect this to lead to stability in public opinion over time on important recurring issues. Furthermore, research suggests that political campaigns may be able to mobilize the Amish counterculture using many of the same techniques that have been applied to the evangelical subculture. For example, Donald Kraybill and Kyle Kopko (2007) discuss how the George W. Bush campaign in 2004 sought to use cultural issues to mobilize Old Order Amish voters in the critical swing state of Ohio.

My theory may also have important implications for nonreligious subcultures. One particularly interesting study may be examining public opinion among the LGBT population. Although gay men in particular have been described as a subculture in the sociology literature (e.g., Herdt 1993), one of the struggles of the LGBT movement has been the decision of whether to stay a subculture or assimilate into the mainstream (e.g., Bernstein and Taylor 2013; Rimmerman 2015). Most of these debates to date have centered on the in-group social distinctiveness of the LGBT movement. However, my subcultural theory suggests the possibility that an additional cost of assimilation may be losing some of the political distinctiveness of the movement, including perhaps losing some of its ability to mobilize when threatened.

Clearly, then, while this investigation has focused on public opinion among evangelicals, the subcultural theory could help us understand public opinion and political behavior among a wide variety of social groups.

Parting Words

From the elections of Ronald Reagan and George W. Bush to the numerous policies passed in state legislatures around the country, evangelicals have played a massive role in American politics over the past few decades. Therefore, developing a better understanding of what drives evangelical political behavior is tremendously important for understanding American politics itself. This study suggests that conceptualizing evangelicalism as a subculture can help us explain patterns of consistency and change in the political attitudes of evangelicals. It is my sincere hope that scholars and practitioners will find my perspectives and analysis helpful in understanding the past, present, and future of evangelicalism's impact on politics.

Appendix

Coding Religious Tradition

One of the most frustrating aspects of doing academic research on religion is achieving a sensible coding scheme for religious tradition. This task was made much more difficult because many of the data sets employ very different versions of the denominational battery used to generate religious tradition.

When setting the coding scheme for each data set, I adhered to a few basic principles:

1. When possible, the preferred approach to building religious tradition is the denomination-based approach suggested in Brian Steensland et al. (2000). When a denomination-based approach was not available, I turned to "born-again" Protestants as a second-best option.
2. When it was unclear from the respondent's denomination which form of Protestantism best characterized the respondent, I used the basic logic employed by Geoffrey Layman and John Green (2005):
   a. Generic Protestants were recoded to black Protestants if they were African American.
   b. Generic Protestants who answered yes to a question about whether they identified as "born-again" were recoded to evangelical Protestants.
   c. Generic Protestants who were not born-again and who displayed low religious engagement (said religion was "not too important" or "not at all important" in their lives, and who attend church "seldom" or "never") were recoded to unaffiliated.
   d. Generic Protestants who did not fall into any of the these groups were labeled mainline Protestants.
3. As discussed in the text, African American evangelical and mainline Protestants were recoded to black Protestants.

1972–2014 GENERAL SOCIAL SURVEY

The classic approach to coding General Social Survey data is the RELTRAD coding scheme (Steensland et al. 2000). I used an updated version of that scheme (Stetzer and Burge 2016), which corrects for a significant error in the original coding, with the exception that I recoded African American evangelicals and mainline Protestants to black Protestants.

2007 AND 2014 PEW RELIGIOUS LANDSCAPE STUDY

My version of religious tradition is based on the standard version of religious tradition that comes in Pew's data set, with one change: I recoded black evangelical and mainline Protestants to black Protestants.

2010–2014 COOPERATIVE CONGRESSIONAL ELECTION STUDY PANEL SURVEY

The Cooperative Congressional Election Study Panel Survey uses a religious denomination battery similar to the Pew Research Center's. Denominations were coded into religious traditions according to the updated religious tradition scheme in Geoffrey Layman and John Green's (2005) appendix. Open-ended responses were hand-coded into the appropriate categories. When open-ended responses indicated that respondents were generic or ambiguous Protestants (e.g., "Just Christian," "Baptist," "Methodist"), the Layman and Green (2005) method was used to code them into final traditions. Each wave of the panel re-asked the denomination battery. As discussed in the text, the analysis in Chapter 5 considers only those who were coded as evangelical Protestants in all three waves.

2012 PUBLIC RELIGION RESEARCH INSTITUTE MILLENNIAL VALUES SURVEY

The Millennial Values Survey variable "relig" does not ask about specific denominations, and therefore it is impossible to use the traditional denomination-based approach to constructing a measure of evangelical Protestantism. Thus, in this data set, evangelicals are those who identified as "Protestant," "Just Christian," or "Something else" and who identified as born-again.

2016 COOPERATIVE CONGRESSIONAL ELECTION STUDY

The Cooperative Congressional Election Study uses a religious denomination battery similar to the Pew Research Center's. Denominations were coded into religious traditions according to the updated religious tradition scheme in the appendix to Layman and Green (2005). Open-ended responses were hand-coded into the appropriate categories. When open-ended responses indicated that respondents were generic or ambiguous Protestants (e.g., "Just Christian," "Baptist," "Methodist"), the Layman and Green (2005) method was used to code them into final traditions.

Chapter 3 Appendix

Tables A3.1–A3.3 show the model results used to construct the figures in Chapter 3. They are included for transparency and as a reference but do not merit further discussion, as the interaction terms mean that the data are much easier to visualize.

TABLE A3.1. MODELS FOR PARTY IDENTIFICATION, IDEOLOGY, ABORTION, GAY MARRIAGE, AND HOMOSEXUALITY

	Party ID	Ideology	Abortion	Gay marriage	Homosexuality
Age	0.012	0.025†	−0.006	0.292†	0.263†
	(0.008)	(0.005)	(0.007)	(0.059)	(0.059)
Age × age	−0.001*	−0.001***	0.001†	−0.005*	−0.002
	(0.000)	(0.000)	(0.000)	(0.003)	(0.002)
Religious commitment	0.381†	0.378†	0.684†	4.743†	5.018†
	(0.054)	(0.035)	(0.048)	(0.412)	(0.424)
Age × religious commitment	−0.005	−0.010**	−0.015**	−0.110*	−0.138**
	(0.008)	(0.005)	(0.007)	(0.058)	(0.059)
Constant	0.315†	0.269†	0.095**	−3.859†	−4.387†
	(0.046)	(0.029)	(0.042)	(0.355)	(0.370)
N	7,920	7,920	7,633	7,358	7,252
R^2	0.029	0.079	0.123		
F test	39.04†	108.36†	180.61†		
Pseudo R^2				.129	.118
Wald χ^2				628.46†	581.24†

Source: 2014 Pew Religious Landscape Study.
Note: Standard errors are in parentheses. *$p < .10$; **$p < .05$; ***$p < .01$; †$p < .001$ (two-tailed tests).

TABLE A3.2. MODELS FOR ENVIRONMENT, WELFARE, IMMIGRATION, DIPLOMACY, AND ISOLATION

	Environment	Welfare	Immigration	Diplomacy	Isolation
Age	0.143***	0.136***	0.186†	0.040†	0.028***
	(0.045)	(0.045)	(0.045)	(0.010)	(0.010)
Age × age	−0.004*	−0.007***	−0.011†	−0.000†	−0.000†
	(0.002)	(0.002)	(0.002)	(0.000)	(0.000)
Religious commitment	1.113†	0.998***	−0.603*	0.011	1.997†
	(0.313)	(0.317)	(0.317)	(0.529)	(0.546)
Age × religious commitment	−0.044	−0.037	0.100**	0.013	−0.008
	(0.045)	(0.045)	(0.045)	(0.010)	(0.010)
Constant	−1.227†	−0.657**	−0.410	−1.438†	−2.138†
	(0.265)	(0.266)	(0.264)	(0.401)	(0.411)
N	7,412	7,434	7,475	7,720	8,359
Pseudo R^2	.015	.008	.048	.009	.014
Wald χ^2	99.21†	47.36†	313.15†	62.86†	119.56†

Source: 2014 Pew Religious Landscape Study (environment, welfare, immigration); 2007 Pew Religious Landscape Study (military, isolationism).
Note: Standard errors are in parentheses. $^*p < .10$; $^{**}p < .05$; $^{***}p < .01$; $^†p < .001$ (two-tailed tests).

TABLE A3.3. MODELS FOR 2012 AND 2016 VOTES

	2012 vote	2016 vote
Age	−0.020	0.016
	(0.023)	(0.018)
Age × age	0.000*	−0.000
	(0.000)	(0.000)
Religious commitment	2.531†	1.490***
	(0.749)	(0.569)
Age × religious commitment	−0.008	0.007
	(0.013)	(0.010)
Constant	−0.465	−0.768
	(0.776)	(0.595)
N	8,059	7,562
Pseudo R^2	.040	.039
Wald χ^2	179.90†	163.05†

Source: 2012 Cooperative Congressional Election Study (2012 vote); 2016 Cooperative Congressional Election Study (2016 vote).
Note: Standard errors in are parentheses. $^*p < .10$; $^{**}p < .05$; $^{***}p < .01$; $^†p < .001$ (two-tailed tests).

Chapter 5 Appendix

Tables A5.1–A5.4 show the model results used to construct the figures in Chapter 5.

TABLE A5.1. THE IMPACT OF RELIGIOUS COMMITMENT ON PARTY IDENTIFICATION, IDEOLOGY, AND ATTITUDES ABOUT ABORTION, GAY MARRIAGE, AND HOMOSEXUALITY

	Party ID	Ideology	Abortion	Gay marriage	Homosexuality
Party ID		0.240†	0.126***	0.380	0.393
		(0.027)	(0.040)	(0.305)	(0.310)
Ideology	0.521†		0.318†	2.574†	2.112†
	(0.054)		(0.066)	(0.479)	(0.495)
Female	−0.047**	−0.015	−0.053**	−0.477***	−0.809†
	(0.023)	(0.016)	(0.022)	(0.181)	(0.187)
Income	0.074*	0.076**	−0.059	0.104	0.174
	(0.043)	(0.033)	(0.041)	(0.334)	(0.340)
Education	0.044	−0.009	−0.112**	−1.083***	−1.388†
	(0.049)	(0.034)	(0.050)	(0.399)	(0.403)
South	0.028	−0.020	0.056**	0.435**	0.182
	(0.023)	(0.016)	(0.022)	(0.178)	(0.182)
Hispanic	−0.036	0.002	0.072*	0.202	−0.037
	(0.039)	(0.024)	(0.037)	(0.285)	(0.273)
Asian	−0.100	−0.075**	−0.071	−0.421	0.273
	(0.077)	(0.035)	(0.049)	(0.522)	(0.572)
Mixed/other	−0.149†	−0.054**	−0.022	0.317	0.347
	(0.038)	(0.024)	(0.036)	(0.292)	(0.274)
Religious commitment	0.312†	0.223†	0.483†	4.015†	3.824†
	(0.075)	(0.047)	(0.074)	(0.636)	(0.645)
Constant	0.078	0.246†	0.047	−4.575†	−4.111†
	(0.069)	(0.042)	(0.062)	(0.561)	(0.571)
N	909	909	895	856	840
R^2	0.274	0.247	0.232		
F test	28.58†	28.08†	20.76†		
Pseudo R^2				.175	.161
Wald χ^2				119.85†	108.08†

Source: 2014 Pew Religious Landscape Study.
Note: Coefficients are OLS for party and ideology, ordered logit for abortion, and logit for homosexuality and gay marriage. Standard errors are in parentheses. *$p < .10$; **$p < .05$; ***$p < .01$; †$p < .001$ (two-tailed tests).

TABLE A5.2. THE IMPACT OF RELIGIOUS COMMITMENT ON ATTITUDES ABOUT ENVIRONMENT, WELFARE, IMMIGRANTS, DIPLOMACY, AND ISOLATION

	Environment	Welfare	Immigrants	Diplomacy	Isolation
Party ID	0.696**	1.185†	0.796**	1.195†	0.605**
	(0.290)	(0.295)	(0.319)	(0.267)	(0.248)
Ideology	0.939**	1.408***	0.254	1.103**	0.624
	(0.418)	(0.447)	(0.455)	(0.433)	(0.403)
Female	−0.334**	−0.531***	−0.098	0.042	−0.415**
	(0.165)	(0.176)	(0.182)	(0.179)	(0.171)
Income	−0.608**	1.224†	0.196	0.036	0.243
	(0.302)	(0.329)	(0.323)	(0.330)	(0.317)
Education	−0.840**	−0.336	−1.458†	−0.752**	1.381†
	(0.388)	(0.409)	(0.408)	(0.372)	(0.353)
South	0.045	−0.107	0.111	0.410**	−0.213
	(0.163)	(0.177)	(0.176)	(0.177)	(0.168)
Hispanic	−0.060	−0.510*	−0.667**	−0.482	0.969†
	(0.248)	(0.260)	(0.315)	(0.305)	(0.279)
Asian	0.029	−2.367†	−1.271**	−2.034*	−0.469
	(0.484)	(0.620)	(0.591)	(1.125)	(0.609)
Mixed/other	0.060	0.155	−0.370	−0.167	−0.405
	(0.242)	(0.257)	(0.284)	(0.338)	(0.347)
Religious commitment	1.123**	0.681	−0.469	−1.075*	0.857
	(0.470)	(0.533)	(0.504)	(0.598)	(0.601)
Constant	−1.329***	−1.806†	−0.331	−0.956**	−2.116†
	(0.425)	(0.492)	(0.467)	(0.445)	(0.467)
N	878	870	863	647	686
Pseudo R^2	.048	.144	.056	.081	.068
Wald χ^2	44.51†	105.31†	43.48†	53.04†	48.70†

Source: 2014 Pew Religious Landscape Study (environment, welfare, immigration), 2007 Pew Religious Landscape Study (military, isolationism).
Note: Coefficients are logistic regression. Standard errors are in parentheses. *$p < .10$; **$p < .05$; ***$p < .01$; †$p < .001$ (two-tailed tests).

TABLE A5.3. THE IMPACT OF RELIGIOUS COMMITMENT ON SALIENCE OF ABORTION, GAY MARRIAGE, IMMIGRATION, AND JOB ISSUES

	Abortion	Gay marriage	Immigration	Jobs/unemployment
Party ID	0.764	1.149	0.716	0.829
	(0.610)	(0.742)	(0.697)	(0.626)
Ideology	2.707***	3.468***	1.565	0.609
	(0.963)	(1.108)	(1.055)	(1.017)
Female	0.003	−0.226	−0.025	−0.514
	(0.350)	(0.390)	(0.349)	(0.353)
Income	−0.711	−1.103	−0.621	−0.809
	(0.749)	(0.806)	(0.761)	(0.818)
Education	−0.637	−0.962	0.042	0.453
	(0.617)	(0.686)	(0.638)	(0.599)
South	0.254	0.194	0.494	0.303
	(0.351)	(0.417)	(0.347)	(0.398)
Hispanic	1.142**	1.198**	0.876*	0.801
	(0.550)	(0.607)	(0.532)	(0.573)
Mixed/other	0.518	0.851	0.460	1.112*
	(0.674)	(0.812)	(0.570)	(0.580)
Religious commitment	1.972*	1.792	−1.267	−1.897
	(1.015)	(1.360)	(0.983)	(1.244)
Constant	−3.775†	−4.505†	−1.065	1.645
	(0.922)	(1.168)	(0.851)	(1.273)
N	350	350	350	350
Pseudo R^2	.142	.182	.046	.056
Wald χ^2	38.98†	36.20†	10.90	15.38*

Source: Public Religion Research Institute Millennial Values Survey, 2012.
Note: Coefficients are logistic regression. Standard errors are in parentheses. *p < .10; **p < .05; ***p < .01; †p < .001 (two-tailed tests).

TABLE A5.4. THE IMPACT OF RELIGIOUS COMMITMENT ON SALIENCE OF WEALTH GAP, EDUCATION, FEDERAL DEFICIT, ENVIRONMENT, AND NATIONAL SECURITY ISSUES

	Gap between rich and poor	Education	Federal deficit	Environment	National security
Party ID	0.030	0.165	0.337	−1.002	1.347*
	(0.706)	(0.701)	(0.574)	(0.708)	(0.737)
Ideology	−0.779	−0.073	0.529	−1.125	0.424
	(1.038)	(0.969)	(1.000)	(1.028)	(1.031)
Female	0.271	0.656**	−0.643*	0.593	0.019
	(0.350)	(0.334)	(0.362)	(0.364)	(0.338)
Income	−1.367*	0.048	−0.356	−0.227	−1.422**
	(0.741)	(0.688)	(0.752)	(0.757)	(0.714)
Education	−1.465**	0.529	0.858	−0.762	0.105
	(0.610)	(0.565)	(0.616)	(0.621)	(0.624)
South	0.428	0.001	0.532	0.260	0.501
	(0.358)	(0.339)	(0.367)	(0.363)	(0.328)
Hispanic	0.228	0.219	−1.363***	0.624	−0.225
	(0.527)	(0.459)	(0.469)	(0.531)	(0.465)
Mixed/other	−0.171	−0.322	−0.524	0.204	1.192**
	(0.603)	(0.601)	(0.605)	(0.573)	(0.598)
Religious commitment	0.261	−0.276	−2.267*	1.677	0.884
	(1.097)	(0.976)	(1.213)	(1.270)	(0.926)
Constant	0.559	−0.716	2.068**	−1.052	−1.747**
	(1.079)	(0.883)	(0.914)	(1.089)	(0.835)
N	350	350	350	350	350
Pseudo R^2	.087	.025	.105	.091	.083
Wald χ^2	17.13**	6.23	22.91***	19.45**	14.68

Source: Public Religion Research Institute Millennial Values Survey, 2012.
Note: Coefficients are logistic regression. Standard errors in parentheses. *$p < .10$; **$p < .05$; ***$p < .01$ (two-tailed tests).

Chapter 6 Appendix

Tables A6.1–A6.4 show the full models used to generate the figures in Chapter 6.

TABLE A6.1. ARE LIBERAL YOUNG EVANGELICALS DISTINCTIVE FROM OTHER YOUNG LIBERALS ON CULTURAL ISSUES?

	Abortion	Gay marriage	Homosexuality
Party ID	0.157***	1.298***	0.989*
	(0.037)	(0.377)	(0.422)
Female	−0.043*	−0.708***	−1.000***
	(0.018)	(0.215)	(0.246)
Income	−0.163***	−1.194**	−0.549
	(0.031)	(0.387)	(0.417)
Education	−0.196***	−2.219***	−2.323***
	(0.038)	(0.660)	(0.614)
South	0.029	0.199	0.157
	(0.019)	(0.217)	(0.247)
Black	0.133***	1.607***	1.590***
	(0.028)	(0.289)	(0.305)
Hispanic	0.087**	0.799**	0.178
	(0.028)	(0.277)	(0.327)
Asian	0.034	−0.536	0.374
	(0.037)	(0.555)	(0.509)
Mixed/other	0.025	0.233	0.258
	(0.030)	(0.291)	(0.339)
Evangelical	0.093**	1.339***	1.802***
	(0.036)	(0.291)	(0.301)
Constant	0.414***	−1.569***	−1.727***
	(0.033)	(0.439)	(0.467)
N	1,472	1,473	1,473
R^2	0.160		
F Test	19.93***		
Pseudo R^2		.193	.174
Wald χ^2		157.22***	115.32***

Source: 2014 Pew Religious Landscape Study.
Note: Respondents were liberals ages eighteen to twenty-nine. Coefficients shown are from OLS regression for abortion and logistic regression for attitudes toward gay marriage and homosexuality. Standard errors are in parentheses. All independent variables are coded to range from 0 to 1. *$p < .05$; **$p < .01$; ***$p < .001$ (two-tailed tests).

TABLE A6.2. ARE LIBERAL YOUNG EVANGELICALS DISTINCTIVE FROM OTHER YOUNG LIBERALS ON NONCULTURAL ISSUES?

	Environment	Welfare	Immigration	Diplomacy	Isolationism
Party ID	1.007†	1.816†	1.034***	0.963***	−0.425
	(0.288)	(0.280)	(0.369)	(0.351)	(0.273)
Female	0.029	−0.041	0.105	0.264	−0.174
	(0.162)	(0.149)	(0.200)	(0.217)	(0.154)
Income	−1.395†	−0.149	−1.007***	0.563	0.194
	(0.285)	(0.247)	(0.332)	(0.400)	(0.272)
Education	−1.880†	−1.046***	−2.644†	−2.103†	0.791***
	(0.411)	(0.344)	(0.583)	(0.499)	(0.294)
South	0.145	−0.068	−0.078	0.254	−0.130
	(0.167)	(0.158)	(0.209)	(0.226)	(0.173)
Black	1.049†	0.705***	0.251	0.376	−0.485*
	(0.221)	(0.218)	(0.293)	(0.313)	(0.249)
Hispanic	0.071	0.557***	−0.373	−0.085	0.524**
	(0.220)	(0.215)	(0.292)	(0.311)	(0.218)
Asian	0.707**	0.484	−0.858	−0.282	−0.497
	(0.316)	(0.296)	(0.538)	(0.732)	(0.469)
Mixed/other	0.329	0.024	−0.333	0.006	−0.219
	(0.226)	(0.228)	(0.299)	(0.363)	(0.291)
Evangelical	0.542**	0.042	1.006†	0.739***	−0.098
	(0.240)	(0.257)	(0.281)	(0.272)	(0.235)
Constant	−0.632**	−1.150†	−0.693*	−1.937†	−0.777†
	(0.299)	(0.272)	(0.362)	(0.352)	(0.235)
N	1,470	1,446	1,464	834	830
Pseudo R^2	.115	.083	.109	.077	.025
Wald χ^2	113.40†	101.62†	80.59†	47.87†	22.44**

Source: 2014 Pew Religious Landscape Study (environment, welfare, immigration), 2007 Pew Religious Landscape Study (diplomacy, isolationism).
Note: Respondents were liberals ages eighteen to twenty-nine. Coefficients shown are from logistic regression. Standard errors are in parentheses. All independent variables are coded to range from 0 to 1. *$p < .10$; **$p < .05$; ***$p < .01$; †$p < .001$ (two-tailed tests).

TABLE A6.3. POLITICAL IDEOLOGY AND SALIENCE OF ABORTION, GAY MARRIAGE, IMMIGRATION, AND JOB ISSUES AMONG LIBERAL EVANGELICALS

	Abortion	Gay marriage	Immigration	Jobs
Ideology	3.120†	3.970†	1.978**	1.107
	(0.880)	(1.009)	(0.955)	(0.971)
Religious commitment	2.282**	2.152	−0.901	−1.543
	(0.985)	(1.308)	(1.025)	(1.267)
Female	0.009	−0.254	0.023	−0.487
	(0.343)	(0.386)	(0.345)	(0.358)
Income	−0.700	−1.138	−0.605	−0.770
	(0.724)	(0.781)	(0.742)	(0.803)
Education	−0.651	−1.009	−0.107	0.379
	(0.609)	(0.691)	(0.622)	(0.608)
Hispanic	0.946*	0.884	0.660	0.589
	(0.529)	(0.565)	(0.499)	(0.545)
Mixed	0.551	0.283	−0.567	0.625
	(0.696)	(0.981)	(0.696)	(0.697)
Other	0.443	1.167	0.920	1.436*
	(1.009)	(1.110)	(0.756)	(0.867)
Constant	−3.607†	−4.099†	−0.816	1.774
	(0.900)	(1.215)	(0.843)	(1.283)
N	350	350	350	350
Pseudo R^2	.134	.171	.037	.046
Wald χ^2	34.68†	30.20†	9.61	10.21

Source: 2012 Public Religion Research Institute Millennial Values Survey.
Note: Coefficients shown are from ordered logistic regression. Standard errors are in parentheses. All independent variables are coded to range from 0 to 1. *$p < .10$; **$p < .05$; ***$p < .01$; †$p < .001$ (two-tailed tests).

TABLE A6.4. POLITICAL IDEOLOGY AND SALIENCE OF EDUCATION, ENVIRONMENT, WEALTH GAP, FEDERAL DEFICIT, AND NATIONAL SECURITY ISSUES AMONG LIBERAL EVANGELICALS

	Education	Environment	Gap between rich and poor	Federal deficit	National security
Ideology	0.024	−1.637*	−0.709	0.777	1.203
	(0.853)	(0.948)	(0.930)	(0.971)	(0.879)
Religious commitment	−0.228	1.368	0.381	−1.960*	1.401
	(0.967)	(1.144)	(1.064)	(1.150)	(0.958)
Female	0.649**	0.680*	0.362	−0.553	0.039
	(0.329)	(0.368)	(0.348)	(0.350)	(0.334)
Income	0.055	−0.314	−1.402*	−0.378	−1.348*
	(0.682)	(0.741)	(0.743)	(0.741)	(0.702)
Education	0.532	−0.864	−1.598**	0.680	0.014
	(0.576)	(0.635)	(0.626)	(0.615)	(0.602)
Hispanic	0.181	0.816*	0.191	−1.448***	−0.539
	(0.434)	(0.478)	(0.463)	(0.470)	(0.452)
Mixed	−0.307	−0.494	−0.954	−1.245*	0.799
	(0.650)	(0.642)	(0.697)	(0.667)	(0.801)
Other	−0.333	0.577	0.258	−0.049	1.292*
	(0.841)	(0.790)	(0.824)	(0.820)	(0.703)
Constant	−0.697	−1.010	0.677	2.191**	−1.445*
	(0.900)	(1.019)	(1.031)	(0.907)	(0.863)
N	350	350	350	350	350
Pseudo R^2	.025	.081	.084	.098	.056
Wald χ^2	6.33	17.61**	17.20**	22.58***	11.35

Source: 2012 Public Religion Research Institute Millennial Values Survey.
Note: Coefficients shown are from ordered logistic regression. Standard errors are in parentheses. All independent variables are coded to range from 0 to 1. *$p < .10$; **$p < .05$; ***$p < .01$ (two-tailed tests).

Notes

INTRODUCTION

1. Political scientists are generally opposed to combining these smaller traditions into an "other" category because doing so defeats the logic of religious traditions (given that they have little in common besides minority status). However, each tradition is too small to have a reliable sample size for analysis, and therefore the most common approach is to leave them out of most analyses.

2. Premillennialism is a belief that the condition of the world will worsen until Jesus Christ physically returns to the earth (i.e., the Second Coming). Premillennialism is often contrasted with postmillennialism, which holds that Christ will return after a long period in which Christianity and Christian ethics prosper. Premillennial dispensationalism divides the history of the earth into several periods, each with its own covenant between God and the people. Premillennial dispensationalism is probably best known for its belief that Christ will return and save his people (the Rapture) before the rise (and subsequent defeat) of the Antichrist (Weber 1999). Premillennial dispensationalism has made its way into pop culture through the *Left Behind* book series written by Tim LaHaye and Jerry B. Jenkins.

3. Religious commitment is a scale comprised of frequency of church attendance, frequency of prayer, and the degree to which religion guides the respondent's life (all recoded to range from 0 to 1). To preserve cases where possible, missing values were replaced with the mean of nonmissing values for each respondent. In principal components factor analysis, the three items loaded strongly on one factor, with an eigenvalue of 2.13, explaining 71 percent of the total variance.

CHAPTER 1

1. The traditional story is that Luther nailed his Ninety-Five Theses to the door of All Saints' Church in Wittenberg. However, there is some debate among historians as to whether Luther actually did so (e.g., Marty 2008).

2. Data from the 2006 National Congregations Study show that 36 percent of churches would prevent openly gay couples from becoming full-fledged members of the congregation and 21 percent of churches would prevent an openly pro-choice person from becoming a full-fledged member of the congregation (ARDA, n.d.; Chaves and Anderson 2008). Naturally, we would expect these limits to be more prevalent in congregations that emphasize a subcultural perspective.

3. Aside from its college ministry activities, the Navigators is known for its NavPress publishing house and *The Message* translation of the Bible.

CHAPTER 2

1. From a premillennial dispensationalist perspective, when the rapture could occur at any moment, individuals should focus on their personal salvation rather than long-term concerns like the environment.

2. As is common practice in the religion and politics literature (e.g., Layman 2001), African American evangelicals have been recoded into the black Protestant tradition for two reasons. First, most churches still experience a high degree of racial segregation. For example, using data from the 2012 National Congregation Study, the Pew Research Center reports that about eight in ten Americans attend a church where one racial or ethnic group makes up more than 80 percent of the congregation (Lipka 2014). Second, black Protestant theology is quite different from white evangelical Protestant theology, including an increased emphasis on social justice (Lincoln and Mamiya 1990). With the exception of recoding African American evangelicals to black Protestant, I include all racial/ethnic groups in my analysis. Traditionally, race has formed an important boundary for the evangelical subculture (e.g., Emerson and Smith 2000; Green 2010, 34; Hatch 1989; Oldfield 1996, 57). However, as my dissertation (Castle 2015a) shows, evangelicals are becoming more racially diverse over time. Furthermore, I find that while Hispanic and Asian evangelicals are more Democratic and more liberal, in terms of issue preferences, they are quite comparable to evangelicals. Ultimately, including nonwhites in my analysis is well-advised, given the changing racial makeup of evangelicalism, and doing so also presents a "tougher" test of my subcultural theory.

3. Surveys tend to overestimate the frequency of presidential vote results because of social desirability bias, among other factors (for an extended discussion on this issue, see Abramson, Aldrich, and Rohde 2011, 94–95). While this generates concerns when trying to estimate turnout, those concerns are somewhat reduced when using the data for the purposes here (namely, comparing group preferences for presidential candidates). Nevertheless, these results should be interpreted with some caution.

4. For the sake of a more reliable analysis, I have not shown the means when the per-generation sample in any given year is less than thirty, as was often the case for Millennials in 2000 and 2002.

5. Unfortunately, the PRRI data did not include the full battery of religious tradition variables. Rather, they used a truncated set of labels that did not distinguish between Protestant traditions. Therefore, for this data set, I define "evangelicals" as "Protestants" or "just Christians" who (1) were not African American and (2) described themselves as born-again Christians. I continue to use the label "evangelicals" to maintain the continuity of my narrative, but readers should be aware that when I used the

PRRI data, the measure I got was not achieved through the standard denominational battery. In short, the varying measures of evangelicalism across the data sets means that my analysis considers overlapping, but not identical, segments of the population.

CHAPTER 3

1. The full models used in constructing the figures discussed in this section are shown in the Chapter 3 Appendix.

2. Religious commitment is an additive index composed of church attendance (six categories ranging from "never" to "more than once a week"), frequency of prayer (seven categories ranging from "never" to "several times a day"), and personal importance of religion (four categories ranging from "not at all important" to "very important"). Each variable was recoded to range from 0 to 1. To preserve cases, missing values were replaced with the mean of the nonmissing values for each respondent. In principal components factor analysis of the 2014 Pew data, these items loaded strongly on one factor, with an eigenvalue of 2.32 explaining 77 percent of the variance. Results for the other data sets were highly similar.

CHAPTER 4

1. One might speculate that as social acceptance of alcohol grew in the wake of Prohibition, the evangelical subculture risked its position in the religious marketplace by continuing to make temperance an important part of its identity.

2. Of course, other traditions also have their own distinctive beliefs. In addition to the formal theological commitments of the Catholic Church, Gregory Allen Smith (2008, 3) explains that Catholicism has consistently emphasized issues including care for the poor, capital punishment, opposition to war, abortion, and sexual morality. David Campbell, John Green, and J. Quin Monson (2014, 55) suggest Mormons are distinctive for their belief in the Book of Mormon, God and Jesus as distinct and corporeal beings (in contrast to the doctrine of the Trinity), Joseph Smith's status as a prophet, and the current president of the Church as a living prophet. In Islam, the Five Pillars summarize some of the core values of the tradition: declaring that there is no God except God and that Muhammad is God's Messenger, ritually praying five times a day, giving wealth to the poor, fasting during Ramadan, and undertaking the pilgrimage to Mecca at least once in a lifetime ("Pillars of Islam," n.d.).

3. Technically, Bush attends a United Methodist Church and is a mainline Protestant. Nevertheless, his use of language and many of his religious beliefs are more representative of evangelical Protestantism. For example, his transformative "born again" experience is more typical of evangelical Protestantism (e.g., Green 2003).

4. The passage the student references appears in Leviticus 18:22.

5. I do not link to the college's website or quote from the policy directly to maintain confidentiality. However, this description remained true to the college's web page as of March 15, 2018.

6. It was unclear from our conversation on what issues this professor was advocating more Democratic views.

7. I do not discuss the exact issue out of an abundance of caution with respect to maintaining the confidentiality of New Faithful's identity.

CHAPTER 5

1. As with all interviewees throughout this study, this is a pseudonym designed to protect the respondent's identity.

2. The Michigan School's funnel model suggests that controlling for ideology in the party model may be inappropriate because party affiliation develops earlier in the causal process (e.g., Campbell et al. 1960). However, scholars are increasingly recognizing that ideology is a social identity in and of itself (Conover and Feldman 1981) and the choice of party and ideology often occurs at the same causal stage (Miller and Shanks 1996). Therefore, I choose to include ideology largely because doing so represents a stricter test of my theory and reduces the potential for omitted variable bias.

3. While frequency of prayer is often a concern in measures of behaving because it may single out evangelical and Protestant denominations more so than Catholics or various other religions, in the context of a sample limited to young evangelicals, its inclusion should be far less controversial.

4. In principal components and factor analysis, the three items strongly loaded one factor with an eigenvalue of 2.22, explaining 74 percent of the variance. Religious commitment is the mean of each respondent's values on the three items. To preserve cases, missing values were replaced with the mean of nonmissing values when possible.

5. As a reminder, when using the PRRI data set, I defined "evangelicals" as "Protestants" or "just Christians" who (1) were not African American and (2) described themselves as born-again Christians. I continued to use the label "evangelicals" to maintain the continuity of my narrative, but when I used the Millennial Values Survey data, the measure was not achieved through the standard religious tradition battery. Thus, the measures of evangelicalism based on religious tradition (in the Pew Religious Landscape and Cooperative Congressional Election data sets) and the measures of evangelicalism based on born-again status capture overlapping but not identical segments of the population.

6. In the unweighted Cooperative Congressional Election Study, limiting the data to evangelicals ages eighteen to twenty-nine yields a sample of approximately thirty-five, which is far too low for reliable structural equation modeling.

7. Church attendance, frequency of prayer, and religious guidance have all been recoded to range from zero to one. In principal components factor analysis, the 2010 values of each variable loaded strongly on one factor, with an eigenvalue of 2.394, explaining 79.8 percent of the variance (results for the 2012 and 2014 analyses were highly comparable). Religious commitment is the mean of each respondent's values on the three items. To preserve cases, missing values were replaced with the mean of nonmissing values when possible.

8. Typically, researchers would report a variety of fit indexes (e.g., comparative fit index [CFI] and Tucker-Lewis Index [TLI]) when working with structural equation models. However, when working with survey data, many of these indexes are not appropriate because the models no longer have a sample likelihood value (StataCorp 2013, 102). Because this is the case for the data here, the only statistic reported is the coefficient of determination (CD), which is equivalent to R^2 for the model.

CHAPTER 6

Much of the material in this chapter is a revised version of Jeremiah J. Castle, "Subcultural Identity and the Evangelical Left: Comparing Liberal Young Evangelicals to

Other Young Liberals," in *The Evangelical Crackup? The Future of the Evangelical-Republican Coalition*, edited by Paul A. Djupe and Ryan L. Claassen (Philadelphia: Temple University Press), 124–143. It is included here with the permission of Temple University Press.

1. Names and nonsubstantive details have been changed to protect confidentiality.

2. An important caveat to this point is that scholars have generally found that it is mainline Protestants and Catholics who are leaving the faith, rather than evangelicals (e.g., Hout and Fischer 2002). First, one reason evangelicals may be less likely to leave their faith is because of the strength of the evangelical subculture as a political and social network (e.g., Campbell 2004; Smith et al. 1998). Second, although at the aggregate level it appears to be primarily mainline Protestants and Catholics who are leaving the faith, this does not preclude the notion that at the individual level one strategy for dealing with cognitive dissonance between competing liberal and evangelical identities is leaving the faith.

3. Researchers have often found that evangelicals tend to have higher scores in terms of religious commitment compared to other denominations. This might be partially because evangelicalism tends to have higher participation demands for members (Campbell 2004; Smith et al. 1998). However, it might also reflect that the items used in the religious commitment scale are biased in favor of finding higher commitment among evangelicals. For example, the use of "religious guidance" and "frequency of prayer" might tend to give evangelicals an advantage compared to other traditions because these are core values of the evangelical tradition (see Chapter 3). To account for this bias, when creating the tertile "bins," I did so by dividing evangelicals into tertiles (rather than using all of the respondents in the sample). The reason the three tertile bins are not equal in size is because young evangelicals tend to have somewhat lower levels of religious commitment compared to older evangelicals.

4. In this case, the two categories of religious commitment are those above and below the fiftieth percentile of religious commitment among evangelicals ages eighteen to twenty-nine. While it might be preferable to divide young evangelicals into tertiles or quartiles of religious commitment, I used two categories because of the relatively small number of liberal evangelicals in this age group in the data set.

5. Campolo uses the term "Red Letter Christians" to identify a group of post–Christian Right elites (most of whom are evangelicals), including himself, Brian McLaren, Richard Rohr, Cheryl Sanders, Noel Castellanos, Jim Wallis, Duane Shank, and their respective followers. The term, which was coined by a radio personality during an interview with Wallis, attempts to highlight the fact that these Christian thinkers emphasize the New Testament and the words and deeds of Jesus in developing their lifestyle and ideology. The term is a reference to the fact that some versions of the Bible print Christ's words in red letters.

6. Unfortunately, the Public Religion Research Institute data does not include the full battery of religious tradition variables. Rather, they use a truncated set of labels that do not distinguish between Protestant traditions. Therefore, for this data set, I define "evangelicals" as "Protestants" or "just Christians" who (1) are not African American and (2) describe themselves as born-again Christians. I continue to use the label "evangelicals" to maintain the continuity of my narrative, but please note that the measure from the Public Religion Research Institute data was not achieved through the standard religious tradition battery.

CONCLUSION

1. Specifically, in this case, the court found that while the government had an interest in ensuring contraceptives would be provided, the mandate was not the "least restrictive means" of ensuring that they would do so.

2. In 1862, Congress rejected a petition to from a majority-Mormon state (to be named Deseret) and subsequently outlawed polygamy in United States territories (including the land that later became Utah) with the Morrill Anti-Bigamy Act. One individual convicted under the Morrill Act was George Reynolds. In *Reynolds v. United States* (1879), the Supreme Court ruled that polygamy was not protected by the free exercise clause.

3. For example, the Cardinal Newman Society annually publishes a list of colleges that are committed to a "faithful Catholic education," including Ave Maria University, Thomas Aquinas College (the one in Santa Paula, California), Wyoming Catholic College, and others (Cardinal Newman Society, n.d.).

References

Abramson, Paul R., John H. Aldrich, and David W. Rohde. 2011. *Change and Continuity in the 2008 and 2012 Elections*. Washington, DC: CQ Press.

Adams, Greg D. 1997. "Abortion: Evidence of an Issue Evolution." *American Journal of Political Science* 41 (3): 718–737.

Adkins, Todd, and Jeremiah J. Castle. 2014. "Moving Pictures? Experimental Evidence of Cinematic Influence on Political Attitudes." *Social Science Quarterly* 95 (5): 1230–1244.

Adkins, Todd, Geoffrey C. Layman, David E. Campbell, and John C. Green. 2013. "Religious Group Cues and Citizen Policy Attitudes in the United States." *Politics and Religion* 6 (2): 235–264.

Ambrosino, Brandon. 2016. "How Trump Is Dividing Jerry Falwell's University." *Politico Magazine*, October 27. Available at http://www.politico.com/magazine/story/2016/10/trump-evangelical-falwell-liberty-university-christian-conservatives-214394.

Ansolabehere, Stephen. 2010a. "CCES Common Content, 2006." Version 4.0. Available at https://dataverse.harvard.edu/dataset.xhtml?persistentId=hdl:1902.1/14002.

———. 2010b. "Guide to the 2006 Cooperative Congressional Election Study." August 20. Available at https://dataverse.harvard.edu/dataset.xhtml?persistentId=hdl:1902.1/14002.

Ansolabehere, Stephen, and Brian Schaffner. 2013. "CCES Common Content, 2012." Available at http://hdl.handle.net/1902.1/21447.

———. 2017. "CCES Common Content, 2016." Available at https://dataverse.harvard.edu/dataset.xhtml?persistentId=doi%3A10.7910/DVN/GDF6Z0.

Apter, David Ernest. 1967. *The Politics of Modernization*. Chicago: University of Chicago Press.

Arceneaux, Kevin, and Robin Kolodny. 2009. "Educating the Least Informed: Group Endorsements in a Grassroots Campaign." *American Journal of Political Science* 53 (4): 755–770.

ARDA (Association of Religion Data Archives). n.d. "National Congregations Study, Panel Dataset (1998 and 2006–2007)." Available at http://www.TheArda.com/Archive/Files/Codebooks/NCSPANEL_CB.asp#V442 (accessed January 18, 2019).

Avery, Alison, Justin Chase, Linda Johansson, Samantha Litvak, Darrel Montero, and Michael Wydra. 2007. "America's Changing Attitudes toward Homosexuality, Civil Unions, and Same-Gender Marriage: 1977–2004." *Social Work* 52 (1): 71–79.

Banerjee, Neela. 2008. "Young Evangelicals Seek Broader Political Agenda." *New York Times*, June 1. Available at http://www.nytimes.com/2008/06/01/world/americas/01iht-01evangelical.13366425.html.

Barker, David C., and Christopher Jan Carman. 2000. "The Spirit of Capitalism? Religious Doctrine, Values, and Economic Attitude Constructs." *Political Behavior* 22 (1): 1–27.

Bartkowski, John. 2007. "Religious Socialization among American Youth: How Faith Shapes Parents, Children, and Adolescents." In *Handbook of the Sociology of Religion*, edited by James Beckford and N. J. Demerath III, 495–509. Thousand Oaks, CA: Sage.

Beck, Paul Allen, and Edward T. Jennings. 1991. "Family Traditions, Political Periods, and the Development of Partisan Orientations." *Journal of Politics* 53 (4): 742–763.

Bellah, Robert N. 1967. "Civil Religion in America." *Daedalus* 96 (1): 1–21.

———. 1970. "Religious Evolution." In *Beyond Belief: Essays on Religion in a Post-traditional World*, 20–50. New York: Harper and Row.

Berelson, Bernard R., Paul F. Lazarsfeld, and William N. McPhee. 1954. *Voting*. Chicago: University of Chicago Press.

Berger, Peter L. 1967. *The Sacred Canopy*. Garden City, NY: Doubleday.

———. 1979. *The Heretical Imperative*. Garden City, NY: Anchor Press.

Berger, Peter L., and Thomas Luckmann. 1966. *The Social Construction of Reality*. Garden City, NY: Doubleday.

Berinsky, Adam J., and Tali Mendelberg. 2005. "The Indirect Effects of Discredited Stereotypes in Judgments of Jewish Leaders." *American Journal of Political Science* 45 (4): 845–864.

Bernstein, Mary, and Verta Taylor, eds. 2013. *The Marrying Kind? Debating Same-Sex Marriage within the Lesbian and Gay Movement*. Minneapolis: University of Minnesota Press.

Bolce, Louis, and Gerald De Maio. 2008. "A Prejudice for the Thinking Classes: Media Exposure, Political Sophistication, and the Anti-Christian Fundamentalist." *American Politics Research* 36 (2): 155–185.

Bruns, Alex. 2012. "Mitt Romney and Evangelical Voters: An Arranged Marriage." *PBS NewsHour*, July 10. Available at http://www.pbs.org/newshour/rundown/mitt-romney-and-evangelical-voters-an-arrainged-marriage.

Burwell v. Hobby Lobby Stores, Inc. 2014. 573 U.S. ___.

Campbell, Alexia Fernandez. 2014. "The Surprising South Carolina Evangelicals Who Support Immigration." *The Atlantic*, July 16. Available at https://www.theatlantic

.com/politics/archive/2014/07/the-surprising-south-carolina-evangelicals-who-support-immigration/431133.

Campbell, Angus, Philip E. Converse, Warren E. Miller, and Donald E. Stokes. 1960. *The American Voter*. Unabridged ed. Chicago: University of Chicago Press.

Campbell, David E. 2002. "The Young and the Realigning: A Test of the Socialization Theory of Realignment." *Public Opinion Quarterly* 66 (2): 209–234.

———. 2004. "Acts of Faith: Churches and Political Engagement." *Political Behavior* 26 (2): 155–180.

———, ed. 2007. *A Matter of Faith: Religion in the 2004 Presidential Election*. Washington, DC: Brookings Institution Press.

Campbell, David E., John C. Green, and Geoffrey C. Layman. 2011. "The Party Faithful: Partisan Images, Candidate Religion, and the Electoral Impact of Party Identification." *American Journal of Political Science* 55 (1): 42–58.

Campbell, David E., John C. Green, and J. Quin Monson. 2014. *Seeking the Promised Land: Mormons and American Politics*. Cambridge: Cambridge University Press.

Campbell, David E., and J. Quin Monson. 2007. "The Case of Bush's Re-election: Did Gay Marriage Do It?" In *A Matter of Faith: Religion in the 2004 Presidential Election*, edited by David E. Campbell, 120–141. Washington, DC: Brookings Institution Press.

Campbell, David E., and Robert D. Putnam. 2011. "Crashing the Tea Party." *New York Times*, August 17, p. A23.

Campolo, Tony. 2008. *Red Letter Christians: A Citizen's Guide to Faith and Politics*. Ventura, CA: Regal.

Capps, Walter H. 1994. *The New Religious Right: Piety, Patriotism, and Politics*. Columbia: University of South Carolina Press.

Cardinal Newman Society. n.d. "Recommended Colleges." Available at https://newmansociety.org/the-newman-guide/recommended-colleges (accessed March 19, 2019).

Carmines, Edward G., and James A. Stimson. 1989. *Issue Evolution: Race and the Transformation of American Politics*. Princeton, NJ: Princeton University Press.

Carroll, Colleen. 2002. *The New Faithful: Why Young Adults Are Embracing Christian Orthodoxy*. Chicago: Loyola Press.

Castle, Jeremiah J. 2015a. "Rock of Ages: Subcultural Religious Identity and Public Opinion among Evangelical Millennials." Ph.D. diss., University of Notre Dame.

———. 2015b. "The Electoral Impact of Public Opinion on Religious Establishment." *Journal for the Scientific Study of Religion* 54 (4): 814–832.

———. 2018a. "Electoral Choice and Religion: United States." In *Oxford Research Encyclopedia of Politics*. Oxford: Oxford University Press. Available at http://oxfordre.com/politics/view/10.1093/acrefore/9780190228637.001.0001/acrefore-9780190228637-e-728?rskey=wTRefh&result=2.

———. 2018b. "New Fronts in the Culture Wars? Religion, Partisanship, and Polarization on Religious Liberty and Transgender Rights in the United States." *American Politics Research*, December 14. Available at https://doi.org/10.1177/1532673X18818169.

———. 2018c. "Subcultural Identity and the Evangelical Left: Comparing Liberal Young Evangelicals to Other Young Liberals." In *The Evangelical Crackup? The*

Future of the Evangelical-Republican Coalition, edited by Paul A. Djupe and Ryan L. Claassen, 124–143. Philadelphia: Temple University Press.

Castle, Jeremiah J., Geoffrey C. Layman, David E. Campbell, and John C. Green. 2012. "A New Party Faithful?" Paper presented at Southern Political Science Association, New Orleans, LA, January 12–14.

———. 2017. "Survey Experiments on Candidate Religiosity, Political Attitudes, and Vote Choice." *Journal for the Scientific Study of Religion* 56 (1): 143–161.

Castle, Jeremiah J., and Patrick L. Schoettmer. 2019. "Secularism and Politics." In *Oxford Research Encyclopedia of Politics*. Oxford: Oxford University Press. Available at http://oxfordre.com/politics/view/10.1093/acrefore/9780190228637.001.0001/acrefore-9780190228637-e-663.

Chaves, Mark. 1993. "Denominations as Dual Structures: An Organizational Analysis." *Sociology of Religion* 54 (2): 147–169.

———. 1994. "Secularization as Declining Religious Authority." *Social Forces* 72 (3): 749–774.

Chaves, Mark, and Shawna Anderson. 2008. "National Congregations Study, Cumulative Dataset (1998 and 2006–2007)." Available at http://www.thearda.com/Archive/Files/Descriptions/NCSCUM.asp.

Claiborne, Shane. 2006. *The Irresistible Revolution*. Grand Rapids, MI: Zondervan.

———. 2013. "A Dialogue on What It Means to Be Pro-Life." *Red Letter Christians*, January 22. Available at http://www.redletterchristians.org/a-dialogue-on-what-it-means-to-be-pro-life.

Claiborne, Shane, and Chris Haw. 2008. *Jesus for President: Politics for Ordinary Radicals*. Grand Rapids, MI: Zondervan.

Clark, Fred. 2013. "Michele Bachmann, Rick Warren Telling Lies for Jesus That Hurt Poor Women." *Patheos*, March 25. Available at https://www.patheos.com/blogs/slacktivist/2013/03/25/michele-bachmann-rick-warren-telling-lies-for-jesus-that-hurt-poor-women.

Conover, Pamela Johnston, and Stanley Feldman. 1981. "The Origins and Meaning of Liberal/Conservative Self-Identifications." *American Journal of Political Science* 25 (4): 617–645.

Converse, Philip E. 1964. "The Nature of Belief Systems in Mass Publics." In *Ideology and Discontent*, edited by David E. Apter, 206–261. New York: Free Press.

Cook, Elizabeth Adell, Ted G. Jelen, and Clyde Wilcox. 1992. *Between Two Absolutes: Public Opinion and the Politics of Abortion*. Boulder, CO: Westview Press.

Cooperman, Alan, and Thomas B. Edsall 2006. "Christian Coalition Shrinks as Debt Grows." *Washington Post*, April 10. Available at http://www.washingtonpost.com/wp-dyn/content/article/2006/04/09/AR2006040901063.html.

Cramer, Katherine J. 2016. *The Politics of Resentment: Rural Consciousness in Wisconsin and the Rise of Scott Walker*. Chicago: University of Chicago Press.

Cru. n.d. "What We Do." Available at https://www.cru.org/us/en/about/what-we-do.html (accessed March 19, 2019).

Danielsen, Sabrina. 2013. "Fracturing over Creation Care? Shifting Environmental Beliefs among Evangelicals, 1984–2010." *Journal for the Scientific Study of Religion* 52 (1): 198–215.

Deckman, Melissa M. 2004. *School Board Battles: The Christian Right in Local Politics*. Washington, DC: Georgetown University Press.

Delli Carpini, Michael X., and Scott Keeter. 1996. *What Americans Know about Politics and Why It Matters*. New Haven, CT: Yale University Press.

DeRogatis, Amy. 2015. *Saving Sex: Sexuality and Salvation in American Evangelicalism*. Oxford: Oxford University Press.

Dierenfield, Bruce J. 2007. *The Battle over School Prayer: How Engel v. Vitale Changed America*. Lawrence: University Press of Kansas.

Djupe, Paul A., and Christopher P. Gilbert. 2002. "The Political Voice of Clergy." *Journal of Politics* 64 (2): 596–609.

———. 2003. *The Prophetic Pulpit: Clergy, Churches, and Communities in American Politics*. Lanham, MD: Rowman and Littlefield.

———. 2009. *The Political Influence of Churches*. Cambridge: Cambridge University Press.

Dokoupil, Tony. 2009. "Why Young Evangelicals Voted for Obama." *Newsweek*, January 16. Available at http://www.newsweek.com/why-young-evangelicals-voted-obama-78485.

Domke, David, and Kevin Coe. 2008. *The God Strategy: How Religion Became a Political Weapon in America*. New York: Oxford University Press.

Douglas, William, and Lesley Clark. 2015. "Pop Culture Helps Change Minds on Gay Rights." *Seattle Times*, January 1. Available at http://www.seattletimes.com/nation-world/pop-culture-helps-change-minds-on-gay-rights.

Downs, Anthony. 1957. *Economic Theory of Democracy*. New York: HarperCollins.

Draper, Electa. 2011. "Focus on the Family Announces More Layoffs." *Denver Post*, September 16. Available at http://www.denverpost.com/2011/09/16/focus-on-the-family-announces-more-layoffs.

Du Noyer, Paul. 2003. "Contemporary Christian Music." In *The Billboard Illustrated Encyclopedia of Music*, 422–423. New York: Billboard Books.

Edwards, Haley. 2008. "Young, Evangelical . . . for Obama?" *Seattle Times*, May 11. Available at http://www.seattletimes.com/politics/young-evangelical-for-obama.

Edwards v. Aguillard. 1987. 482 U.S. 578.

Emerson, Michael O., and Christian Smith. 2000. *Divided by Faith: Evangelical Religion and the Problem of Race in America*. Oxford: Oxford University Press.

Engel v. Vitale. 1962. 370 U.S. 421.

Epperson v. Arkansas. 1968. 393 U.S. 97.

Evans, Christopher H. 2017. *The Social Gospel in American Religion: A History*. New York: New York University Press.

Evans, Rachel Held. 2013. "Ask Shane Claiborne . . . (Response)." *Rachel Held Evans Blog*, February 27. Available at http://rachelheldevans.com/blog/ask-shane-claiborne-response.

Farrell, Justin. 2011. "The Young and the Restless? The Liberalization of Young Evangelicals." *Journal for the Scientific Study of Religion* 50 (3): 517–532.

Fellowship of Christian Athletes. 2016. "Rise: 2016 Ministry Report." Available at http://2016.fca.org/wp-content/uploads/sites/5/2017/01/FCA-Annual-Report-2016_ForWeb.pdf.

Festinger, Leon. 1957. *A Theory of Cognitive Dissonance*. Stanford, CA: Stanford University Press.

Finke, Roger, and Rodney Stark. 2005. *The Churchgoing of America, 1776–2005*. New Brunswick, NJ: Rutgers University Press.

Fiorina, Morris P., with Samuel J. Abrams and Jeremy C. Pope. 2010. *Culture War? The Myth of a Polarized America*. 3rd ed. New York: Pearson Longman.

FitzGerald, Frances. 2017. *The Evangelicals: The Struggle to Shape America*. New York: Simon and Schuster.

Ford, Zack, and Annie-Rose Strasser. 2012. "Rick Warren: I Regret Coming Out in Support of California's Anti–Gay Marriage Proposition." *ThinkProgress*, November 28. Available at http://thinkprogress.org/lgbt/2012/11/28/1250921/rick-warren-i-regret-coming-out-in-support-of-californias-anti-gay-marriage-proposition.

Fox News. 2005. "The Role of Faith in President Jimmy Carter's Life." *Fox News*, December 27. Available at http://www.foxnews.com/story/2005/12/27/role-faith-in-president-jimmy-carter-life.

Gay, David A., Christopher G. Ellison, and Daniel A. Powers. 1996. "In Search of Denominational Subcultures: Religious Affiliation and 'Pro-Family' Issues Revisited." *Review of Religious Research* 38 (1): 3–17.

Gelder, Ken. 2005. *The Subcultures Reader*. 2nd ed. New York: Routledge.

Gelman, Andrew, Jeffrey Lax, and Justin Phillips. 2010. "Over Time, a Gay Marriage Groundswell." *New York Times*, August 21. Available at http://www.nytimes.com/2010/08/22/weekinreview/22gay.html.

Gilens, Martin, and Naomi Murakawa. 2002. "Elite Cues and Political Decision-Making." In *Research in Micropolitics*, vol. 6, edited by Michael X. Delli Carpini, Leonie Huddy, and Robert Y. Shapiro, 15–49. Amsterdam: JAI.

Graham, Efren. 2015. "'God's Not Dead' Creators Hope for Double Blessing." *CBN News*, March 17. Available at http://www1.cbn.com/cbnnews/us/2015/March/Gods-Not-Dead-Creators-Hope-for-Double-Blessing.

Green, Donald, Bradley Palmquist, and Eric Schickler. 2002. *Partisan Hearts and Minds: Political Parties and the Social Identities of Voters*. New Haven, CT: Yale University Press.

Green, John C. 2003. "The President and His Faith: Interview with John Green." *PBS FrontLine*, December 5. Available at http://www.pbs.org/wgbh/pages/frontline/shows/jesus/interviews/green.html.

———. 2010. *The Faith Factor: How Religion Influences American Elections*. Westport, CT: Praeger.

Green, John C., Lyman A. Kellstedt, Corwin E. Smidt, and James L. Guth. 2007. "How the Faithful Voted: Religious Communities and the Presidential Vote." In *A Matter of Faith: Religion in the 2004 Presidential Election*, edited by David E. Campbell, 15–36. Washington, DC: Brookings Institution Press.

Greene, Steven. 1999. "Understanding Party Identification: A Social Identity Approach." *Political Psychology* 20 (2): 393–403.

———. 2004. "Social Identity Theory and Party Identification." *Social Science Quarterly* 85 (1): 136–153.

Guerra, Kristine, and Tim Evans. 2015. "How Indiana's RFRA Differs from Federal Version." *Indianapolis Star*, April 2. Available at http://www.indystar.com/story/news/politics/2015/03/31/indianas-rfra-similar-federal-rfra/70729888.

Guth, James L. 2009. "Religion and American Public Opinion: Foreign Policy Issues." In *The Oxford Handbook of Religion and American Politics*, edited by Corwin E. Smidt, Lyman A. Kellstedt, and James A. Guth, 243–266. New York: Oxford University Press.

Guth, James L., Cleveland R. Fraser, John C. Green, Lyman A. Kellstedt, and Corwin E. Smidt. 1996. "Religion and Foreign Policy Attitudes: The Case of Christian Zionism." In *Religion and the Culture Wars*, edited by John C. Green, James L. Guth, Corwin E. Smidt, and Lyman A. Kellstedt, 330–360. Lanham, MD: Rowman and Littlefield.

Guth, James L., John C. Green, Lyman A. Kellstedt, and Corwin E. Smidt. 1995. "Faith and the Environment: Religious Beliefs and Attitudes on Environmental Policy." *American Journal of Political Science* 39 (2): 364–382.

Guth, James L., John C. Green, Corwin E. Smidt, Lyman A. Kellstedt, and Margaret M. Poloma. 1997. *The Bully Pulpit: The Politics of Protestant Clergy*. Lawrence: University Press of Kansas.

Guth, James L., Lyman A. Kellstedt, Corwin E. Smidt, and John C. Green. 2006. "Religious Influences in the 2004 Presidential Election." *Presidential Studies Quarterly* 36 (2): 223–242.

Hadden, Jeffrey K. 1969. *The Gathering Storm in Churches*. Garden City, NY: Doubleday.

———. 1993. "The Rise and Fall of American Televangelism." *Annals of the American Academy of Political and Social Science* 527 (1): 113–130.

Hadden, Jeffrey K., and Anson D. Shupe. 1988. *Televangelism, Power, and Politics on God's Frontier*. New York: Henry Holt.

Haenfler, Ross. 2013. *Subcultures: The Basics*. New York: Routledge.

Hargrove, Barbara. 1989. *The Sociology of Religion: Classic and Contemporary Approaches*. Arlington Heights, IL: Harlan Davidson.

Harris, Dan. 2008. "Are Young Evangelicals Skewing More Liberal?" *ABC News*, February 10. Available at http://abcnews.go.com/Politics/Vote2008/story?id=4269824&page=1.

Hatch, Nathan O. 1989. *The Democratization of American Christianity*. New Haven, CT: Yale University Press.

Hebdige, Dick. 1979. *Subculture: The Meaning of Style*. New York: Routledge.

Herdt, Gilbert H., ed. 1993. *Gay Culture in America: Essays from the Field*. Boston: Beacon Press.

Hersh, Eitan D., and Gabrielle Malina. 2017. "Partisan Pastor: The Politics of 130,000 American Religious Leaders." Available at http://www.eitanhersh.com/uploads/7/9/7/5/7975685/hersh_malina_draft_061117.pdf.

Hess, Robert, and Judith Torney. 1967. *The Development of Political Attitudes in Children*. Garden City, NY: Doubleday.

Hirschkorn, Phil, and Jennifer Pinto. 2012. "White Evangelicals Are Half of GOP Primary Voters." *CBS News*, March 15. Available at http://www.cbsnews.com/news/white-evangelicals-are-half-of-gop-primary-voters.

Holmes, David L. 2012. *The Faiths of the Postwar Presidents: From Truman to Obama*. Athens: University of Georgia Press.

Hostetler, John A. 1993. *Amish Society*. 4th ed. Baltimore: Johns Hopkins University Press.

Hout, Michael, and Claude S. Fischer. 2002. "Why More Americans Have No Religious Preference: Politics and Generations." *American Sociological Review* 67 (2): 165–190.

Howard, Jay R., and John M. Streck. 1999. *Apostles of Rock: The Splintered World of Contemporary Christian Music*. Lexington: University Press of Kentucky.

Howe, Neil, and William Strauss. 2000. *Millennials Rising: The Next Great Generation*. New York: Vintage Books.
Huddy, Lione, and Nadya Terkildsen. 1993. "Gender Stereotypes and the Perception of Male and Female Candidates." *American Journal of Political Science* 37 (1): 119–147.
Hunter, James Davison. 1983. *American Evangelicalism*. New Brunswick, NJ: Rutgers University Press.
———. 1987. *Evangelicalism: The Coming Generation*. Chicago: University of Chicago Press.
———. 1991. *Culture War: The Struggle to Define America*. New York: Basic Books.
InterVarsity. n.d. "Ministry Impact." Available at http://www.intervarsity.org/about/our/vital-statistics (accessed January 18, 2019).
Irons, Peter. 2007. *God on Trial: Landmark Cases from America's Religious Battlefields*. New York: Viking/Penguin Books.
Iyengar, Shanto, Guarov Sood, and Yphtach Lelkes. 2012. "Affect, Not Ideology: A Social Identity Perspective on Polarization." *Public Opinion Quarterly* 76 (3): 405–431.
Jelen, Ted G. 1991. *The Political Mobilization of Religious Beliefs*. New York: Praeger.
———. 1993. *The Political World of the Clergy*. Westport, CT: Praeger.
———. 2009. "Religion and American Public Opinion: Social Issues." In *The Oxford Handbook of Religion and American Politics*, edited by Corwin E. Smidt, Lyman A. Kellstedt, and James A. Guth, 217–243. New York: Oxford University Press.
Jelen, Ted G., Corwin E. Smidt, and Clyde Wilcox. 1993. "The Political Effects of the Born-Again Phenomenon." In *Rediscovering the Religious Factor in American Politics*, edited by David C. Leege and Lyman A. Kellstedt, 199–215. Armonk, NY: M. E. Sharpe.
Jelen, Ted G., and Clyde Wilcox. 2003. "Causes and Consequences of Public Attitudes toward Abortion: A Review and Research Agenda." *Political Research Quarterly* 56 (4): 489–500.
Jennings, M. Kent, and Richard G. Niemi. 1981. *Generations and Politics: A Panel Study of Young Adults and Their Parents*. Princeton, NJ: Princeton University Press.
Jennings, M. Kent, Laura Stoker, and Jake Bowers. 1999. "Politics across Generations: Family Transmission Re-examined." Paper presented at the annual meeting of the American Political Science Association, Atlanta, GA, September 3–5.
Johnson, Janet B., H. T. Reynolds, and Jason D. Mycoff. 2008. *Political Science Research Methods*. 6th ed. Washington, DC: CQ Press.
Johnstone, Ronald L. 1988. *Religion in Society: A Sociology of Religion*. Englewood Cliffs, NJ: Prentice-Hall.
Jones, Robert P. 2016. *The End of White Christian America*. New York: Simon and Schuster.
Kaleem, Jaweed. 2013. "Jim Wallis Talks Faith's Role in Politics, Gay Marriage, and Immigration." *Huffington Post*, April 5. Available at http://www.huffingtonpost.com/2013/04/05/jim-wallis-faith-politics-immigration_n_3024458.html.
Katz, Elihu, and Paul F. Lazarsfeld. 1955. *Personal Influence: The Part Played by People in the Flow of Mass Communications*. New York: Free Press.
Kellstedt, Lyman A., John C. Green, James L. Guth, and Corwin E. Smidt. 1996. "Grasping the Essentials: The Social Embodiment of Religion and Political Be-

havior." In *Religion and the Culture Wars*, edited by John C. Green, James L. Guth, Corwin E. Smidt, and Lyman A. Kellstedt, 174–192. Lanham, MD: Rowman and Littlefield.
Kellstedt, Lyman A., John C. Green, Corwin E. Smidt, and James L. Guth. 1996. "The Puzzle of Evangelical Protestantism." In *Religion and the Culture Wars*, edited by John C. Green, James L. Guth, Corwin E. Smidt, and Lyman A. Kellstedt, 240–266. Lanham, MD: Rowman and Littlefield.
Kellstedt, Lyman A., and Corwin E. Smidt. 1996. "Measuring Fundamentalism: An Analysis of Different Operational Strategies." In *Religion and the Culture Wars*, edited by John C. Green, James L. Guth, Corwin E. Smidt, and Lyman A. Kellstedt, 193–218. Lanham, MD: Rowman and Littlefield.
Kidd, Thomas S. 2008. "Jonathan Edwards and the Great Awakening." In *The Oxford Handbook of Early American Literature*, edited by Kevin J. Hayes, 169–188. Oxford: Oxford University Press.
Killian, Mitchell, and Clyde Wilcox. 2008. "Do Abortion Attitudes Lead to Party Switching?" *Political Research Quarterly* 61 (4): 561–573.
Kinder, Donald R., and Cindy D. Kam. 2009. *Us versus Them: Ethnocentric Foundations of American Public Opinion*. Chicago: University of Chicago Press.
Kinnaman, David. 2011. *You Lost Me: Why Young Christians Are Leaving Church . . . and Rethinking Faith*. Grand Rapids, MI: Baker.
Kleppner, Paul. 1970. *The Cross of Culture: A Social Analysis of Midwestern Politics, 1850–1900*. New York: Free Press.
———. 1979. *The Third Electoral System, 1853–1892*. Chapel Hill: University of North Carolina Press.
Kohut, Andrew, John C. Green, Scott Keeter, and Robert C. Toth. 2000. *The Diminishing Divide: Religion's Changing Role in American Politics*. Washington, DC: Brookings Institution.
Krattenmaker, Tom. 2013. *The Evangelicals You Don't Know: Introducing the Next Generation of Christians*. Lanham, MD: Rowman and Littlefield.
Kraybill, Donald B. 2001. *The Riddle of Amish Culture*. Rev. ed. Baltimore: Johns Hopkins University Press.
Kraybill, Donald B., and Kyle C. Kopko. 2007. "Bush Fever: Amish and Old Order Mennonites in the 2004 Presidential Election." *Mennonite Quarterly Review* 81 (April): 165–205.
Krohe, James, Jr. 2010. "Taking the Christian Out of the YMCA." *Illinois Times*, August 12. Available at http://illinoistimes.com/article-7621-taking-the-christian-out-of-the-ymca.html.
Larson, Edward J. 2006. *Summer of the Gods: The Scopes Trial and America's Continuing Debate over Science and Religion*. New York: Basic Books.
Layman, Geoffrey C. 2001. *The Great Divide: Religious and Cultural Conflict in American Party Politics*. New York: Columbia University Press.
Layman, Geoffrey C., and John C. Green. 2005. "Wars and Rumours of Wars: The Contexts of Cultural Conflict in American Political Behavior." *British Journal of Political Science* 36 (1): 61–89.
Lazarsfeld, Paul F., Bernard Berelson, and Hazel Gaudet. 1944. *The People's Choice: How the Voter Makes Up His Mind in a Presidential Campaign*. New York: Columbia University Press.

Lebo, Lauri. 2008. *The Devil in Dover: An Insider's Account of Dogma v. Darwin in Small-Town America*. New York: New Press.

Lee, Deborah Jain. 2015. "Why the Young Religious Right Is Leaning Left." *Time*, October 20. Available at http://time.com/4078909/evangelical-millennials.

Lee, M. J. 2017. "God and the Don." *State*, June. Available at https://www.cnn.com/interactive/2017/politics/state/donald-trump-religion.

Leege, David C., and Lyman A. Kellstedt, eds. 1993. *Rediscovering the Religious Factor in American Politics*. Armonk, NY: M. E. Sharpe.

Leege, David C., Kenneth D. Wald, Brian S. Krueger, and Paul D. Mueller. 2002. *The Politics of Cultural Differences: Social Change and Voter Mobilization Strategies in the Post–New Deal Period*. Princeton, NJ: Princeton University Press.

Levendusky, Matthew. 2009. *The Partisan Sort: How Liberals Become Democrats and Conservatives Became Republicans*. Chicago: University of Chicago Press.

Lewis-Beck, Michael S., William G. Jacoby, Helmut Norpoth, and Herbert F. Weisberg. 2008. *The American Voter Revisited*. Ann Arbor: University of Michigan Press.

Lincoln, C. Eric, and Lawrence Mamiya. 1990. *The Black Church in the African American Experience*. Durham, NC: Duke University Press.

Lipka, Michael. 2014. "Many U.S. Congregations Are Still Racially Segregated, but Things Are Changing." *Pew Research Center*, December 8. Available at http://www.pewresearch.org/fact-tank/2014/12/08/many-u-s-congregations-are-still-racially-segregated-but-things-are-changing-2.

Lyons, Gabe. 2012. *The Next Christians: Seven Ways You Can Live the Gospel and Restore the World*. Colorado Springs, CO: Multnomah Books.

Magolda, Peter M., and Kelsey Ebben Gross. 2009. *It's All About Jesus! Faith as an Oppositional Collegiate Subculture*. Sterling, VA: Stylus.

Manson, Jamie L. 2011. "Tainted Love: The Cost of Sojourners' Refusal to Take Sides on LGBT Issues." *Religion Dispatches*, May 16. Available at http://religiondispatches.org/tainted-love-the-cost-of-sojourners-refusal-to-take-sides-on-lgbt-issues.

Marsden, George. 1980. *Fundamentalism and American Culture: The Shaping of Twentieth-Century Evangelicalism, 1870–1925*. New York: Oxford University Press.

Martin, William. 2005. *With God on Our Side: The Rise of the Religious Right in America*. New York: Broadway Books.

Marty, Martin E. 2008. *Martin Luther: A Life*. New York: Penguin Books.

Marwell, Gerald, and N. J. Demerath III. 2003. "'Secularization' by Any Other Name." *American Sociological Review* 68 (2): 314–316.

Masterpiece Cakeshop v. Colorado Civil Rights Commission. 2018. 584 U.S. ___.

McDaniel, Eric L. 2008. *Politics in the Pews: The Political Mobilization of Black Churches*. Ann Arbor: University of Michigan Press.

McDermott, Monika L. 2009. "Religious Stereotyping and Voter Support for Evangelical Candidates." *Political Research Quarterly* 62 (2): 340–354.

McLeod, Saul. 2018. "Cognitive Dissonance." *Simply Psychology*, February 5. Available at http://www.simplypsychology.org/cognitive-dissonance.html.

McMurtrie, Beth. 2001. "Crusading for Christ, amid Keg Parties and Secularism." *Chronicle of Higher Education*, May 18, p. A-42.

Meacham, Jon. 2009a. "The End of Christian America." *Newsweek*, April 3. Available at http://www.newsweek.com/meacham-end-christian-america-77125.

———. 2009b. "We Didn't Attack Christianity." *Newsweek*, April 7. Available at http://www.newsweek.com/jon-meacham-we-didnt-attack-christianity-77475.

Medhurst, Martin J. 2008. "George W. Bush, Public Faith, and the Culture War over Same-Sex Marriage." In *The Prospect of Presidential Rhetoric*, edited by James Arnt Aune and Martin J. Medhurst, 209–237. College Station: Texas A&M University Press.

Mendenhall, Vanessa. 2006. "Are Young Evangelicals Leaning Left?" *PBS NewsHour*, November 21.

Miller, Warren E., and Merrill Shanks. 1996. *The New American Voter*. Cambridge, MA: Harvard University Press.

Mondak, Jeffrey J. 1993. "Source Cues and Policy Approval: The Cognitive Dynamics of Public Support for the Reagan Agenda." *American Journal of Political Science* 37 (1): 186–212.

Montanaro, Domenico. 2015. "Indiana Law: Sorting Fact from Fiction from Politics." *NPR*, April 1. Available at http://www.npr.org/blogs/itsallpolitics/2015/04/01/395613897/sorting-fact-from-fiction-from-politics-on-the-indiana-law.

Moon, Ruth. 2013. "Why Pope Francis Excites (Most) Evangelical Leaders." *Christianity Today*, March 14. Available at http://www.christianitytoday.com/ct/2013/march-web-only/why-pope-francis-excites-most-evangelical-leaders-bergoglio.html.

Murashko, Alex. 2014. "David Platt: Young Evangelicals Passionate about Poor, Enslaved but Strangely Quiet on Abortion, Same-Sex Marriage." *Christian Post*, March 22. Available at http://www.christianpost.com/news/david-platt-young-evangelicals-passionate-about-poor-enslaved-but-strangely-quiet-on-abortion-same-sex-marriage-116623.

Nazworth, Napp. 2014. "Russell Moore: Young Evangelicals Reject Christian Right, but Not Moving Left, Prefer to Be Freakish." *Christian Post*, March 29. Available at http://m.christianpost.com/news/russell-moore-young-evangelicals-reject-christian-right-but-not-moving-left-prefer-to-be-freakish-117056.

Nelson, Thomas E., and Donald R. Kinder. 1996. "Issue Frames and Group-Centrism in American Public Opinion." *Journal of Politics* 58 (4): 1055–1078.

Neundorf, Anja, and Kaat Smets. 2017. "Political Socialization and the Making of Citizens." *Oxford Research Handbooks Online*. Available at http://www.oxfordhandbooks.com/view/10.1093/oxfordhb/9780199935307.001.0001/oxfordhb-9780199935307-e-98.

Noll, Mark. 1983. "From the Great Awakening to the War for Independence: Christian Values in the American Revolution." *Christian Scholar's Review* 12 (2): 99–110.

Obergefell v. Hodges. 2015. 576 U.S. ____.

Oldfield, Duane M. 1996. *The Right and the Righteous*. Lanham, MD: Rowman and Littlefield.

Olson, Laura R. 2009. "Clergy and American Politics." In *The Oxford Handbook of Religion and American Politics*, edited by Corwin E. Smidt, Lyman A. Kellstedt, and James A. Guth, 371–393. New York: Oxford University Press.

Pally, Marcia. 2011. *The New Evangelicals: Expanding the Vision of the Common Good*. Grand Rapids, MI: Eerdmans.

Parsons, Talcott. 1964. "Christianity in Modern Industrial Society." In *Sociological Theory, Values, and Sociocultural Change*, edited by Edward Tiryakian, 233–270. Glencoe, IL: Free Press.

Patrikios, Stratos. 2008. "American Republican Religion? Disentangling the Causal Link Between Religion and Politics in the U.S." *Political Behavior* 30 (3): 367–389.

Pearson-Merkowitz, Shanna, and James G. Gimpel. 2009. "Religion and Political Socialization." In *The Oxford Handbook of Religion and American Politics*, edited by Corwin E. Smidt, Lyman A. Kellstedt, and James A. Guth, 164–190. New York: Oxford University Press.

Pelz, Mikael L., and Corwin E. Smidt. 2015. "Generational Conversion? The Role of Religiosity in the Politics of Evangelicals." *Journal for the Scientific Study of Religion* 54 (2): 380–401.

Penning, James M., and Corwin E. Smidt. 2002. *Evangelicalism: The Next Generation*. Grand Rapids, MI: Baker Academic.

Pew Research Center. 2007. "U.S. Religious Landscape Survey." Available at http://www.pewforum.org/dataset/u-s-religious-landscape-survey.

———. 2009. "A Conversation with Pastor Rick Warren." Available at http://www.pewresearch.org/2009/11/13/a-conversation-with-pastor-rick-warren.

———. 2014. "Pew Research Center 2014 U.S. Religious Landscape Study." Available at http://www.pewforum.org/dataset/pew-research-center-2014-u-s-religious-landscape-study.

"Pillars of Islam." n.d. *Oxford Islamic Studies Online*. Available at http://www.oxfordislamicstudies.com/article/opr/t125/e1859 (accessed January 18, 2019).

Popkin, Samuel L. 1994. *The Reasoning Voter: Communication and Persuasion in Presidential Campaigns*. 2nd ed. Chicago: University of Chicago Press.

Powell, Mark Allan. 2002. *Encyclopedia of Contemporary Christian Music*. Peabody, MA: Hendrickson.

Prendergast, William B. 1999. *The Catholic Voter in American Politics: The Passing of the Democratic Monolith*. Washington, DC: Georgetown University Press.

Public Religion Research Institute. 2012. "Millennial Values Survey, 2012." Available at http://www.thearda.com/Archive/Files/Downloads/MILVAL12_DL2.asp.

Putnam, Robert D. 2000. *Bowling Alone*. New York: Simon and Schuster.

Putnam, Robert D., and David E. Campbell. 2010. *American Grace: How Religion Divides and Unites Us*. New York: Simon and Schuster.

Pyle, Ralph E. 1993. "Faith and Commitment to the Poor: Theological Orientation and Support for Government Assistance Measures." *Sociology of Religion* 54 (4): 385–401.

Quinley, Harold E. 1974. *The Prophetic Clergy: Social Activism among Protestant Ministers*. New York: Wiley.

Reynolds v. United States. 1878. 98 U.S. (8 Otto.) 145.

Rimmerman, Craig A. 2015. *The Lesbian and Gay Movements: Assimilation or Liberation?* 2nd ed. Boulder, CO: Westview Press.

Rising, Bill. 2012. "In the Spotlight: Marginsplot." *Stata News* 27 (4): 2–3.

Rivers, Douglas. 2006. "Understanding People: Sample Matching." YouGov Polimetrix white paper. Available at http://www.websm.org/uploadi/editor/1368187057Rivers_2006_Sample_matching_Representative_sampling_from_Internet_panels.pdf.

Roberts, Keith A. 2004. *Religion in Sociological Perspective*. 4th ed. Belmont, CA: Wadsworth.

Roberts, Tom. 2010. "Urban Monk Works to See 'The Church We Dream Of.'" *National Catholic Reporter*, November 1. Available at http://ncronline.org/news/faith-parish/urban-monk-works-see-church-we-dream.

Roe v. Wade. 1973. 410 U.S. 113.

Rousseau, Jean-Jacques. 1893. *The Social Contract*. Translated by Rose M. Harrington. New York: G. P. Putnam's Sons.

Ryder, Norman B. 1965. "The Cohort as a Concept in the Study of Social Change." *American Sociological Review* 30 (6): 843–861.

Sanburn, Josh. 2014. "4 Ways Millennials Have It Worse Than Their Parents." *Time*, December 4. Available at http://time.com/3618322/census-millennials-poverty-unemployment.

Scanzoni, Letha Dawson. n.d. "When Evangelicals Were Open to Differing Views on Abortion." *Christian Feminism Today*. Available at http://www.eewc.com/FemFaith/evangelicals-open-differing-views-abortion (accessed January 18, 2019).

Schaeffer, Francis. 1976. *How Then Should We Live: The Rise and Decline of Western Thought and Culture*. Westchester, IL: Crossway Books.

Schaffner, Brian, and Stephen Ansolabehere. 2015. "2010–2014 Cooperative Congressional Election Study Panel Survey." Version 10.0. Available at https://dataverse.harvard.edu/dataset.xhtml?persistentId=doi%3A10.7910/DVN/TOE8I1.

Schultze, Quentin J. 1988. "Evangelical Radio and the Rise of the Electronic Church, 1921–1948." *Journal of Broadcasting and Electronic Media* 32 (3): 289–306.

Scott, Eugenie. 1997. "Antievolution and Creationism in the United States." *Annual Review of Anthropology* 26:263–289.

Sears, David O., and Sheri Levy. 2003. "Childhood and Adult Political Development." In *Oxford Handbook of Political Psychology*, edited by David O. Sears, Leonie Huddy, and Robert Jervis, 60–109. New York: Oxford University Press.

"7 Burning Issues: Gay Rights." 2008. *Relevant*, June 5. Available at http://www.relevantmagazine.com/god/church/features/1457-7-burning-issues-gay-rights.

Sider, Ronald J. 2008. *The Scandal of Evangelical Politics: Why Are Christians Missing the Chance to Really Change the World?* Grand Rapids, MI: Baker.

Smidt, Corwin E., ed. 2004. *Pulpit and Politics: Clergy in American Politics at the Advent of the Millennium*. Waco, TX: Baylor University Press.

Smidt, Corwin E. 2007. "Evangelical and Mainline Protestants at the Turn of the Millennium: Taking Stock and Looking Forward." In *From Pews to Polling Places: Faith and Politics in the American Religious Mosaic*, edited by J. Matthew Wilson, 29–52. Washington, DC: Georgetown University Press.

———. 2013. *American Evangelicals Today*. Lanham, MD: Rowman and Littlefield.

Smidt, Corwin E., John C. Green, Lyman A. Kellstedt, and James L. Guth. 1996. "The Spirit-Filled Movements and American Politics." In *Religion and the Culture Wars*, edited by John C. Green, James L. Guth, Corwin E. Smidt, and Lyman A. Kellstedt, 219–239. Lanham, MD: Rowman and Littlefield.

Smidt, Corwin E., Lyman A. Kellstedt, and James L. Guth. 2009. "The Role of Religion in American Politics: Explanatory Theories and Associated Analytical and Measurement Issues." In *The Oxford Handbook of Religion and American Politics*, edited by Corwin E. Smidt, Lyman A. Kellstedt, and James A. Guth, 3–42. New York: Oxford University Press.

Smith, Buster G., and Byron Johnson. 2010. "The Liberalization of Young Evangelicals: A Research Note." *Journal for the Scientific Study of Religion* 49 (2): 351–360.

Smith, Christian, Michael Emerson, Sally Gallagher, Paul Kennedy, and David Sikkink. 1998. *American Evangelicalism: Embattled and Thriving*. Chicago: University of Chicago Press.

Smith, Christian, and Patricia Snell. 2009. *Souls in Transition: The Religious and Spiritual Lives of Emerging Adults*. Oxford: Oxford University Press.

Smith, Gregory Allen. 2008. *Politics in the Parish: The Political Influence of Catholic Priests*. Washington, DC: Georgetown University Press.

Smith, Tom W., Michael Hout, and Peter Marsden. 2016. "General Social Survey, 1972–2014." Available at https://www.icpsr.umich.edu/icpsrweb/ICPSR/studies/36319.

Sniderman, Paul M., Richard A. Brody, and Philip E. Tetlock. 1991. *Reasoning and Choice: Explorations in Political Psychology*. Cambridge: Cambridge University Press.

StataCorp. 2013. *Stata Structural Equation Modeling Reference Manual, Release 13*. College Station, TX: StataCorp.

Steensland, Brian, Jerry Z. Park, Mark D. Regnerus, Lynn D. Robinson, W. Bradford Wilcox, and Robert D. Woodbury. 2000. "The Measure of American Religion: Toward Improving the State of the Art." *Social Forces* 79 (1): 291–318.

Steinfels, Peter. 2007. "Roman Catholics and American Politics, 1960–2004." In *Religion and American Politics: From the Colonial Period to the Present*, 2nd ed., edited by Mark A. Noll and Luke E. Harlow, 345–366. Oxford: Oxford University Press.

Stetzer, Ed, and Ryan Burge. 2016. "Research Report: Reltrad Coding Problems and a New Repository." *Politics and Religion* 9 (1): 187–190.

Strachan, Owen. 2015. *Awakening the Evangelical Mind: An Intellectual History of the Neo-evangelical Movement*. Grand Rapids, MI: Zondervan.

"Subculture." n.d. *Oxford English Dictionary*. Available at http://www.oxforddictionaries.com/us/definition/american_english/subculture (accessed January 18, 2019).

Taber, Charles S., and Milton Lodge. 2006. "Motivated Skepticism in the Evaluation of Political Beliefs." *American Journal of Political Science* 50 (3): 755–769.

Tajfel, Henri. 1981. *Human Groups and Social Categories: Studies in Social Psychology*. Cambridge: Cambridge University Press.

———. 1982. "Social Psychology of Intergroup Relations." *Annual Review of Psychology* 33 (1): 1–39.

Tschannen, Olivier. 1991. "The Secularization Paradigm: A Systematization." *Journal for the Scientific Study of Religion* 30 (4): 395–415.

Vavreck, Lynn, and Douglas Rivers. 2008. "The 2006 Cooperative Congressional Election Study." *Journal of Elections, Public Opinion, and Parties* 18 (4): 355–366.

Verba, Sidney, Kay Lehman Schlozman, and Henry Brady. 1995. *Voice and Equality: Civic Voluntarism in American Politics*. Cambridge, MA: Harvard University Press.

Vicari, Chelsen. 2014a. "Are Young Evangelicals Kissing the Culture War Goodbye?" *Christian Post*, January 27. Available at http://www.christianpost.com/news/are-young-evangelicals-kissing-the-culture-wars-goodbye-113432.

———. 2014b. *Distortion: How the New Christian Left Is Twisting the Gospel and Damaging the Faith*. Lake Mary, FL: FrontLine.

Wald, Kenneth D., and Allison Calhoun-Brown. 2014. *Religion and Politics in the United States*. 7th ed. Lanham, MD: Rowman and Littlefield.

Wald, Kenneth D., Dennis E. Owen, and Samuel S. Hill Jr. 1988. "Churches as Political Communities." *American Political Science Review* 82 (2): 531–548.

———. 1990. "Political Cohesion in Churches." *Journal of Politics* 52 (1): 197–215.

Wallis, Jim. 2006. *God's Politics: Why the Right Gets It Wrong and the Left Doesn't Get It*. New York: HarperCollins.

Warner, Jessica. 2009. "Temperance, Alcohol, and the American Evangelical: A Reassessment." *Addiction* 104:1075–1084.

Wear, Michael. 2014. "The Changing Face of Christian Politics." *The Atlantic*, February 17. Available at http://www.theatlantic.com/politics/archive/2014/02/the-changing-face-of-christian-politics/283859.

Weber, Max. 1930. *The Protestant Ethic and the Spirit of Capitalism*. Translated by Talcott Parsons. New York: Scribner.

Weber, Timothy. 1999. "Dispensational Premillennialism: The Dispensationalist Era." *Christianity Today*, January. Available at http://www.christianitytoday.com/history/issues/issue-61/dispensational-premillennialism-dispensationalist-era.html.

Wehner, Peter. 2007. "Among Evangelicals, a Transformation." *National Review* 59 (24). Available at http://eppc.org/publications/among-evangelicals-a-transformation.

———. 2015. "Why Evangelicals Should Love the Pope." *New York Times*, April 4. Available at http://www.nytimes.com/2015/04/05/opinion/sunday/why-evangelicals-should-love-the-pope.html.

Weissman, Jordan. 2014. "Indisputable Evidence That Millennials Have It Worse Than Any Generation in 50 Years." *The Atlantic*, February 11. Available at http://www.theatlantic.com/business/archive/2014/02/indisputable-evidence-that-millennials-have-it-worse-than-any-generation-in-50-years/283752.

Wilcox, Clyde. 1988. "The Christian Right in Twentieth Century America: Continuity and Change." *Review of Politics* 50 (4): 659–681.

———. 1992. *God's Warriors: The Christian Right in Twentieth-Century America*. Baltimore: Johns Hopkins University Press.

Wilcox, Clyde, and Carin Robinson. 2010. *Onward Christian Soldiers? The Religious Right in American Politics*. 4th ed. Boulder, CO: Westview Press.

Wilcox, W. Bradford. 2009. "How Focused on the Family? Evangelical Protestants, the Family, and Sexuality." In *Evangelicals and Democracy in America*, vol. 1, *Religion and Society*, edited by Steven Brint and Jean Reith Schroedel, 251–275. New York: Sage.

Will, Jeffry A., and John K. Cochran. 1995. "God Helps Those Who Help Themselves? The Effects of Religious Affiliations, Religiosity, and Deservedness on Generosity toward the Poor." *Sociology of Religion* 56 (3): 327–338.

Williams, Daniel K. 2010. *God's Own Party: The Making of the Christian Right*. New York: Oxford University Press.

Wilson, J. Matthew. 1999. "'Blessed Are the Poor?': American Protestantism and Attitudes toward Poverty and Welfare." *Southeastern Political Review* 27 (3): 421–437.

———. 2007. "The Changing Catholic Voter: Comparing Responses to John Kennedy in 1960 and John Kerry in 2004." In *A Matter of Faith: Religion in the 2004*

Presidential Election, edited by David E. Campbell, 162–179. Washington, DC: Brookings Institution Press.

———. 2009. "Religion and American Public Opinion: Economic Issues." In *The Oxford Handbook of Religion and American Politics*, edited by Corwin E. Smidt, Lyman A. Kellstedt, and James A. Guth, 191–216. New York: Oxford University Press.

Winograd, Morley, and Michael D. Hais. 2008. *Millennial Makeover: Myspace, YouTube, and the Future of American Politics*. New Brunswick, NJ: Rutgers University Press.

———. 2011. *Millennial Momentum: How a New Generation Is Remaking America*. New Brunswick, NJ: Rutgers University Press.

Wuthnow, Robert. 1988. *The Restructuring of American Religion*. Princeton, NJ: Princeton University Press.

———. 1994. *God and Mammon in America*. New York: Free Press.

———. 2007. *After the Baby Boomers: How Twenty- and Thirty-Somethings Are Shaping the Future of American Religion*. Princeton, NJ: Princeton University Press.

Zaller, John. 1990. "Political Awareness, Elite Opinion Leadership, and the Mass Survey Response." *Social Cognition* 8 (1): 125–153.

———. 1992. *The Nature and Origins of Mass Opinion*. Cambridge: Cambridge University Press.

Zaller, John, and Stanley Feldman. 1992. "A Simple Theory of Survey Response: Answering Questions versus Revealing Preferences." *American Journal of Political Science* 36 (3): 579–616.

Zogoby, John. 2009. "Young Evangelicals Cheer Obama—for Now." *Forbes*, January 22. Available at http://www.forbes.com/2009/01/21/evangelicals-polls-obama-oped-cx_jz_0122zogby.html.

Zukin, Cliff, Scott Keeter, Molly Andolina, Krista Jenkins, and Michael X. Delli Carpini. 2006. *A New Engagement? Political Participation, Civic Life, and the Changing American Citizen*. Oxford: Oxford University Press.

Index

Page numbers in italics indicate material in figures or tables.

abortion, 114; age and views on, 51, *52*, 66–68, *67*; biblical views on, 122; black Protestants on, *153*, 154; Campolo on, 166; Catholicism on, 154, 195n2 (chap. 4); church events regarding, 123–125; commitment hypothesis and, 74, *78*, 78–79, 133, 152–154, *153*; economic causes of, 166; evangelical leaders and, 23, 28–29, 39, 73, 151; evangelicals and, 5, 10, 23–24, 28–29, 39; framing of, 124–125; as future issue, 174–175; immersion and, 137–139, *138*; issue hypothesis and, 29, 39, 41, 65; issue salience and, 66–68, *67*, 147, *169*, 169–170, *170*; Jesus and, 151; Jimmy Carter on, 150–151; liberal evangelicals and, 152–154, *153*, 158, *162*, 162–164, 166, 169; March for Life, 28; millennials and, 79, 169; New Christian Right and, 177; "partial-birth" abortions, 51; in presidential elections, 45–47; Protestantism and, 154; public opinion on, 50–51, *51*; religious commitment and, *78*, 86, *134*, 134–135, 142–143, *144*; Republican Party on, 5; *Roe v. Wade* decision on, 21; sexual attitudes and, 114; statistical models for, *183*, *186*, *187*, *189*, *191*; student clubs on, 129; as "unofficial litmus test," 150; young evangelicals and, 1, 12, 51, *52*, 65–69, *67*, 121, 147, *153*
Access Hollywood video, 47
activists, 23, 90, 146, 176
Affordable Care Act, 175
African Americans, 147, 181–182, 194n2 (chap. 2), 194–195n5, 196n5, 197n6. *See also* black Protestants
"aftershocks" in New Christian Right, 72
age groups: and abortion, 51, *52;* age effects, 10, 45, 47–49, *48*, *49*, 56, 65; data and methods, 42–43; and environmental attitudes, 54, *55*; and homosexuality/gay marriage, 51, *53*; and ideology, *46*; and immigration, 56, *58*, 59; and military/foreign policy, 59, *60*, *62*; and partisanship, *44*, 75; and presidential vote (2012), *48*; race/ethnicity by, *8*; and welfare, 56, *57*. *See also* young evangelicals
alcohol consumption, 104, 195n1 (chap. 4)
Amish subculture, 179
ANES (American National Election Study), 43, 141
Answers in Genesis, 22, 24
Apostles' Creed, 26
Ark Encounter, 22, 24
Asian evangelicals, *8*, 8–9, 133, 162, *185–186*, *189–190*, 194n2 (chap. 2)

Bakker, Jim and Tammy Faye, 21
baptism, 26

believing, behaving, belonging dimensions, 2–5, 30
Berelson, Bernard, 35, 140
biblical literalism, 3, 5, 18, 20, 27, 40, *105*, 105–106, 165
bidirectional causation, 140, 145
black Protestants, 3, 6, *7*, 30, 194n2 (chap. 2). *See also* African Americans; religious denominations' traditions and beliefs
Bob Jones College, 32
Boomer generation, 61, *63–64*, 65
born-again/conversion experience, 5, 18–19, 27, 106, *107*
Bryan, William Jennings, 20
Burwell v. Hobby Lobby, 177
Bush, George H. W., 39
Bush, George W., 1, 9, 39, 120, 175, 179–180, 195n3
Butler Act (Tennessee), 20

Campbell, David, 35, 51, 72, 79, 175, 178, 195n2 (chap. 4)
Campolo, Tony, 4, 86, 147–148, 151, 166
Campus Crusade for Christ (Cru), 33–34
campus organizations, 33–34
Carroll, Colleen, 2, 37
Carter, Jimmy, 147, 150–151
Carter, Rachel, 146, 163–165, 167–168
cartoons, Christian, 22
Casting Crowns, 22
Castle, Darrell, 50
Catholics/Catholicism, 69, 195n2 (chap. 4); decline in, by age, 6–8, *7*; in Democratic and Republican parties, 30; and entertainment industry, 116, *117*; as immigrants, 40–41; leaving the faith, 197n2; and Martin Luther, 19; and political religion hypothesis, 140–141; and private schools, 32; returning to orthodoxy, 2; subcultures within, 179; as threat to fundamentalism, 20. *See also* religious denominations' traditions and beliefs
causal claims, 90, 132, 137, 139–141, *143–144*
CCES (Cooperative Congressional Election Study), 35, 59, 74; evangelical liberal-conservative identification, 2; evangelical race/ethnicity by age group, 8; Panel Survey, 132, 141–144, *143*, *144*, 182; party-ideology causal relationship, *143*, *144*; presidential vote (2012), 47–50, *48*, *49*, *50*; presidential vote (2016), 2, 13, 42, 47, *49*, 49–50, *50*, 182, 196nn5–6; two-party presidential votes, *77*
CCM (contemporary Christian music), 21–22
Center for Science and Culture, 24

CFI (comparative fit index), 196n8
change from outside versus inside, 13, 70–72
Chapman, Steven Curtis, 22
charismatic movement, 3–4, 18, 106
Christian Broadcasting Network University, 32
Christian Coalition, 23, 39, 73
Christianity Today, 4
Christian Right, 5, 24, 72–73, 83. *See also* New Christian Right
churches: and identity building, 26; as providing political cues, 28, 123–124; youth groups based in, 100
Cizik, Richard, 40
Claiborne, Shane, 111, 147, 149, 151, 166
clergy/pastors, 28–29, 32, 40–41, 73–74, 125–126, 151–152
Clinton, Bill, 1
Clinton, Hillary, 47, 49, 75
coding scheme, 181–182
cognitive dissonance, 147–149, 150, 163, 166, 169, 197n2
cohabitation, 11, 12
cohort effects, 10–11, 61, *63–64*, 65, 71, 83
colleges and universities, evangelical, 32–34, 91–97. *See also individual colleges*
Columbia School perspective, 100
commitment, religious, 195n2 (chap. 3); and attitudes, 133–137, *134*; defined, 193n3; and evangelicalism, 197n3; impact of, on cultural issues, 133–137, *134*; and noncultural issues, *134*, 136–137; over time, 5–8, *7*; and partisanship, 141–145, *143*, *144*; and same-sex marriage views, *134*, 135; among young evangelicals, *7*, 8
commitment hypothesis, 30–31, 34, 71, 132, 142–143, *143*, 172; testing of, 74–84, *76*, *77*, *78*, *80*, *82*, *84*, 133–139, *134*, *138*
comparative fit index (CFI), 196n8
Constitution, U.S., 21, 165, 175, 177
contemporary Christian music (CCM), 21–22
contraceptives, 166, 177, 198n1
conversion/born-again experience, 5, 18–19, 27, 106, *107*
Cooperative Congressional Election Study. *See* CCES (Cooperative Congressional Election Study)
core values/beliefs, 197n3; and abortion, 39; community promotion of, 26–27; contradictions in, 19; emphasis on, 29; and environmental conservatism, 40; and immigration, 168; of Islam, 195n2 (chap. 4); preserving, 18; threats to, 24; transmitting, 31–32, 35, 86, 99, 104

Courageous (film), 22
Cramer, Katherine, 90
creation care, 167
creationism, 22, 24, 125, 177
critical issues, 66–68, *67*, 137–139, *138*, 168–171, *169*, *170*
cross-sectional data issues, 12–13, 43, 69, 90, 137
Cru (Campus Crusade for Christ), 33–34
cultural modernism, 3, 5, 9, 26, 30, 176
"culture wars," 177–179; background of, 112; at colleges, 128; and conflation of religion and politics, 35, 121; fatigue over, 2, 73, 172; liberals as winners of, 175; media and, 115
Cyrus, Miley, 118

Darrow, Clarence, 20
Darwinian evolution, 20, 24, 26, 105
data and methods, 42–43
dc Talk, 22
Defense of Marriage Act, 39
Democrats/Democratic Party, 5; and Barack Obama's success, 175; composition of, 30, 147, 194n2 (chap. 2); and cultural modernism, 5, 176; demographic trends in, 11, 30; effect of, on evangelical views, 134; and evangelicals, *76*; example of, 146; Jimmy Carter as exemplar of, 151; popular vote losses by, 1; professor identifying as, 128; and social identity theory, 140; and young evangelicals, 1–2, 9, 27, 43–50, *44*, *48*, *49*, 73, 86
denominational churches, 3
Directional State University, 97, 128–129
Discovery Institute, 24
distinctive beliefs/core values, 27; of evangelical subculture, 104–114, *105*, *107*, *109–110*, *113*, 122–123, 129; as heuristics, 29; immersion and, 71; of Islam, 195n2 (chap. 4); of liberal evangelicals, 164, 167–168; of Mormons, 178, 195n2 (chap. 4)
Dobson, James, 23, 39, 73, 120
Don't Ask, Don't Tell, 39
Duck Dynasty (TV series), 32

early-life socialization, 31
economic policies: church programs for poor, 28; evangelical views on, 10, 24, 40, 122–123, 138, 166–167; and liberalism, 166
education, 12, *138*, 139; profiles of featured colleges, 92–97; teacher-led prayer, 21, 123, 175, 177
Edwards, Jonathan, 19

Edwards v. Aguillard, 125
employment, 66, 169, *187*
"The End of Christian America" (Meacham), 72
Engel v. Vitale, 21
Enlightenment, 19
environment: attitudes among liberals on, *156*; attitudes on, by age, 54, *55*, 81, *82*; black Protestants on, 154, *158*; and creation care, 167; immersion and, 137, *138*; and issue salience, 29, *67*, 68; jobs trade-off with, 54, 81, 136, 154; mercury poisoning, 40; predicted views on, among evangelicals by religious commitment, *82*; and religious commitment, 139; young evangelicals' opinions on, 12, 54–56, *55*
Epperson v. Arkansas, 125
evangelical colleges, 32–34; and building evangelical identity, 100–105; chapel services at, 101; deepening of religion at, 102; degree of political advocacy at, 126–129; and incorporating religion in coursework, 101, 118. *See also* New Faithful College; Old Faithful College
evangelicalism, 5; and age, 6–8, *7*; distinctive beliefs within, 18, 104–114, *105*, *107*, *109–110*, *113*; effect of, on public opinion, 17, 25–27; evangelical Protestantism, 2–6, *7*, 18–20, 39, 71, 105, 111, 181; as future political minority, 177; and political activity over time, 9; and political affiliation, 1, 9, 27–28, 43–50, *44*, *48*, *49*, 141, 149; progressivism within, 4; race and ethnicity in, *8*, 8–9, 194n2 (chap. 2); as resisting modernization, 20; and secularization, 6; and theological exclusivism, 108, *109*. *See also* New Faithful College; Old Faithful College; religious denominations' traditions and beliefs; social group identity; young evangelicals
evangelizing, 106, *107*, 111
evolution, 20, 24, 26, 105, 111, 114
external versus internal factors, 2, 11, 17, 66, 70–71, 78–81, 84–86

Facing the Giants (film), 22
faith healing, 4
Falwell, Jerry: and abortion, 39; death of, 10, 73; as encouraging engagement in society, 4, 111, 176; and Liberty University, 32; and Moral Majority, 23, 39; and New Christian Right, 27; political positions of, 120, 151; and Republican Party, 39; television ministry of, 21, 28

Falwell, Jerry, Jr., 175
families: James Dobson's emphasis on, 23, 73; Mormon emphasis on, 179; and political socialization, 31; and religious holidays, 26; separation of, with deportation, 168
Family Research Council, 23
Family Talk (radio series), 73
Farrell, Justin, 11, 12, 86
FCA (Fellowship of Christian Athletes), 33
federal deficit, 66–68, *67*, *138*, 138–139, *169–170*, *188*, *192*
Festinger, Leon, 148, 163
films, evangelical, 22, 79
Fireproof (film), 22
First Great Awakening, 19
Fischer, Claude, 6, 35, 140, 174
fit indexes, 196n8
Five Pillars of Islam, 195n2 (chap. 4)
Focus on the Family, 23, 39, 73
foreign policy issues, 12, 30, 41–42, 59–65, *62*, *64*, 163
Francis, Pope, 73
Franklin, Paul, 131–132
Fuller, Charles, 21
Fuller Theological Seminary, 4
fundamentalist movement, 3–4, 20, 24, 32, 104, 114, 175
Fundamentals: A Testimony to the Truth, 20
funnel model, 196n2

gay marriage, 29; Catholic Church and, 154; college students on, 121–123, 126; "culture wars" over, 112; Defense of Marriage Act, 39; evangelical opinion on, 5, 126, 152, 165, 176–177; GSS data on, 61, *63*; immersion and, 137; issue hypothesis and, 39; issue salience of, 10, 29, 66–68, *67*, 137–139, *138*, *170*, 170–171; Jimmy Carter on, 151; Jim Wallis on, 152; liberal evangelicals and, 158, *162*, 164–166, 169, 173; *Obergefell v. Hodges* on, 175, 177; Pew Religious Landscape Study questions on, 51–54, *53*; public opinion on, 51–54, *53*, 61, *63*; and religious commitment, 79–81, *80*, 86, 132–136, *134*, *138*, 139, 143–144, *144*, 154, *155*; scripture used in support of, 164; Shane Claiborne on, 151–152; as 2004 election issue, 39; young evangelical opinion on, 11–12, 65, 135–136, 154, 173, 176–177. *See also* homosexuality
gender: controlling for in results, 136, 138, 162, 170; and development of partisanship, 140
General Social Survey. *See* GSS (General Social Survey)

Gen X, 61, *63–64*
Gingrich, Newt, 45
Glee (TV series), 79
glossolalia/speaking in tongues, 4, 18, 106
God's Not Dead (film), 22
God's Politics (Wallis), 24
government: and aid to needy, 12, 56, 136; and *Burwell v. Hobby Lobby*, 187; Christian perspective on, 101; and constitutional rights, 165; and "culture wars," 177; and gay marriage, 165; and LDS and polygamy, 178; Mormonism and, 81
Graham, Billy, 4, 21, 40, 111, 176
Grant, Amy, 22
Great Books College, 96–97, 100, 102, 122–123, 125, 129
Greatest Adventure: Stories from the Bible (Hanna-Barbera), 22
Green, John, 175, 178, 181–182, 195n2 (chap. 4)
Green Lantern, 79
group identity, 4–5, 17, 23, 26–27, 29, 99–104
GSS (General Social Survey), 12, 182; abortion views, *52*; environment views, 54–56, *55*; gay marriage views, *53*, 54, 61, *63*; ideological trends, 45, *46*; immigration views, *58*, 59, *64*; LGBT views, *53*; military and foreign policy views, 59–62, *60*, *62*, *64*; party identification, 43–45, *44*; premarital sex views, 112, *113*; religious affiliation over time, 6, *7*; religious commitment, *7*, *8*; time-series data, 43, 54, 59, 61, 65, 69; welfare views, 56, *57*, *63*
Guth, James, 41

Hais, Michael, 71
Ham, Ken, 4, 24
Hanna-Barbera, 22
Harris, Dan, 1
Hersh, Eitan, 28
heuristics, 4, 25–27, 29, 100
HHS (Department of Health and Human Services) contraceptive mandate, 177
Hispanic evangelicals, 8, 8–9, *185–192*, 194n2 (chap. 2)
Hollywood as threat to values, 116, *117*
homosexuality: and attraction without sexual activity, 127; Christian views on, 23, 122; college stances on, 125–127; and "culture wars," 112; evangelical views on, 11–12, 29, 39, 51–54, *53*, 165, 176–177; gay evangelicals, 125–126; generational views on, *63*, 65, 79; liberal evangelical views on, 151, 158, 162; public opinion on, 51–54, *53*, 176–177;

and refusal of service, 177–178; and religious commitment, 79–81, *80*, 86, 133–135, *134*, 137; as subculture, 180; views on, at Old Faithful College, 127; and Westboro Baptist Church, 151; young evangelical views on, *53*, 54, 61, 65–66, 73, 122. *See also* gay marriage; model results
Hout, Michael, 6, 35, 140, 174
Huckabee, Mike, 120
Hunter, James Davison, 11, 115
Hunter, Joel, 73

identity building, 26, 100–104
ideology: and church attendance, *150*; and issue salience, *170*; and partisanship, 43–50, *44*, *46*, *48*, *49*, *50*, 142; party-ideology causal relationship, *143*, *144*; and religious commitment, 76, 142–143, *143*; as social identity, 196n2; young evangelical trends in, 45, *46*
immersion, subcultural: as cause of conservatism, 131–132, 138, 140, 145; defined, 91; impact of, on cultural issues, 133–137, *134*; and issue salience, 137–139, *138*; and negative views, 118; and partisanship, 141–145, *143*, *144*
immigration views, 29–30, 114; by age group, 56, *58*, 59; by cohort, *64*, 65; core values and, 168; and fears of Catholics and Jews, 40–41; Jesus and, 41; of liberal young evangelicals, 158, *159*, 167–168; of liberal young people, 158, *159–161*; of New Christian Right, 168; over time, *58*; and religious commitment, 83–84, *84*, 137–139, *138*; of young evangelicals, *58*, 59, *64*, 68. *See also* religious denominations' traditions and beliefs
individual salvation, 19
inequality issues, 10, 126, 151
infrequent attendees, 79, 86, 132, 176
intelligent design, 22, 24, 125, 177
internal versus external factors, 2, 11, 17, 66, 70–71, 78–81, 84–86
internationalism, 41, 61, *62*, 158, *161*
InterVarsity, 34, 102, 129
interviews, 13; on biblical guidance, 122; on building group identity, 100–104; on church and politics, 123–126; on cognitive dissonance, 163–164; on college and politics, 127–129; on colleges, 94–97; on creationism, 125; on economics, 123; on gay marriage, 164–165; issues stressed by liberal evangelicals in, 166–167, 171; on meaning of "evangelicals," 108–111, 115–116; on popular culture, 118–119; of Rachel, 163–164;

on Republican Party, 121–122; selection of interviewees, 91–92; on student clubs, 129
Islam, 195n2 (chap. 4)
isolationism, 61, *184*; and liberal young people, *161*, *190*; and religion, 41; and religious commitment, 84–86, *85*, 133–134, *134*, 137, 158, *161*, *186*; and young evangelicals, *62*, *162*, 162–163
issue attitudes among liberal evangelicals, 149–158, *153*, *155–157*
issue-based sorting, 5
issue hypothesis, 29, 34, 39–42, 65, 131–133, 137–139, *138*, 172
issue salience (PRRI): among eighteen- to twenty-nine-year olds, *169*, 169–171, *170*; among liberal evangelicals, 147, 165–171, *169*, *191–19*; Millennial Values Survey, 66, 182, 196n5, 197n62; and religious commitment, *138*, *187–188*; subcultural immersion and, 137–138; among young evangelicals, 67, 67–68, 137–139, *138*

Jelen, Ted, 51, 175
Jenkins, Jerry B., 193n2
Jesus: and abortion, 151; on distributing your wealth, 167; on equality, 126; and immigrants, 41; media caricatures of, 119; Mormonism and, 178, 195n2 (chap. 4); and Obama, 164; as only way to salvation, 3; personal relationship with, 111; and Red Letter Christians, 197n5; Second Coming of, 193n2; on social justice and stewardship, 148; treatment of people by, 164
Jews/Judaism: and attitudes about Torah, *105*, 106; and politics, 30; and Protestant nativism, 40; and religious influence, *110*, 111; on religious tradition, *30*. *See also* religious denominations' traditions and beliefs
jobs: environment trade-off with, 54, 81, 136, 154; and issue salience, *138*, 139, *170*, *187*, *191*; and unemployment, 66–68, *67*, 169
Johnson, Byron, 12, 43, 69
Johnson, Gary, 49
Johnson, Janet, 90
Josh (in *God's Not Dead*), 22
"Juno generation," 79
"just Christians," 194–195n5, 196n5, 197n6
justice: biblical, 168; economic, 24; social, 4, 24, 40, 148, 168, 179, 194n2 (chap. 2)

Kennedy, John F., 179
Know-Nothing Party, 41
Kopko, Kyle, 179
Kraybill, Donald, 179

LaHaye, Tim, 193n2
Layman, Geoffrey, 181–182
Lazarsfeld, Paul, 35, 140
LDS (Church of Jesus Christ of Latter-Day Saints), 178–179. *See also* Mormons
Left Behind series (LaHaye and Jenkins), 193n2
LGBTQ issues. *See* homosexuality
liberal evangelicals: cognitive dissonance in, 147–148; demographics of, 149, *150*; on gay marriage, 146–147, 154–155, *155*; interviews of, 163–165; issue attitudes of, 149–158, *155, 156, 157,* 165–168; Jimmy Carter, 147, 150–151; Jim Wallis, 4, 24, 86, 111, 147–148, 151–152, 166; in Millennial Values Survey (2012), 168–171, *169, 170*; and multivariate analysis, 158–163, *159–162*
liberalism, ideological, 26, 86, 140, 147
Libertarian Party, 49
Liberty University, 32, 47, 94
Luther, Martin, 19, 193n1 (chap. 1)
Lutheranism, 3, 26, 28

Maier, Walter, 21
mainline religion, 181–182, 197n2; future of, 69; liberals leaving, 140; prevalence of, 6, *7*; and Protestantism, 19–20; and Republican Party, 30; split of, with evangelicalism, 20–21, 23, 29–32, *105*, 105–106; and use of military, 158, *160*. *See also* Great Books College; religious denominations' traditions and beliefs; Top 100 College
Malina, Gabrielle, 28
March for Life, 28
marriage. *See* gay marriage
marriage, delayed, 12
Masterpiece Cakeshop v. Colorado Civil Rights Commission, 177
Maturen, Mike, 50
McGovern, George, 5
McMullin, Evan, 49, *50*
McPhee, William, 35, 140
McPherson, Aimee Semple, 21
Meacham, Jon, 72
media bias, 114–115
Mencken, H. L., 20
Michigan perspective, 100, 196n2
military attitudes, 33, 41, 59–62, *60*, 137; and liberal young evangelicals, 158, *160*; and liberal young people, 158, *159–161*; and religious commitment, 83–86, *85*
Millennial generation, 61, *62–64*, 65; approach of, to religion, 6; and commitment and salience, *187–188, 191*; declining religious affiliation of, 72; employment crisis among, 169; liberalism/secularism among, 9, 71, 114; Paul Franklin, 131–132; as percentage of voting-age population, 11; and politicization of religious affiliation, 72; as pro-life "Juno generation," 79; PRRI Millennial Values Survey (2012), 66, *67*, 137–138, *138*, 147, 168–171, *169*, 182, 196n5, 197n6. *See also* GSS (General Social Survey)
mixed-methods approach, 90–92, 97
model results, *183–192*
modernization, influence of, 3, 10–11, 20–21, 71, 105
"Monkey Trial"/Scopes Trial, 20, 111, 114, 175
Monson, J. Quin, 175, 178, 195n2 (chap. 4)
Moore, Russell, 2, 37
moral authority, 11, 12, 86
Moral Majority, 23, 39, 73
moral relativism/absolutism views, 112–114, *113*
Mormons, 178–179, 195n2 (chap. 4)
multivariate analysis, 158–163, *159–162*
music, 21–22, 26, 119
Mycoff, Jason, 90

National Congregations Study (2006), 194n2 (chap. 1)
National Freedom to Marry Day, 128
nationally representative survey data, 42, 90, 122, 139
national security, 41, *67*, *138*, 139, *169–170*, *188, 192*
Navigators, 34, 194n3 (chap. 1)
negative reference groups, 23, 140
"neoevangelical" movement, 4
"New Birth," 19
New Christian Right: "aftershocks" in, 72–73; criticisms of, 166; evangelicals and, 4, 24; and immigration, 168; liberal exceptions to, 168; and linking of conservatism and religion, 147; as losing "culture war," 175; new leadership of, 10; political activism of, 23, 41, 72, 171; Republican Party and, 9, 147; use of government institutions by, 177; use of media by, 27; young evangelicals and, 2, 70
"new evangelicals," 73
The New Faithful (Carroll), 2
New Faithful College: chapel services at, 101; and politics, 128; profile of, 94–95; and religion and pop culture, 119; religion courses at, 100–101, 115–116; student interviews, 108–109, 118–119, 121, 124, 131, 146
Noah's Ark, 22
nondenominational churches, 3–4

Obama, Barack, 1, 45–47, *48*, 75, 164, 175
Obergefell v. Hodges, 175, 177
Old Faithful College: chapel services at, 101; coursework at, 100–101; profile of, 92–94, 97; student interviews, 93–94, 102–103, 115, 118–119, 121–122, 124
On the Origin of Species (Darwin), 105
Oral Roberts University, 32
organized religion, decline in, 6, 12, 72
orthodoxy (in religious beliefs), 2, 26, 30, 102
Osteen, Joel, 10, 73
"other" religions, 193n1 (intro.)

Palin, Sarah, 9, 121
panel data, 13, 35, 132, 141, 182. *See also* CCES (Cooperative Congressional Election Study)
"partial-birth" abortions, 51
partisanship: and ideology, 43–50, *44*, *46*, *48*, *49*, *50*, 142; Michigan perspective on, 100, 196n2; party identity, 10, 43, 100, 140 (*see also* Democrats/Democratic Party; Republicans/Republican Party); as stable over time, 10, 31, 142
Patrikios, Stratos, 35, 140–141
Patty, Sandi, 22
Pelz, Mikael, 12, 43, 69
Pence, Mike, 177
Penning, James, 11
Pentecostalism, 3–4, 18, 104, 106
"perceptual screens," 27
period effects, 10, 61, *64*, 65
Perry, Rick, 121
personal conversion experiences, 5, 18–19, 27
Pew Religious Landscape Studies, 34, 42; on abortion, *52*, *76*, *153*; on being born again, *107*; church attendance and ideology, *150*; effect of evangelicalism on liberals, *162*; effect of ideology on issue salience, *170*; on environment, *55*, *156*; on eternal life, *109*; on gay marriage, *53*, *155*; on Hollywood, *117*; on immigration, *58*, *159*; on isolationism, *62*, *161*; on LGBT issues, *53*; on military, *60*, *160*; models for figures, *183–192*; on one true faith, *109*; on out-of-wedlock children, *113*; partisanship and attitudes, *76*; on premarital sex, *113*; on religion and modern society, *117*; on religion and politics, *109*; on religion keeping tradition, *117*; religious commitment and attitudes, *76*, 133–137, *134*, *138*; on sharing faith, *107*; on welfare, *57*, *63*, *157*
Phillips, Jack, 177–178
"pick your battles" strategy, 30

Planned Parenthood, 28
"plausibility structures," 26
P.O.D., 22
political views/behavior, 5–6; in churches, *110*, 111, 123–126; in evangelical colleges, 126–129; heuristics and, 25; and parties as negative reference groups, 140; political religion hypothesis, 140–143, *143*; political science theory, 10; as social identity, 196n2
polygamy, 81, 178–179, 198n2
pop culture as negative, 116–119, *117*, 193n2
pornography, 11, 12, 22–23
Post-American/Sojourners, 24
postmillennialism, 193n2
poverty, *67*, 68; evangelicals and, 4, 10, 28, 29, 37, 40; liberal evangelicals and, 166; "new evangelicals" and, 41, 73; Social Gospel on, 20; and welfare, 56; young evangelicals and, 66–68, *67*
prayer: in colleges, 96; frequency of, 7, 111, 133, 142, 193n3, 195n2 (chap. 3), 196n3, 197n3; in public schools, 21, 123, 175, 177
predicted views among evangelicals by religious commitment, *76–78*, *82*, *84*, *85*, *90*
premarital sex, 11, 12, 112–114, *113*
premillennial dispensationalism, 3, 40, 193n2, 194n1
presidential elections and young evangelicals, 45–50, *46*, *48*, *49–50*
progressivism within evangelicalism, 4, 96
pro-life activism, 28, 39, 41, 123–124. *See also* abortion
pro-life attitudes, 51, 79, 81, 121–124, 163–164. *See also* abortion
prophesy/prophets, 4, 178, 195n2 (chap. 4)
Protestants/Protestantism, 2; decline in, by age, 6–8, *7*; leaving the faith, 197n2; mainline-evangelical split within, 19–20; and political religion hypothesis, 140–141; "Protestant ethic," 40; as subculture, 19. *See also* black Protestants; evangelicalism
PRRI Millennial Values Survey (2012), 66, 182, 196n5, 197n6. *See also* issue salience (PRRI)
Putnam, Robert, 35, 51, 72, 79

race/ethnicity, 129; controlling for, in results, 136, 138, 162, 170, 194n2 (chap. 2); and development of partisanship, 140; of evangelicals by age, *8*, 8–9; and segregation in church, 194n2 (chap. 2); white proportion as shrinking, 11. *See also* black Protestants
Rachel, 146, 163–165, 167–168

radio and television ministries, 21–22, 27, 73
Rapture, 193n2, 194n1
RAS (receive-accept-sample) model, 25–27, 29–30, 99, 115, 172
"rational choice" perspective, 100
Reagan, Ronald, 1, 9, 39, 73, 120, 180
Red Letter Christians, 4, 166, 197n5
Redman, Matt, 22
Reed, Ralph, 23
religion as multidimensional, 2–3, 6, 9, 30
religious commitment. *See* commitment hypothesis
religious denominations' traditions and beliefs, 3; on abortion, *153*, 154, 195n2 (chap. 4); as in conflict with modern society, 116–118, *117*; environmental attitudes, 154, *156*; foundational beliefs, *105*, 105–106; guidance on right and wrong, *110*, 111; Hollywood as threatening, *117*; immigration attitudes, 158, *159*; isolationism attitudes, *161*; military attitudes, *160*; preservation of, *117*; proportion born again, *107*; proportion sharing faith, *107*; on role of religion in politics, *110*, 111; on sexual morality, 112–114, *113*, 154, *155*; theological exclusivism, 106–108, *109*; welfare attitudes, *157*
Religious Freedom Restoration Act, 177
Religious Landscape Studies. *See* Pew Religious Landscape Studies
RELTRAD coding scheme, 182
Republicans/Republican Party: and abortion, 5; and demographic trends, 11; effect of, on evangelical views, 132–135, *134*; interviews on, 121–122; and Jerry Falwell, 39; and mainline religion, 30; and nativism, 41; and New Christian Right, 9, 147; in presidential politics, 1, 5, 9–11, 39, 43–50, *44*, *48*, *49*; and social identity theory, 140; and young evangelicals, 1–2, 9–11, 27, 43–50, *44*, *48*, *49*, 86
Reynolds, George, 198n2
Reynolds, H. T., 90
Roberts, Keith, 71, 119
Roberts, Oral, 21, 32
Robertson, Pat, 120, 151; and abortion, 39; and Christian Coalition, 23, 73; and politics, 23, 28, 39, 111, 120; television ministry of, 21, 27, 32, 73, 151
Robinson, Carin, 40
Rochester perspective, 100
rock music and culture, 18, 21–22
Roe v. Wade, 21, 150, 175
Romney, Mitt, 45, 47, *48*, 75, *77*, 176, 178

salvation, personal, 3, 19, 194n1
same-sex marriage. *See* gay marriage
Sanctity of Human Life Sunday, 28
Santorum, Rick, 45
Schaeffer, Francis, 39, 111, 176
Schlafly, Phyllis, 10, 39, 73, 120, 151
scholarship on young evangelicals, 12–13, 42–43
schools: evangelicals on boards, 23; evolution taught in, 20; incorporation of faith into classrooms, 101; and political socialization, 31–34; prayer in, 21, 123; sex education in, 112; teacher-led prayer, 21, 123, 175, 177. *See also* colleges and universities, evangelical
Scopes Trial, 20, 111, 114, 175
Second Great Awakening, 19, 32
secularism: and culture as redeemable, 115; and Democratic Party, 30; increase in, by age, 6–8, *7*; influence of, 10–11
semistructured interviews, 13, 90–91, 131
separation of church and state, 3, 165
September 11 attacks, 8
Serrie, Jonathan, 150
The 700 Club (TV series), 73
Sherwood Pictures, 22
Sider, Ronald, 86, 111, 147–149, 166
Silent generation, 61, *63–64*, 65
"Sinners in the Hands of an Angry God" (Edwards), 19
Smidt, Corwin E., 3, 11, 12, 19, 43, 69
Smith, Buster, 12, 43, 69
Smith, Christian, 23, 114, 172
Smith, Gregory Allen, 179, 195n5 (chap. 4)
Smith, Joseph, 195n2 (chap. 4)
Smith, Michael W., 22
Social Gospel, 20
social group identity, 4–5, 17; building/maintaining in-group identity, 23, 26–29, 99–103, 129, 173; cultural issues in, 145
social identity theory, 140
socialization, sources of, 17–18, 31–34
social justice, 4, 24, 40, 148, 179, 194n2 (chap. 2)
social-psychological perspective, 10, 26, 100, 140
sociological perspective, 9, 26, 100, 140
Sojourners, 4, 24–25
sola scriptura doctrine, 19
sorting effects, 20, 35–36, 102, 122, 140–141, 145
Southern white evangelicals, 30
speaking in tongues/glossolalia, 4, 18, 106
"spirit-filled" movement, 4

stewardship, 73, 148
Stryper, 22
subcultural immersion: as cause of conservatism, 131–132, 138, 140, 145; defined, 91; impact of, on cultural issues, 133–137, *134*; and issue salience, 137–139, *138*; and negative views, 118; and partisanship, 141–145, *143*, *144*
subcultural theory of public opinion, 17, 25–31, 34, 66, 90–91, 141, 145, 172
Supreme Court cases: *Burwell v. Hobby Lobby*, 187; *Engel v. Vitale*, 21; *Masterpiece Cakeshop v. Colorado Civil Rights Commission*, 177; *Obergefell v. Hodges*, 175, 177; *Reynolds v. United States*, 198n2; *Roe v. Wade*, 21, 150–151, 175
survey research issues, 35, 90–91, 140
Swaggart, Jimmy, 21

teacher-led prayer, 21, 123, 175, 177
Teach the Controversy campaign, 24
television, 10, 21–22, 27, 32
temperance, 195n1 (chap. 4)
tertile categories, 149, *150*, 197n3
theme parks, Bible-based, 22, 32
theological exclusivism, 18, 106–108, *109*
Third Day, 22
time-series data: versus cross-sectional data, 12–13, 69; GSS data analysis, 43, 54, 59, 61, 65, 69; and sorting effect, 141
TLI (Tucker-Lewis Index), 196n8
Tomlin, Chris, 22
Top 100 College, 95–97, 119, 125, 128–129, 164–165, 167
Trinity Evangelical Divinity School, 24
Trotman, Dawson, 34
Trump, Donald, 47–50, 75–78, *77*, 90, 175–176

unaffiliated religious designation, 3, 6, 7, 69, 111–112, *153*, 154–158, *155*, *156*, *157*
unemployment, 66, 169, *187*
unidirectional religion-politics relationship, 35, 140

Veggie Tales (TV series), 22

Wallis, Jim: on abortion, 151; as author, 148; on gay marriage, 152; as liberal evangelical elite, 86, 111, 166, 197n5; as Sojourners founder, 4, 24, 147

Warren, Rick, 10, 28, 40–41, 73
wealth as religious issue, 167, 195n2 (chap. 4)
wealth gap, *67*, 68–69, *138*, 139, 147, *170*, 175, *188*, *192*
Weber, Max, 122
wedlock, births out of, *113*, 114
welfare: and age groups, 56, *57*; public opinion on, *63*, 65; and religious commitment, 81–83, *82*, 137; young evangelicals and, 56, *57*, *63*, 66–68, *67*, 154, *157*
Westboro Baptist Church, 151
Whitefield, George, 19
Wilcox, Clyde, 40
Will and Grace (TV series), 79
Williams, George, 33
Willie's Redneck Rodeo curriculum, 32
Winograd, Morley, 71
withdrawal strategies, 175–176
Woodruff, Wilford, 178

YMCA/YWCA, 33
YouGov internet survey, 141
young evangelicals, 45, *46*, 84–87; on abortion, 1, 12, 51, *52*, 65–69, *67*, 121, 147, *153*; on cultural issues, 50–54, *52*, *53*; data and methods, 42–43; and Democrats/Democratic Party, 1–2, 9, 27, 43–50, *44*, *48*, *49*, 73, 86; on environment, 12, 54–56, *55*; on foreign policy, 59–66, *60*, *62*–*64*; on gay marriage, 11–12, 51–54, *53*, 65, 135–136, 154, 173, 176–177; on homosexuality, *53*, 54, 61, 65–66, 73, 122; on immigration, 56–59, *58*, *64*, 68; on isolationism, *62*, *162*, 162–163; issue salience among, 66–68, *67*; and New Christian Right, 2, 70; and noncultural issues, 54–59, *55*, *57*, *58*; partisanship and ideology of, 43–45, *44*; place of, in society, 115–116; political beliefs of, 10, 121, 134; on poverty and welfare, 56, *57*, 66–68, *67*, 154; presidential elections and, 45–50, *46*, *48*, *49*–*50*; public opinion among, 37–42, 68–69; religious commitment among, 7, 8; on secular society as negative, 116–119, *117*; self-identification by, 92; and subculture, 25–31, 99; theoretical changes in political views of, 9–11. *See also* GSS (General Social Survey); liberal evangelicals
Young Life, 33
Youth for Christ, 33

Zaller, John, 25, 30, 99, 104, 115, 172

Jeremiah J. Castle is a Lecturer in the Department of Political Science and Public Administration at Central Michigan University.